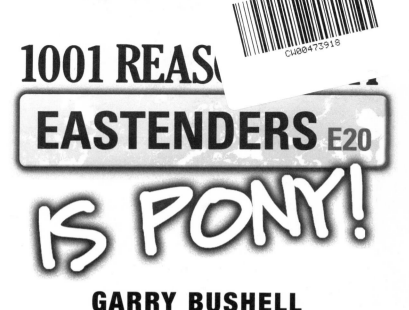

1001 REAS

EASTENDERS E20

IS PONY!

GARRY BUSHELL

Pennant Books

First published in paperback 2009
by Pennant Books

Cover illustration by Joe Wise

British Library Cataloguing-in-Publication Data:
A catalogue record for this book is available on request from
The British Library

ISBN 978-1-906015-40-4

Design & Typeset by Envy Design Ltd

Printed and bound in Great Britain by Clays Ltd, St Ives plc

Every reasonable effort has been made to acknowledge the ownership of
copyright material included in this book. Any errors that have inadvertently
occurred will be corrected in subsequent editions provided
notification is sent to the publisher.

Pennant Books
PO Box 5675
London W1A 3FB

www.pennantbooks.com

1001 REASONS WHY

EASTENDERS E20

IS PONY!

CONTENTS

FOREWORD

Most books written about television soaps are nothing more than extended fan letters. As soap operas are incredibly popular, so authors shamelessly attempt to ingratiate themselves with their audiences.

The resulting books are as critical as a pampered lapdog, as questioning as a showroom dummy or, perhaps, as trustworthy as Nick Cotton. Blinded by love – or in some cases greed – such authors choose to ignore the many irritating contradictions, cock-ups and character rewrites that plague even the best soaps. Instead, they fill their pages with extravagant praise, trivia, recycled press releases, CVs of overrated cast members and other assorted old cobblers.

My book is different. I'm setting out not to praise *EastEnders*, but to bury it.

"Why, Gal?" you ask. "Why be so harsh about a much-loved, BAFTA-winning TV programme? Are you not a Londoner? Do you not feel pride in BBC1's mightiest achievement?"

It's certainly true that, when *EastEnders* began, the show was impressive. Albert Square felt real back in 1985; characters like Dirty Den and Angie Watts were three-dimensional and convincing. The whole set-up seemed drawn from everyday life, as indeed it was. The soap's creators were producer Julia Smith and writer Tony Holland, a genuine East Londoner who modelled early characters on people and families he'd known and grown up with.

Compared to the camp, cosy comedy of *Coronation Street*, early *EastEnders* felt like something new, grittier and altogether more meaningful. It was a challenge to ITV's complacency, a proper punch up the trousers.

17 million people watched the first episode, when poor old Reg Cox was discovered brown bread. Viewing figures continued to rise throughout 1986, regularly attracting more than 20 million. When Den gave Angie her divorce papers at Christmas, the two episodes in question were watched by 29.5 and 31.1 million people respectively. They remain two of the Top Ten all-time most-watched British TV shows, beaten only by the 1966 World Cup final, the funeral of Princess Diana and a 1969 documentary called *The Royal Family*, which gave viewers their first proper tele-visual access to Buckingham Palace.

This book sets out to explain how that all went wrong; how a soap with its finger on the pulse of modern urban London slowly degenerated into a badly-written, error-strewn, melodramatic embarrassment. It will take delight in every ridiculous twist, continuity clanger and inconsistency of character inflicted on the denizens of Walford by the show's blinkered producers, its right-on agenda, poor scripting and lazy plotting, and in those moments when the cast's real-life shenanigans made the scripted fictions look tame.

The rot set in when the soap went to three episodes a week in 1994, accelerating downhill to four per week in 2001. Blown off-course by faster deadlines and growing budgetary restrictions, it began to lose whatever grip on reality it still had and, increasingly, its moral compass.

One key point in *EastEnders*' decline was the decision to bring Lesley Grantham's character Dirty Den back from the grave. This wasn't just the show's 'jump-the-shark' moment, it jet-skied over the whole ruddy aquarium!

It was bonkers for two main reasons: 1) Dennis Watts was dead – and we'd seen him die. 2) Grantham's personal scandals were to completely overshadow the show, allowing thousands to conclude that the soap was much more entertaining off-screen than on.

It has never fully recovered.

In July 2008 the soap plummeted to just 4.9 million viewers, its second lowest ratings ever. I felt vindicated. For years I'd felt like the small boy at the emperor's coronation; I could see he had no clothes on, but the crowd continued to believe he was fully decked in all his magisterial trappings.

But were the viewing public now cottoning on at last?

EastEnders reacted to the crisis by ordering ever more bizarre storylines. Blameless housewife Tanya Branning buried her cheating husband alive. Alleged hard-man and crackpot Sean Slater started torturing poor street cleaner Gus Smith, for no apparent reason. Peggy Mitchell, would-be councillor and hitherto a respectable landlady, began ordering hits like Tony Soprano with a cob on. This was the 'reality' of the madhouse.

EastEnders always goes for big shocks and hopes you don't notice how the plots have more holes than Dot's twitching lace curtain. They crank up the melodrama without ever checking to ensure the storylines make sense. Given the thoroughly middleclass backgrounds of the writers, it doesn't look like getting any more authentic anytime soon.

After years of resurrected publicans and unconvincing gangsters, the BBC still earnestly maintains that *EastEnders* is about real-life – even though, in 2009, few Albert Square citizens possess a washing machine and it's the only part of East London without a kebab shop, or a Bengali, or – crucially, given the number of tragic road deaths – speed bumps. (They only got yellow lines in the Square a couple of years ago.) There has never been a Chinese community in Walford and very few Jewish characters. Local businesses like the nightclub, the Vic, the car-lot/cab firm and the bookies change hands without rhyme or reason (or paperwork). Perfectly normal people simply disappear into the ether, never to be seen again, and no one ever misses them. Where else in Britain does the local GP – when he condescends to show his face – give consultations on the swings?

EastEnders is a laughter-free mess devoted to misery, betrayal, hate and recrimination, unleavened by any sparkle of hope or joy.

When Danielle Jones was run down and killed in April 2009, just moments after finally convincing Ronnie Mitchell that she was her daughter, there was an outcry from fans who demanded to know why the story couldn't have had a happy ending. But had these people never actually watched *EastEnders* before? There is more chance of finding the Pope selling condoms out of a briefcase in George Street market than of this sorry soap embracing a cheerful storyline.

None of the characteristics associated with cockneys is to be found. There is no wit. No banter. None of the bulldog spirit – that ability to keep smiling through that has been the hallmark of London people over the decades, if not centuries.

EastEnders is, in fact, a colossal libel on Londoners.

This is partly due to the background of the writers, and their social worker's worldview, but mostly it's due to laziness. Misery is easy to write. Our lives hover constantly on the verge of pain, illness, disappointment, loss and despair; "in the midst of life we are in death." And so it doesn't take much to make a viewer cry. But the ability to make us laugh is a rare and cherished gift – a gift that the BBC's wretched soap scribes just do not possess.

If life were like *EastEnders*, there wouldn't be a lamppost left to hang yourself from. You'd be reading the obituaries in the *Walford Gazette*, hoping to see your own name.

Garry Bushell

Where in the World Is Walford?

A lbert Square was originally modelled on Fassett Square, just off Dalston Lane in Hackney, northeast London, and the Vic was based on the Queen Elizabeth boozer in Fassett Square. The market was based on Ridley Road market in Dalston, and one of the show's working titles before it started was *East 8* – which is central Hackney's postcode. However, in the 90s, when it became obvious that the Square's ethnic mix did not reflect E8, soap bosses maintained that Walford was more to the east, between Walthamstow and Leytonstone. (Walford takes its name from Walthamstow and Stratford, where the creators were born.) Now though, according to the show's own rail map, Walford is much closer to the river. Walford tube station appears two stops to the west of Canning Town, between East India Dock Road and Blackwall, and New Road, which is physically situated to the southwest of the Square, off Victoria Road, has an E1 postcode.

Walford moves, much like the island on *Lost*, except in infinitely more mysterious ways. If it's just north of the Isle of Dogs, why was the area completely unaffected by Dockland Development? Up until 1998, the LDDC was busy regenerating an area of eight and a half square miles stretching across huge swathes of Southwark, Tower Hamlets and Newham. The Square didn't even get a lick of paint!

(It'll be doubly unlucky if Walford misses out on the Olympic regeneration too ...)

All of which leads to an even bigger mystery. If Walford is situated between Blackwall and East India, why, when the camera pans around the Square, do we never see Canary Wharf or the HSBC and Citibank towers which dominate the entire area? And why do you never hear the sound of planes flying past to nearby City Airport?

In fact, when the funfair paid a surprise visit to the Square in the summer of 2004, the mounted cameras revealed neither the mini-Manhattan of the Isle of Dogs nor the grit and grime of inner-city London. Instead, they treated us to a sweeping panorama of rural Hertfordshire.

My theory is that *EastEnders*' true location is just to the east of Slough – the slough of despond.

(Incidentally, despite the fact that the door numbers go up to 45, careful study reveals that there are only actually 13 houses in Albert Square. This suggests that half of the homes exist in a parallel dimension, which would certainly explain a lot. When Dr Legg apparently vanished for months on end in the 1990s, he was simply tending patients in another universe, see?)

The Soap's Ten Greatest Characters ... and How They Ruined Them

In its 25-year history, *EastEnders* has created some of the most memorable characters ever seen in British soaps. Whether rough and ready, devious, dangerous or engagingly cheeky, these giant personalities have captivated the viewing nation. But sadly, great as they were, every single one of them has been nobbled at some point in their history, either by carelessness, ignorance or plain bad writing. Here is my guide to Albert Square's finest creations, and how they were ruined.

Dirty Den and Angie Watts

Dennis Watts was arguably the most convincing male figure ever to walk the mean streets of Walford. Played by Leslie Grantham, a convicted murderer, Den was a sour, selfish man with a violent streak, but he could also be kind and generous. He was the cock of the walk, a local boy done good who relished being a big fish in a small pond. A ducker and diver by instinct, Den was an incorrigible love rat by inclination with a hustler's gift of the gab. He ran a good pub but also traded in the black economy, somewhere between legitimate business and organised crime.

His wife Angie was just as wonderfully drawn. Played by Anita Dobson, a genuine East Ender from Mile End, cockney sparrow Ange fought the pain of being married to Den with a trowel load of slap, a gallon of gin and a grin as wide as Stratford Broadway. The song lyric, 'smile while your heart is breaking,' could have been penned just for her. She was the first Walford alcoholic, and the best. Chemistry sparked off the two of them. Together, they were electric.

Uniquely, we cared about the Watts because we believed in them.

Dennis – who was nicknamed 'Dirty Den' by the press – handed Angie their divorce papers on Christmas Day 1986. This memorable episode was watched by a record-breaking 30.1 million viewers.

Tony Holland had worked in pubs in his youth and based the characters on people he'd encountered, originally calling them Jack and Pearl. In his pre-show notes on the characters, Holland described them as having been married for 15 years but they "haven't had sex for 13 of them". Their marriage is "a front for the sake of the pub's image" and for their adopted daughter, Sharon. Jack/Den has "had a mistress for five years … very upmarket, a lady, real class".

Den and Angie were teenage sweethearts, but he'd always been over the side. She too had affairs (Tony, Andy the Yuppie) but she'd never stopped loving Den. Angie drank to combat the emptiness of being trapped in a marriage with a man who did not love her in kind. She knew he was playing away with Jan Hammond, his bit of posh, and her pain was tangible. Disappointment stuck to her like Velcro.

In February 1986, Angie sat in the Queen Vic kitchen, stuffed handfuls of pills into her mouth and washed them down with gin.

It was brilliantly acted and utterly believable.

Anita Dobson quit *EastEnders* in 1988. Up until then, she made us care about the tragic figure of Angie Watts, her unrequited love for Den and her battles with the booze and the loathsome James Willmott-Brown. Angie finally left the Square in May of '88 to run a bar in Majorca, with the husband of her best friend.

She was truly a soap giant.

Leslie Grantham had also decided that he wanted to move on, but producer Julia Smith didn't want the programme to suffer the double blow of losing both of the Watts, its king and queen, at the same time. The solution to the problem was one of the soap's most complex and unrewarding exercises.

To keep Den onscreen for an extra year while letting him quit after a few months, they arranged for the character to be banged up in chokey for a year. This meant that a year's worth of scenes could be shot away from the Square in a fraction of the time the storyline would take to unfold. In order to keep viewers on Den's side, they made his crime a 'good' one – he torched the Dagmar wine bar in revenge for the rape of Ian Beale's mother Kathy by the yuppie bar's dastardly (and posh) owner Willmott-Brown. First Den got in way over his head with the soap's original criminal organisation, the Firm (not to be confused with Ethel Skinner and Dot Cotton, who were the Infirm). After he burnt the place to the ground, the Firm wanted to make Den take the blame and do the time for the crime. He refused and went on the run, but the pressure of heavies on his tail eventually convinced Den to turn himself in.

He was remanded in custody at Dickins Hill prison (actually shot at HMP Dartmoor), where his scenes with a small group of new criminal characters and Nick Cotton dragged on as a not entirely successful soap-within-a-soap for another five months.

But before he bowed out, Den was to return to one of the previous great subplots. Back in 1985, Michelle Fowler, 16-year-old friend of his adopted daughter Sharon 'Princess' Watts, found out she was pregnant. Who was the father? The soap had built up the tension expertly, putting several local low-rent Lotharios in the frame. Under suspicion were Andy the Yuppie, Ali Osman, Tony Carpenter and, of course, Dennis Watts. ('Chelle had had the hots for Kelvin Carpenter early doors, but soon realised older men were her thing.) Viewers were kept in the dark until October of that year, in an episode (number 66) written by Tony Holland and directed by Julia Smith where the father was revealed as Den. He'd knocked up his schoolgirl lover on the floor of the Queen Vic.

Over the next few months the canal bank became their meeting point – something that was to prove Dirty Den's undoing, when he was finally allowed to bow out on 23 February 1989. After escaping from custody, instead of legging it directly to the Costa del Crime, he met up with Michelle down at the canal bank for one last fond farewell.

It was a fatal mistake. He wasn't to know that the Firm had Michelle under surveillance. At the canal, 'Chelle poured out her heart to him, assuring him that she would wait for him to return and that one day they would be together with baby Vicki as a family.

20 million viewers watched their emotional goodbye and then gasped in horror as we saw Den gunned down by a villain carrying his handgun concealed in a bunch of daffodils. Den fell into the canal in what was intended by Tony Holland and Julia Smith to be his death scene. (Den actually hit the water in a tank, because the canal water was deemed unsafe.) However, BBC1 controller Jonathan Powell ordered that this final shot be cut from the episode when it screened – to leave the door open for Den to return at a future date.

Furious, Holland and Smith both had their names taken off that episode's credits in protest. Den's exit would be their last contribution to the show.

To viewers, cast and crew alike Dirty Den was dead. Which is how he remained for 14 years, until a new executive producer, Louise Berridge, decided to resurrect him.

It was a toss-up as to who was more desperate for this to work, Berridge or Leslie Grantham. It's true that Grantham has real screen presence, but he's basically very good at playing Leslie Grantham. It's also true that he'd made a number of decent shows since quitting the soap – that number being precisely two, *The Paradise Club* in 1989 and Sky One's *The Stretch* in 2000. He played a Den-like character in both and he teamed up with Anita 'Angie' Dobson for the latter. Coming back without her was like Punch turning up without Judy.

The cover story/explanation for his return (see 'Into the Noughties') was that Den had faked his own death before scarpering to Spain. But why did he never bother to let his loved ones know he was okay? It wasn't as if the Firm was still sniffing around the Square, they hadn't been heard of in years. It didn't make sense, but then, as I pointed out at the time, no soap has ever resurrected a key character without fatally damaging its credibility.

To add insult to injury, Berridge brought Dirty Den back as the gangland character he never was. Den was an adulterer; he was dodgy, a bit flash; he dealt in stolen goods and black-market booze. He ran a few errands for the local faces, but that was it. He was never that *bad*.

Yet to Louise Berridge he was her "new alpha male". (Grantham was pushing 60. He was more likely to be the new Alfie Garnett.) He made his grand comeback for a reported £200,000 a year on 29 September 2003, walking into Sharon's nightclub, Angie's Den, and greeting her with, "Hello, Princess." More than 16 million viewers watched his return – 62 per cent of the viewing public. And so the soap got on with building a family around him. They reunited him with his adopted daughter, Sharon, his real daughter, Vicki, and introduced him to a son Den didn't know he had, Dennis Rickman, with his inexhaustible supply of brown jumpers.

But Den was never the same. His storylines stank like Heather Trott's gusset after a two-hour karaoke session. He blackmailed Zoë Slater into bed – the smell of stale beer and Worthers Originals on his breath must have really got her going – and, because no one in Walford knows about contraception, managed to knock her up too. Zoë was then persuaded – ridiculously quickly, considering that she too was the product of rape – to have an abortion.

This wasn't the Den we knew. This wasn't just dirty, it was sad and sleazy. And when *The People* exposed Leslie Grantham's real-life involvement in an internet sex scandal, the writing was on the wall. (See 'Soap Babylon – Actors Behaving Badly'.) It might have been argued that the scandal merely coincided with the soap's ratings decline, and that the star wasn't directly to blame, but there was no way that the opinions Grantham expressed about the other cast members could be easily forgotten or forgiven.

The real man was dirtier than Den could ever be. For the BBC, the public disgrace and his clear contempt for his co-stars

– who duly sent him to Coventry on set – meant that Grantham had to go.

New executive producer Kathleen Hutchison decided to axe his character. Den was subsequently bludgeoned to death with a dog-shaped doorstop and his body buried in the Queen Vic's cellar. (See 'Into the Noughties'.) A stone-cold, hard-faced bitch had finally got the better of him.

But enough about Chrissie.

Grant and Phil Mitchell

The Mitchell brothers dominated the soap throughout the 1990s. I once jokingly likened Grant and Phil to "the cheeks of one hideous arse"; others compared them to the Weetabix TV advert skinheads. But there is no doubting their impact on the show or the enduring strength of their characters. The 'Bruvs' were macho, unpredictable and the lords of their manor – worthy successors to Den Watts. And their decade was a riot of passion, punch-ups, piss-ups and pain.

Monkey boy Ross Kemp seemed an unlikely hard man at first. Before joining the Square he was best known for his eye-popping roll in the Kellogg's Fruit & Fibre telly advert. (All together: "Apples, hazelnuts, sultanas, raisins, coconuts, bananas ...") But, as Grant Mitchell, Kemp would cast a giant shadow over Walford for a decade. He was that rare thing in the soap – a proper bloke.

At his best Grant was impulsive, impregnating various strumpets on the Queen Vic floor; at worst, he was plainly psychotic – when he was in a rage the Square would be full of low-flying coppers. Ex-Para Grant – or, as his mum called him, 'Gwant' – was so hard he probably performed his own caesarean birth with a Stanley knife. He certainly had a screw loose – he did try to rejoin the Army at one stage but failed the psychiatric tests – and yet Grant was a rock of testosterone in an ocean of wimps.

But he was vulnerable too; he showed his pain. The classic 'Sharongate' episode was his finest hour. Confronted by proof of wife Sharon's infidelity with his own screen brother, Kemp gave a performance of such power and conviction that it remains choking to this day.

Phil, played by Steve McFadden, was just as tough if not quite as volatile. McFadden's first appearance had been in the excellent Alan Clarke film *The Firm*, based on West Ham's notorious ICF hooligans. Phil has a quiet menace about him. He sighs constantly like a balloon deflating and struggles with his weight. Grant was let down by his women – he was married three times – but Phil's greatest love has always been the bottle. Kemp is one of the many who believe McFadden pulled off the "best portrayal of an alcoholic ever seen on British screens". It must help that he looks like the Michelin Man's fatter brother, but, unlike most drunks, even when he's on the sauce he can still get it up – in 2009, during his latest fall from the wagon, Phil managed to service Shirley Carter frequently, despite being as drunk as a thousand sailors on shore leave.

The Mitchell brothers made their first appearance in February 1990. They were the sons of a boxer, they ran the local garage, the Arches, and prided themselves on their toughness. Viewers loved them and the Bruvs rapidly began to dominate the show as effectively as the Watts family had done in the 1980s. They had a beautiful younger sister, Sam, who became larger and less beautiful after her head transplant, and a loyal mum who did the opposite. Their 1994 fall-out over Sharon – Grant's wife, Phil's lover – had been planned right from the start according to Tony Jordan, the soap's finest writer during this period. In the aftermath, when the brothers fought, 26 million viewers watched Grant smash Phil to a pulp. Jordan is rightly proud of 'Sharongate'.

Ross Kemp, a self-confessed "bit of an ugly pug", became an unlikely sex object off-screen, as his onscreen character married Tiffany Raymond and then bedded her mum, Louise, not to mention Mad Joe's mother, Lorraine Wicks. It was a testimony to the strength of his position on the soap that when Ross turned down a plotline – he was being lined up to rape Tiff at Christmas 1997, which would have been completely out of character – the producers listened.

When he did bow out, two years later, it was as the result of a falling out with Phil. It was supposed to be high drama, but Ian Hyland of the *Sunday Mirror* was one of many critics who found it farcical. He mocked the stunts, noting that Phil and Grant "ended up looking like two little kids playing on a building site" and concluding it was "hardly a fitting exit for Walford's dodgiest geezer since Den", rather than the "heart-wrenching farewell" it could have been. Grant Mitchell departed in 1999, taking his daughter Courtney off to Brazil. He would have been one of the few soap characters never to have 'jumped the shark' ... if he hadn't come back.

So where did the Mitchells go wrong?

In my opinion, the writers started mucking up Phil's character first way back in 1993 when they had him marry Nadia Borovac, an illegal immigrant – not the sort of behaviour you'd expect from an East End hard-nut. Years later, Steve McFadden told me, "When I got that storyline, I thought if I can make this cack work, I can make anything work. It was so stupid." His character had driven to Southampton for a day with Michelle; as McFadden recalls, "While I was having a coffee I met a Romanian refugee, and by the end of the week, I'd married her. Ludicrous."

Then they turned him into a grass – phoning up the cops anonymously to inform on various rivals – then a killer, then a gullible mug. They also subjected him to a series of wildly unsuitable women: you could believe in his fling with dangerous Annie Palmer and his falling for gorgeous sad-eyed Lisa Shaw, but his relationship with undercover cop/manicurist Kate Morton never had a whiff of reality about it. And what was he supposed to have seen in solicitor Stella Crawford? The pair had so little onscreen chemistry that they got engaged without ever managing to so much as kiss each other.

Somewhere along the line, the writers decided to turn him from a hard-nut into a hood and so Phil became an armed robber for a week, one of the few middle-aged villains who live with their mums. Phil's son Ben is another cruel prank played on the character by the writers: a weak, half-dead, bed-wetting, show-tune loving wimp of a boy who doesn't have an ounce of Mitchell DNA about him. But the biggest problem for Phil Mitchell occurred off-screen, when McFadden became embroiled in a lurid dogging scandal that made Leslie Grantham's antics seem almost tame. (See 'Soap Babylon – Actors Behaving Badly'.)

As to Grant, after a disappointing run of ITV drama appearances – including one show where he starred as a kind of monkey-boy barrister – it was perhaps inevitable that Ross Kemp would eventually agree to return to Walford again. And so the Bruvs screeched back into the Square in October 2005 – their differences (like the small matter of Phil nearly killing Grant in 1999, and Grant nearly killing Phil five years earlier) all forgotten. They were on a mission to save Peggy from plastic gangsters and, by extension, to revive the flagging soap.

"Hello Mum," Grant growled, arching his eyebrow as only he and Nookie Bear can do, before the credits rolled. Ratings shot up, and I have to admit even I cheered. But it couldn't ever be the same.

Grant was older, fatter and out of condition. He was also dressing like a security man at Heaven nightclub. Tony Jordan cleverly got the jibes in first in a self-mocking script, with one feller likening the Bruvs to Right Said Fred. Phil battered the bloke in a khazi for singing 'I'm Too Sexy' at him, but frankly the Freds should have sued. (Especially as Phil's version would be 'I'm Too Heavy for My Scales'.)

The Mitchells swiftly dominated the Square again with their head-cracking presence. Highlights included Grunt slinging unconvincing tough-guy Little Dennis Rickman all over the Vic. (Dennis: "I don't want to have to hurt you." Grunt: "Well that's hardly likely, is it?")

Three things didn't ring true, though: Grant's calm reaction when Sharon told him she'd aborted his child; Grant having had 'ferapy' (*leave it aht* – a bloke like Grant would no more see a shrink than he'd eat quiche or sleep with Pat Butcher – whoops, there I go, giving them ideas again!); and Phil being described as "the one with the brains". Eh? This is the same Phil Mitchell who married a bag lady, dated an undercover cop and killed a man by torching his own car lot? ...

In November 2005 it even dawned on Billy Mitchell that something didn't add up. Phil had walked free after being nicked for armed robbery, escaping from a prison van, assaulting three cops and going on the run for a year. Billy spoke for all of us when he asked, "Hang on a minute, how is Phil not in prison?"

"It's just one of life's little mysteries," mumbled Grant by way of reply. And that was the end of the matter.

Ross Kemp had only signed up to return for three weeks but his contract was hastily extended for another three months starting the following spring. After his original impact, however, the soap ran out of stories for him and Grant was saddled with an unlikely affair with Jane Collins, the future Mrs Ian Beale. His third wife, lying Brazilian Carla, never convinced and the most useful thing he did was take on Johnny Allen, although the episodes were poorly written. (See 'Into the Noughties'.) After he left in June 2006, soap bosses tried to resurrect the spirit of the Gruntster via the character of Sean Slater who was also ex-army, promiscuous and impetuous. Actor Rob Kalinsky even aped Ross Kemp's mannerisms but was never as convincing, although women viewers loved him.

(Stop press: the rumour mill claims that Ross will be returning to Walford again in time for Christmas 2009. I really wish he wouldn't ...)

Francis Aloysius Butcher

A truly brilliant character. Played by the cockney comic Mike Reid, Frank Butcher was a small-time wheeler-dealer and con-man in a trilby titfer who could charm the birds off the trees and the underwear off some of the least desirable birds in Albert Square. Being a genuine East Londoner, born in Hackney, Reid brought the soap some of the qualities it traditionally lacks – such as humour, realism, a credible accent and authentic sounding dialogue. Reid peppered the often lacklustre scripts with colourful phrases of his own, classics like:

"What are you, some kind of double yoker?"

"What do you take me for, some kind of pilchard?" (Alternatively: "What do you take me for, some kind of ice cream?")

"What am I, some kind of donut?"

Frank accurately accused Robbie Jackson's teenage gang of being "one wave short of an ocean", called wife Peggy "my little handbrake" and told many an idiot, "I'll tell ya what, pal, talk to me like that again and you're gonna get a dry slap." Where did he get these colourful phrases? We can only guess but, given the size of his ears, Mike could probably eavesdrop on every cockney in London.

He was marvellous, one of those characters who light up the screen. But Reidy – not being particularly charged with the Protestant work ethic – found the filming schedule overtaxing and periodically left the soap, returning only when he knew he'd be releasing a comedy video or DVD the following Christmas and needed to up his profile.

His character Frank's lifelong love for Fat Pat took some swallowing though (insert your own Mike Reid penis joke here). As Reidy once joked: "When Pat goes into a room, the mice jump up on chairs. The police issued nude pictures of her as part of their campaign to deter sex offenders. Last year on holiday she went for a dip in Loch Ness and the monster had to be put under sedation."

Inevitably, the soap decided to make Frank suffer from depression, putting a strain on Mike that had a similar effect in real life. He was a funny guy and the constant bombardment of joyless storylines made him at first despondent and then ill. But the show's executives rightly valued him and, in 1998, begged Reid to come back. He went in for a meeting with his agent, David Hahn, and told them he would come back only if he was guaranteed upbeat stories. The producers agreed and Frank Butcher sauntered back. Unfortunately, the agent didn't bother to get the promise put in writing, and Frank's first major story upon his return was running down Tiffany Mitchell in his car on New Year's Eve, killing her.

Not too surprisingly, he quit again in 2000, complaining of "nervous exhaustion". Overall, however, Frank Butcher remains one of the most convincing *EastEnders* characters. Even when he turned up at Pat's wearing nothing but a revolving bowtie ...

In November 2000 Peggy found out about his affair and that was it. He had to leave, he'd burnt so many bridges Blue Watch was on red alert. (If he'd stayed any longer, BT would have had to change Walford's dialling code to 0-0-0-Pat.)

In 2005, brilliant *Guardian* columnist Grace Dent accurately noted, "Britain adores Frank Butcher, associating him with a golden era of the Square, despite the fact he spent the best part of a decade mainly loitering around a car-yard with a beetroot face, wearing a sheepskin coat and golfing breeks, squeezing the soft nodule of skin between his eyes and yelling 'Ricccccccky! Get off my motors!' over and over again."

(Mike Reid was actually the second choice to play Frank Butcher, the role offered first to Derek 'Charlie Slater' Martin, who turned it down because he was committed to a second series of ITV's debt-collector drama *King & Castle*. Derek, who'd also been on the short list to play Dirty Den, tells me that he would have played Frank a lot differently to the comedian. "I would have been much more aggressive," he says. "If anyone had taken liberties with me or mine, I would have been after them. And you would have been stuffed for big ears jokes, Garry.")

Alfie Moon

Another of the all-time classic characters. I chart Alfie's decline elsewhere in this book, but Shane Richie gave the show a real boost when he joined in November 2002 and single-handedly kept it afloat during the barren days of 2004. Alfie had a good heart; he called Peggy 'the Duchess' and, despite spending three years banged up for credit card fraud, couldn't steal from her. Alfie will be remembered for his personalised West Ham top (Moon 6), the three-quarter-length leather coat he wore, no matter how hot it was, and for his witty catchphrase of "Shut up, you muppet!" He'll also be remembered for winning Sexiest Soap Male, despite persistently sporting a manky old dressing gown that many homeless people would have turned their noses up at.

Peggy Mitchell

I have to declare a special interest in Peggy. I campaigned for Barbara Windsor to join the soap's cast before the BBC signed her, inspiring Chris Evans to do the same on his radio show. Surely, I reasoned, the star so associated in the public memory for her groundbreaking, bra-busting roles in the *Carry On* films could only dispel the fog of misery hanging over the soap. So what did they do? They signed her up and cut off her breast! In 1999, Peggy became the first soap character to have a mastectomy. As potent symbols of Englishness go, this was like booking Trafalgar Square and demolishing Nelson's column.

Margaret Ann Mitchell did establish herself as a proper East End matriarch, however. She was staunchly loyal to her morally incontinent offspring and a firm advocate of 'fam'lee' values (which sometimes stretched to include Billy, the out-and-out runt of the extended Mitchell clan).

Bar, born in Bethnal Green, made Peggy a stronger, better-dressed character than her original incarnation. (Peggy had been played by the rather larger Jo Warne when we first saw her, for a three-month period in 1991.) She based Peg on women she'd seen in East End pubs "whose hair is great and their outfits more Walthamstow market ... they get it slightly wrong." She took some of Peggy's qualities from her own mum, Rose, a dressmaker who Bar describes as "an East End snob". "I saw her as much ballsier than they did," she says, "they wanted her to be this rather sad, vulnerable lady who spent all her time worrying about her children. And her clothes to begin with weren't right, they were too downmarket. They had to be flasher and more aspirational. Peggy is old school, she's tough and she doesn't take any crap from anyone. But she isn't perfect. She can be blinkered, especially when it comes to her family."

The actors who played her screen sons were delighted by Bar's arrival. "She personifies the East End," Ross Kemp told me. "It could only get better if Bob Hoskins turned up as my uncle." (If only!)

With the blessing of new soap boss Corinne Hollingworth, the character of Peggy Mitchell was toughened up and she took over the Queen Vic. The Mitchell clan became one of the central planks of the show, true soap royalty. Sadly, but inevitably, the writers then started chipping away at the character's credibility. There were ludicrous boyfriends (Fat Harry Slater – why?!), her logic-defying friendship with Pat, the woman who betrayed her trust and shagged her husband, and, most ridiculously of all, Peggy's 2009 transformation into Ma Barker. That March Peggy had entered local politics in a bid to cleanse Walford of sin, but at Easter she started behaving like Al Capone with a toothache, telling Phil to murder his uncle, and Peg's new husband Archie Mitchell (brother of her first husband, Eric). "End this nightmare once and for all," she said. "Kill 'im!" It was completely out of character. Even Violet Kray didn't order assassinations. Besides, what exactly had Archie *done* except make her dress her age?

Okay, he told a few pork pies with tragic unintended consequences; but Johnny Allen threatened her life, Frank Butcher broke her heart ... and Peggy never wanted to feed their gizzards to the lizards.

Similarly, Phil may have been an armed robber for a week in the 90s, but he had never been a murderer (not intentionally, at any rate). The resulting Wrong Good Friday saw Phil threaten to torture and top Archie. He turned down £50K to release him and then let him go (for nothing) after giving him a soaking ... In other words, he'd managed to piss off a vengeful millionaire with no scruples who'd think nothing of spending £5K on a professional killer. Nice one, Einstein.

No one as streetwise as Phil Mitchell would do this. But then no one remotely streetwise is involved in writing *EastEnders* ...

Appalling Pauline Fowler

Pauline Fowler, brilliantly played by Wendy Richard, was one of the stand-out characters of the soap. With her sour face, constant moaning and endless interfering, Pauline came to symbolise the worst elements of womanhood inside or outside of the East End. Critics queued up to pour abuse on the character: Pauline had "a face like a month of wet weekends", she was "the Boadicea of battle-axes", a hag who had "a voice that could curdle milk". Lucy Mangon in *The Guardian* called her "one of the oddest soap creations ever ... a character without humour, charisma or any redeeming features." And yet, right at the start of the soap, Pauline wasn't like that. She was actually quite likeable.

I'm sure I can remember her smiling – at least once ...

Julia Smith and Tony Holland wrote of her: "She's very conventional, and the salt of the earth. *Jolly*" – my emphasis – "and rounded. Someone you can get your arms round. She doesn't trust skinny people ..."

Pauline's descent into the bossy, permanently complaining Wicked Witch of Walford began in earnest after her Mum, old Lou Beale, popped her clogs at the end of July 1988. Almost immediately, Pauline seemed to adopt her joyless personality. She was the matriarch of the Fowler family now, and she would never be the same.

For her next few years Pauline seemed to be welded to her cardigan. But she had some magnificent moments, not least in 1993 when she had to 'crown' husband Arthur with a frying pan after finding out that he had been over the side with lonely divorcee Christine 'Hot-lips' Hewitt. She threw a TV set at him too.

Her greatest storylines included giving birth to Martin, her late baby, supporting Arthur when he had his mental breakdown, the fight for her grandchild Rebecca and her understandable war of attrition against her dozy, switch-hitting, sometimes straight, sometimes gay daughter-in-law Sonia.

Pauline's strengths were her stoicism, her loyalty and her fighting spirit; her weakness was her control-freak puppeteer approach to the family she claimed to love. Her husband couldn't have been more henpecked if he'd covered his head with corn and taken up residence in a chicken coop. Her children had to emigrate to escape her relentless interfering.

How did they ruin her? By making her too bloody miserable. In the end there was nothing to like about Fowler the Growler, so why should any viewer care about her? One observer noted how, "she became more of a sucking chest wound than the heart of the show". By this point, if she'd tried to smile her face would have been in traction till Christmas. In real life everyone related to her would have topped themselves.

Even the writers seemed to give up on Pauline, making her even more unpleasant by having her lie about having a tumour.

Biggest load of cobblers? Her unlikely second marriage to Joe Macer, who murdered her ... if you don't count the whole logic-defying HIV storyline and the endless string of customers in that poxy launderette.

Typical quote: "Shut up Arthur Fowler, no one interrupts Pauline Beale when she's in full flow!"

Dot Cotton, a.k.a. Dot Branning, a.k.a. Skeletor

Chain-smoking God-botherer Dot is a prudish busybody who has become one of the few joys of the often dreary soap and a fully-fledged national institution. Played brilliantly by June Brown, the first lady of the launderette has been likened to "a malnourished bird raised in city smog" and "Skeletor in a head-scarf", although she reminds me most of Albert Steptoe in drag. *Oh I say!*

Riddled with prejudices, Dot is the comic cornerstone of Walford, despite suffering the slings and arrows of a godless world for the last quarter of a century – most of them, it must be said, aimed at her by her godless son, Panto Nick, and her late, parasitical pickpocket husband, Cheatin' Charlie Cotton. Like Wendy Richard, June Brown had the integrity to quit the soap in 1993 when she thought that her character wasn't being written properly, but she was talked back in 1997 with assurances that Dot would return to the way she was, and should always be, portrayed. She's been there ever since, fag in hand, always ready to gossip or to cast aspersions.

Having been memorably paired with Ethel Skinner in the show's greatest ever comedy double act, in 2002 Dot married Jim Branning, played by the wonderful John Bardon, an equally accomplished comic actor. The duo became the best thing in the soap until John had a major stroke in 2007. But June Brown is so accomplished that drainpipe-thin Dot has risen above most of the setbacks suffered by other characters. The abortion back-story that the soap saddled her with never felt true, but the biggest flaw in her story is the boringly repetitive nature of her relationship with her son. (See 'The Best of the Worst'.)

Kat Slater, the tart with the heart from Planet Tango

Jesse Wallace was terrific as trashy, gobby Kathleen, the feistiest and most well-rounded (in every sense) member of the dysfunctional Slater family. Yes, she was a slapper – Kat had dropped more flies than a bug-zapper – but she had a warm heart, was loyal and genuinely loved by those around her. Kat, another fine Tony Jordan creation, was the last great soap incarnation of the tart-with-a-heart character, as exemplified by Elsie Tanner and Bet Lynch on *Coronation Street*.

Covered in slap – every day was Pancake Day for Kat – she paraded around Walford in her micro-skirts, fake tan and leopard print tops, sleeping with whoever took her fancy and hollering, "Oi! What you looking at?" at everyone else. *The Guardian*'s Grace Dent called her "a frightening Cockney woman in clown make-up", but she wore her heart on her sleeve and was easy to love. Kat was made for that amiable rogue Alfie Moon, but viewers had to suffer several months of nonsense involving Andy Hunter, the plastic gangster who offered to clear Alfie's £7,000 debt to him in exchange for a night in the sack with her (shades of *Indecent Proposal*).

This storyline never made sense, however. Firstly, because Kat would have dropped her drawers for a cider and black, and secondly because she was never exactly Demi Moore. No disrespect, but while *Corrie*'s Suranne 'Karen McDonald' Jones oozed animal magnetism, Kat looked more like comedy actor Terry Scott in a Ronnie Wood wig. She piled on the pounds too, becoming Fat Kat – or, as she would certainly have been dubbed in the real East End, 'Big Pussy'.

When Andy made damn sure that Alfie saw the tape of him having sex with Kat, the pair split and Kat went on the missing list. She was heartbroken and drinking heavily, but the idiot Slater family didn't seem at all bothered. Moronic Little Mo Morgan reckoned, "She's probably sunning herself in Lanzarote," while Big Mo, never likely to win *Mastermind* herself, agreed. "That's right!" she said. "Or she'll have found herself some rich feller!"

In fact, Kat had ended up in prison for 'assaulting a policeman' – possibly the writer's little joke; in real life, Jesse had been stitched up by the red-tops and her copper boyfriend, Dave Morgan.

After an unconvincing relationship with Kat's simpleton sister, Little Moan (a twice-raped, wife-beaten dimwit with whom he had zero in common), Alfie was eventually reconciled with Kathleen and for once they had a happy ending – leaving Walford together on Christmas Day 2005, to follow Alfie's dream of touring the USA. They haven't been seen since – but, judging by Kat's boat-race, their future's bright, their future's orange.

What never rang true about Kat? There was Andy Hunter's indecent proposal; Kat nearly marrying him; and her relationship with shy, middleclass local GP Anthony Trueman. (And why wasn't he struck off about that, by the way?)

The Best of the Worst

Cindy Beale, Queen of Tarts

Cindy Beale was the soap's most shameless slapper. She was like the Pillsbury Doughboy – always ready for a poke. Cindy cheated on Ian with both of his half-brothers, having never really loved her husband; she only married him to try and make Simon Wicks jealous (Cindy always did like big wicks) – her son Steven was Simon's, although she pretended he was Ian's, and the revelation of her betrayal broke Ian's hard little heart.

When Cindy returned to the Square, in 1992, she tried to make a go of their marriage and had Ian's twins, but she couldn't help herself. Before long, Matt the swimming pool lifeguard was getting busy down her deep end, and then it was the turn of Simon's brother, tragic Lothario David Wicks, to slip into the saddle. Their steamy affair raged for a year before Ian's private dick uncovered it.

In 1996, Cindy hired a hitman to top her weasel-like husband, kidnapped her own kids and fled to Italy. A year later, Ian and the Mitchell bruvvas kidnapped them back, so Cindy returned to Walford with yet another feller. This time around Ian turned the tables on her and had her nicked for attempted murder. Pregnant for the fourth time, Cindy Beale died in November 1998, after giving birth behind bars, and was cremated – going from Cindy to cinders.

Nearly nine years later, her 'ghost' was apparently haunting

Albert Square. Ian thought he could smell her perfume, a heady blend of gin and other men. He found writing on a mirror saying, "Ian, I'm back." Would it be ectoplasm next? I speculated that if he started finding mysterious damp patches around the house, it wouldn't be the first time.

(The real explanation was nothing so exciting. 'Cindy' was actually Steven Beale manipulating his sister Lucy.)

Ian Beale

Greasy spoon boss and occasional gay wedding coordinator, Beale 'the Squeal' is a longstanding joke. He is a spineless creep; a bore and a tightwad; a rat in human form, and a user who lives by the sweat of his frau.

The soap's sopping wet writers have always had it in for Ian because he wants to make a few bob and better himself, and for them that's the cardinal sin. The extent of the Beale business empire is uncertain and is generally subject to change: at one stage he had two fish and chip shops, the café and a bric-a-brac store, which everyone forgot about. He got unstuck when he moved into property. Now Ian only owns one chip shop, a share of the caff and another part share of the Masoods' curry business. Duncan Bannatyne he ain't.

Sneaky, snivelling and untrustworthy, Beale has suffered at the hands of drunken bully Phil Mitchell and blackmailing brass Janine Butcher. But he was at his most wretched back in August 2006, when he hired dishy Dawn Swann to pose as his wife Jane. By the end of the week he was begging the original Jane – the real love cheat – not to leave him in a pathetic high-pitched whine. It was typical Beale. Only he could have a glamorous pretend-wife he wasn't shagging, a mistress he didn't even try to get on a mattress.

Beale's business endeavours to date: the café, a knitting company (!?), mobile disco DJ, loan shark, catering firm, fish shop, bric-a-brac shop, flat construction and renovation, mobile food van ... and he's still pinching pennies in godforsaken Walford.

In 2008 Ian ludicrously pretended to have a butler and wore his grandad's war medals to try and impress some posh bird he didn't know – all at home in his East London hovel! But Beale's least likely storyline remains his romance with beautiful Melanie Healey – he even tricked her into marrying him on New Year's Eve 1999. It was the lowest point in a life spent stooping lower than a worm's belly: lying to Mel that his daughter Lucy was dying, in order to get her down the aisle. The marriage lasted until midnight. But at least you could understand why he went to all that trouble – the butler made no sense at all.

Strangest fact: Ian celebrated his 18th birthday in 1988. Two years later, in 1990, he had his 21st. The soap claimed this was a deliberate mistake because they needed Ian to be older for the storylines they had in store.

Yeah, 'cos that one year makes such a crucial difference...

Kathy Beale

Hair by Wurzel Gummidge, voice by Arthur Mullard, played by Gillian Taylforth. Kath – of Kath's caff – will always be remembered more for her off-screen antics than her onscreen storylines. Gillian's big mistake was to sue *The Sun* for libel in January 1994, after they ran a story claiming she had performed a 'sexual act' on boyfriend Geoff Knights in their Range Rover on an M25 slip-road. It became a high-profile legal case. Taylforth maintained that Knights had suffered an acute attack of pancreatitis and that she was merely massaging his stomach to soothe his pain. The Old Bill said she was giving him a blowjob. During the court case, *The Sun* entered as evidence a 35-minute home video of Gillian "suggestively posing with a large sausage" and "graphically simulating masturbation with a wine bottle". She boasted to the camera, "I give very good head." The jury returned a ten-to-two majority verdict in favour of *The Sun*, after which poor Gillian collapsed and had to be whisked off in an ambulance (which sounds like something she might have done to Knights).

For a while, even fellow actors would jokingly ask for a G & T – meaning not gin and tonic but a 'Gillian Taylforth', i.e. fellatio.

Taylforth's stormy relationship kept her in the news. In November 2006, Knights was arrested and slung in the cells for 18 hours after allegedly punching her over a sofa. The actress required three stitches in her head. Just over two years later, Knights was nicked again for allegedly assaulting Darren Welsh, the ex-boyfriend of their daughter Jessica; Welsh was arrested in turn for allegedly assaulting Jessica.

Taylforth and Knights are now said to have split after 23 tempestuous years together.

Mark Fowler

This mono-brow market man had more hair in his eyebrows than Grant ever had on his head. His incredible range of emotions encompassed every facial expression between frowning and frowning really hard, before he was fatally nobbled by his unlikely and never fully explained HIV storyline.

Mark Fowler was a great character to begin with, a leather-jacketed delinquent chock full of attitude. He was dangerous and sexy, the nearest E20 would ever get to an Elvis. That was when he was played by David Scarboro – a great teen actor with piercing James Dean eyes. Scarboro tragically committed suicide, throwing himself off of Beachy Head in 1988, aged just 20, unable to cope with the pressures of working on the show and then being sacked from it; he also hated the aggressive press coverage that the high-profile role brought with it. (Scarboro was 'allowed to go' after he refused to play Mark as a racist, and entered a psychiatric unit soon after.) In 1990, he was replaced by popular Todd Carty, a children's TV favourite. The HIV storyline came a year later, restricting and overshadowing everything to do with the character that followed.

Todd Carty's finest moment? Playing Tucker Jenkins in *Grange Hill*.

Nasty Nick Cotton

Or Panto Nick, as I prefer to call him, due to the complete absence of dramatic realism in John Altman's cartoon-like performance.

Nick is a charmless murderer – he killed Reg Cox, the pensioner who was found in the show's very first episode, and Eddie Royal, the Queen Vic publican, in 1991 – but his biggest problem is terminal plot-loop syndrome. The most rotten of the Cottons lives life like *Groundhog Day* in a grubby leather jacket. It's always the same story with him: Nick comes back, tries to con his ma, gets outsmarted, leaves, comes back, tries to con his ma ... You wouldn't mind so much if Dot had anything worth nicking, but if she died then what would he actually inherit? A few bob, Grandad Jim's clapped-out Austin Traveller and a hovel in an undesirable neighborhood. Nick is a ridiculous played-out character, a hammy monolithic oaf who has about as much credibility as a Heather Trott storyline. The one interesting thing about him is his neck tattoo which, despite being clearly visible when he returned around Christmastime 2008, has since become a smudge.

Grandad Jim Branning

A wonderful character played by the accomplished comic actor John Bardon (whose one-man Max Miller show was one of the great joys of Channel 4's opening night schedule). Grandad Jim married Dot Cotton and John became a perfect comedy foil for June Brown. Sadly, their double act was cut short when the great man suffered a major stroke in 2007. He has been back on screen a couple of times, but it made for uncomfortable viewing – a stricken old man played by a likeable actor we know to have had a stroke himself.

Jim is another EastEnder who has undergone a complete character rewrite. When he first appeared in 1996, he was an out-and-out racist who totally opposed daughter Carol's marriage to the very black Alan Jackson. He took one look at Alan and sniffed, "You're not marrying that, are yer?"

Soap bosses could never put up with a likeable soap character so shockingly prejudiced, so in his second incarnation Jim was cleansed of bigotry and became best buddies with Patrick Trueman (as well as helping Dot spirit illegal immigrant and prostitute Anya away from the authorities). As this allowed Jim to become a soap regular and a reliable source of joy, it's a hard decision to object to, but it's still more a case of liberal wish fulfilment than of the soap's watchword, 'reality'.

According to John though, "West Indian ladies of a certain age love Jim Branning. Every time they see me in the street they fall about laughing. But it is a bit of a struggle getting round Tesco's now." Jim also touched a chord with kids, who wrote to John asking if he'd be their grandad as their real one had died. "It's heartbreaking," he told me.

Daftest plot: apart from his character transplant, the grim and unlikely back-story that Jim and his mates had once locked his son Max, then 13, in a coffin overnight. Runner-up: Jim at the lap-dancing club.

Fat Pat Butcher

One of the most fearsome female characters in the soap, Pat was seen by the show's creators as "a vicious shrew". A hard-faced, morally incontinent ex-prostitute, Pat was brought in to "toughen the soap up" and "add a new hardness to the atmosphere". She whored herself again and got Mary the Punk to do the same. She was jailed for killing an unfortunate pedestrian while driving drunk. She also stole Frank Butcher from Peggy Mitchell, and yet, insanely, the two women remain bosom buddies. (Remind me again why we're supposed to *like* her.)

Even Pam St Clement, the wonderful actress who plays her, was aghast. She told the *Walford Gazette* (an *EastEnders* fanzine, not the fictional local paper): "I remember saying to Julia Smith, 'How can this character be watchable long-term? She's so full of venom, she hates everybody except Angie Watts and maybe Roly the poodle.'"

Pat's various jobs outside of streetwalking – or, in her case, street-waddling – have included pub landlady, manager of the bookies, cab operator and Easter Island statue. (I may have dreamt that last one.) And the most nonsensical storyline attached to her – other than the fact that Walford's menfolk find her irresistible – came in the 1990s when Pat, East London's biggest tart, insisted on Kathy as a chaperone before she would go on a date with the earnest, harmless Roy Evans.

(Poor impotent Roy couldn't get it up for her. Now that I *do* believe. He used to sit in the caff and weep every time anyone said, "Knob of butter?")

As Pam St Clement admits, "Early on Pat's biography was changed quite heavily by one particular script editor to make her more consumer friendly, to blend into the community and help the audience root for her relationship with Frank." Frankly (no pun intended), it had to be. The original Fat Pat was so hard-faced and stony of heart, you could imagine Les Dawson saying, "Strong men faint in the street as Pat goes by; if she's facing into the wind, weather vanes turn round in self-defence."

Paul Trueman

A good boy turned bad whose heart was in the right place. As actor Gary Beadle tells me: "*EastEnders* were quite ground-breaking with Paul Trueman. He was the first black character who wasn't a doctor or a lawyer. They allowed him to be politically incorrect. But there were reasons for him being bad. He had a mum who didn't love him and a dad who wasn't his real father; he had a baby taken away from him and a girlfriend who died from drugs.

"That's why all the grans want to take me home, they understand why Paul was like he was and they want to make it right."

Paul was topped by the Walford Firm in revenge for him grassing up Andy Hunter to the Filth. He would have done a runner but realised his family would suffer if he did. Paul left the Square in a taxi – driven by Hunter's hitman. His last words were, "Make it quick, mate." (Which, by way of coincidence, is what Janine said when she slept with Ian Beale.)

Billy Mitchell

Played by the best actor in the show, genuine East Londoner Perry Fenwick, but weighed down with dreary storylines apparently garnered from the Samaritans' late-night log. Poor Billy is the least fortunate man alive. If he slept with a nun he'd catch a dose. Black cats believe that it's unlucky to cross his path. Abused at a children's home, his first wife, Little Mo, was raped and refused to abort the child; his second wife had a Down Syndrome baby – Petal – and left him. Billy has lost his home, his family and his self-respect. If he fell asleep with a fag in his hand someone would light it.

Dr Legg

Harold Legg, the soap's first GP, had mystical powers as he would often disappear for months on end. Played by Leonard Fenton, Dr Legg was one of the show's surprisingly few Jewish characters. The doc always talked softly, so as not to wake up the squirrels kipping above his eyes, and was forced to go when it was felt he was making the soap too eyebrow. (See *Doctors* in 'Random *EastEnders* Irritations'.)

Big Mo Harris

Scarier than Vinnie Jones, gobbier than Mrs Merton, Mo makes the Slater men look feminine. And next to her, they are.

When she first appeared in the show, I launched a Mo Must Go campaign, dubbing her a "Big Daddy look-alike" and complaining, "the last time we saw a face this hard on TV it was in a documentary on Mount Everest." But nine years on Mo has become one of my favourites: a rare ray of sunshine in the increasingly bizarre soap world. She is a female Del Boy, which can only be a good thing, with a string of little-seen contacts such as Fat Elvis, Chinese Walter and Dagenham Dave (who, bafflingly, wasn't from Dagenham at all). She is 73, with a face like a squashed cabbage, and has more of a sex-life than any of the show's teenagers. What's her secret? Less K-Y Jelly and more Poli-Grip, I shouldn't wonder, but it doesn't really bear thinking about.

Sonia bloody Jackson

Teetotal/alcoholic/straight/bisexual/lesbian/unemployed student/nurse Sonia was one of the soap's most mixed-up creations. Allegedly a bright girl, the teenage Sonia was actually so dumb she didn't even realise she was pregnant until she gave birth to Chloe (the daughter also known as Rebecca) in October 2000. A plain girl, she won the heart of Jamie Mitchell (how, exactly?) before marrying Martin Fowler, the lanky moron who killed him.

While working as a nurse, Sonia became a part-time lesbian with the rather stern Naomi (who looked like *Doctor Who*'s Face of Boe – although for Martin she was more a face you'd boo). She then reunited with Martin and fell out permanently and tediously with his mum, Appalling Pauline.

Talking about Pauline's depression, Sonia told Martin, "There ain't nothing wrong with your mother that a smack in the mouth wouldn't fix." What a great advert for the struggling NHS! But still, I'd like to see her kind of treatment catch on at Walford General: "Chronic fatigue? A Chinese burn will sort you out, pal! Stomach ulcer? Take two slaps and a kick in the goolies …"

Nurse Sonia did eventually slap her mother-in-law on the day she died, and was briefly suspected of murder and arrested. Sadly, no miscarriage of justice took place and Sonia was released. In her final episode, in 2007, she was inexplicably reunited with the lanky moron and their daughter. The potless family has apparently been touring the USA ever since.

Michelle Fowler

A great character, as played by Susan Tully, Michelle didn't seem to have a single ounce of her mother's DNA in her. 'Chelle was impregnated by Dirty Den, her best friend's dad, when she was still a 16-year-old schoolgirl. But she didn't moan about it, like Pauline would have done, she just got on with her life – even taking one of her school exams in the maternity ward. Despite her unfortunate affliction (Michelle suffered from permanent PMS – Pizza Mush Syndrome), she attracted the attentions of George 'Lofty' Holloway, the Square's likeable misfit – jilting him at the altar in 1986, only to finally relent and marry him before breaking his heart by aborting their child. Michelle hated Grant Mitchell for the way he treated her best mate Sharon, and in 1995 the pair had a blazing row which ended up with them shagging in the Queen Vic. Nine months later, after emigrating to Alabama, she gave birth to Mark Junior – the son the Gruntster never knew he had. The kid is now 13 and is surely destined to turn up in Albert Square sometime soon ...

Johnny Allen

Arguably the most rounded gangster ever seen in Albert Square, and (at first) easily the most believable. Johnny was played with softly-spoken authority by East London-born actor Billy Murray. He was brought in by executive producer Kathleen Hutchinson specifically to counter the years of plastic gangsters, but a change of execs put the kibosh on his entire story arc. Walford-born and bred, businessman Johnny was a former villain whose criminal past had made him rich and had successfully built up his own company, J.A. Enterprises. Johnny returned to E20 in 2005, with his daughter Ruby, after his wife Stephanie and daughter Scarlet died in an arson attack by rival gangsters. He bought the Square's nightclub, then called Angie's Den, which he renamed Scarlet's in his late daughter's honour. Johnny's character would be ruined by a sloppy timeline (see 'Big Swinging Cobblers') and a ludicrously unlikely final encounter with the Mitchell bruvs in their 'Get Johnny Week', March 2006 (see 'Into the Noughties').

His finest moment? Throwing Andy Hunter off a South London flyover.

Bianca Jackson

Only two manmade structures are visible from space. One is the Great Wall of China; the other is Bianca Jackson's gob. Best known for her appalling dress sense and for shouting, "Rickayyyyy!" at her on-off feller Fick Rick Butcher in a voice that could shatter cut glass.

Tiffany Raymond

A true dark-eyed, raven-haired soap beauty, played by Martine McCutcheon. In any chart of 1990s soap babes, it was always Tiff at the top. Just don't mention the moustache ...

Stacey Slater

Or Tiff Mark III – if we count Janine as Mark II – with extra attitude. Brunette sex-pot Stacey was introduced in 2004 as chunky Charlie's great-niece. She had a string of great storylines, including betraying boyfriend Bradley Branning with his bad dad Max, and was generally acknowledged to be one of the most interesting characters in the soap. So what on earth persuaded the producers to make her bipolar like her mum, Mad Jean, who is the soap's least interesting and most irritating character? Bisexual I could have coped with. Bionic I might have enjoyed. But bipolar? There's no way back from this. Stacey is ruined ...

Jamie Mitchell

Good-looking second cousin to the Mitchell bruvs, who was ruined by having his character rewritten – when Jamie went from tearaway to trainee social worker overnight, *The Guardian* commented on his new "Zen-like" wisdom. *The Sun* was more interested in the urgent need to get his eyes tested, 'cos Jamie turned down Zoe Slater for Sonia bloody Jackson.

Big Dan Sullivan

One of the few Walford hard-men who looked the part, Big Dan was played by movie star and former Millwall bruiser Craig Fairbrass. Naturally, they ruined him by having Dan get chinned by Frank Butcher.

Sharon '40' Watts

Pouting Miss Piggy look-alike, Den and Angie's adopted bizarrely orange daughter and spoilt 'princess', Sharon did her best acting with her incredibly mobile eyebrows. Highs: Sharongate (see 'The Nineties – The Mitchell Era'). Biggest cobblers: it was a soap given that Sharon was infertile throughout the 1990s, while shagging the über-male Mitchell bruvs. Then, at Christmas 2005, they made her pregnant by Dennis Rickman, just to crank up the misery when he was murdered a week later. Career low: Letitia Dean mistaking breathy whispering for acting.

15 of the Most Ridiculous Storylines Ever

1) **The strange case of Gita Kapoor.** In October 1997 Gita took off to stay at her sister's with her daughter, little Chinchilla. (Sorry, I mean Shamilla. A chinchilla is a horrible little hairy-faced thing. I was thinking of Gita.) She was due to return the following January. Husband Sanjay went to meet them at the station but they never arrived. After a few days of worry he alerted the police, who became convinced that stall-owner Sanjay was behind their disappearance. It was a harrowing nightmare for him. His family had vanished; Gita had made no attempt to contact him; Walford Plod suspected him of murder. He was taken in for questioning and accused of the dastardly deed. No charges were brought, but can you imagine how that felt? His whole world was falling apart.

But then, mercifully, the cops forgot about the missing persons. And so did Sanjay. He went back to his normal life and didn't even mention them for months. No one did ... until July 1998, when Gita returned from Birmingham, clutching another man's baby in her arms. When her poor, long-suffering husband asked why she hadn't even phoned him to let him know they were alright, Gita looked him in the eye and replied, "Oh Sanjay, don't be so unreasonable!"

She'd deserted him. She'd had another bloke's kid. She'd done a bunk, leaving him to worry about what had happened to his family and to be suspected of their murder. Yet *he* was being unreasonable. And they've got the cheek to call this 'reality' ...

2) **Peggy and the Paedo.** Creepy Harry Slater was the secret father of his niece Kat Slater's secret daughter, Zoe, having molested Kat when she was 14. He was played by the alcoholic Michael Elphick, whose best work was decades behind him – *Enders* booked him after seeing his picture in a copy of *Spotlight* that was years out of date. They expected the handsome star of *Boon*; instead they got the Elephant Man: a dribbling, blubbery beast of a bloke who looked like something Picasso forgot to paint.

In August 2001, beer monster Harry and Peggy Mitchell went 'back for coffee'. How could she? I mean, physically – how *could* she?

She would have had to go on top, for sure, probably backwards to avoid asphyxiation from his alcohol-sodden breathing. (H's breath could rotate windmills on a landscape painting.) Clothed, he resembled half a ton of condemned veal in a Hawaiian shirt; unclothed doesn't bear thinking about. His face looked like he spent his spare time bobbing for pancake rolls.

But, incredibly, the soap persisted with the storyline that glamorous Peggy would fall for the bloated gut-bucket. "He ain't heavy, he's Peggy's fella," laughed the press, and Barbara Windsor was understandably furious. Yet onscreen Peggy nearly married the booze-sodden hefferlump ... until brother Charlie ran him out of Walford. Harry kept trying to contact Zoe, much to her disgust, but his death by heart attack was the best 18th birthday present a girl could wish for. (In real life, widower Elphick was a quiet, kindly man. Sadly, he drank himself to death in 2002.)

3) **Mark Fowler's HIV.** At the beginning of the 90s, the soap decided to launch an educational storyline about AIDS and associated social prejudices. They wanted one major character to contract HIV and so, inevitably, they chose a heterosexual market trader who wasn't an intravenous drug user. As a delinquent teenager Mark Fowler, later recast as Todd Carty, had been one of the soap's livelier characters, and Todd was much loved for his previous incarnation as Peter 'Tucker' Jenkins in the kids' show *Grange Hill*.

But Mark suffered because the soap wanted to push the then-fashionable, but clearly wrongheaded, we-are-all-equally-at-risk line. (The same false logic that panicked the Tory government into sending matronly spinsters leaflets on the dangers of vigorous anal sex.) He found out he was infected in 1991 and informed the family on Boxing Day – Merry Christmas everybody! We had to assume that his ex-girlfriend Gill had infected him, but how she contracted it was never made clear. Gill subsequently developed full-blown AIDS and died, in typical *Enders* style, the day after he married her.

It would be easy to dismiss this as another example of the soap pushing its middleclass liberal right-on fantasies, but in many ways the Fowler AIDS storyline was touching and quite miraculous. For Mark was the only person ever to be HIV positive for ten years and still put on weight.

4) **Backwards Day.** People think I'm making this one up, but I swear it happened. In 1992, when AIDS sufferer Gill was dying, the entire cast decided to do everything backwards for a day. This insane episode ended with half of 'em doing a reverse conga out of the Vic and round the Square.

5) **Plain Girls, Fit Boys.** Being primarily aimed at women, the soap periodically serves up unlikely romantic storylines – the most absurd being Jamie Mitchell's lust for Sonia Jackson. He fell for her first in 2000 and was still sniffing around her two years later. Why? What did he see in this unattractive girl who, as well as being chunky, was so dim that she didn't even realise she was pregnant until the moment she gave birth? Jamie (played by Jack Ryder) was handsome and bright; in the later stages of his role he was almost Zen-like in his wisdom. So what explained the attraction? On screen he said he liked Sonia because she made him laugh. To which I remarked that Sonia had better hope that Ken Dodd never plays Walford, as he's not only funnier but he's prettier too.

Sonia gave birth to Martin Fowler's baby, Chloe, while she was going out with Jamie. He didn't mind. She gave the baby away, but then kidnapped her afterwards. Jamie proposed to her, but it all went tits-up when he slept with Zoe Slater, one of the prettiest women in the Square, though naturally he preferred Sonia to Zoe ...

In the summer of 2002, Jamie made another play for her, allowing Sonia to give him the brush-off – yeah, right – in favour of Gus the road sweeper. They did get engaged again, when Sonia nursed Jamie back to health after Phil had battered him. But Jamie died shortly afterwards, run down by Martin Fowler, on – you'll never guess when?! – Christmas Day. Naturally, Sonia married Martin.

So what was the secret of her appeal? I did ask one of the show's leading writers to explain it, but he just looked blank for 30 seconds and shrugged his shoulders. My own theory involves her years as a musician. If she could blow anything else as well as she blew that trumpet, then *(cut! – Ed)* ...

6) In 2006, Pauline Fowler married Joe Macer, a man she didn't appear to like, had no sexual feelings for and later admitted she had never loved. She didn't even take his name. Their salsa-based relationship rang about as true as a politician's promise. Wendy Richard cited the absurd plot development as one of the reasons she quit the show. The only explanation for their wedding was that the soap's desperate bosses needed an onscreen event to coincide with its 21st anniversary.

7) That wasn't the least likely Walford wedding though. In 1993, hard-nut Phil Mitchell married Nadia, a Romanian bag lady.

8) **Ronny Ferreira's kidney saga.** The least gripping long-running storyline in the soap's history wasn't entirely the writers' fault. At the end of 2003 actor Dalip Tahil, who played Elvis-loving father Dan Ferreira, had to be axed when it emerged that he'd been employed without a proper work permit. He was actually marched off the *EastEnders* set by immigration officials, just as the Ferreiras were on the verge of their most dramatic moment

ever. Writer Tony Jordan told me that Dan was going to be exposed as a horrible, oppressive bully and his family was scheduled to bump him off. "It was all scripted," said Jordan wistfully. "They were going to bury him in a shallow grave. And then Dalip got bloody deported."

This left a major hole in the soap's plotlines, with around 50 episodes to rewrite on the hurry-up. So the big murder story had to be replaced with the lame tale of Ronny needing a kidney transplant from Tariq, who turned out to be his half-brother (and consequently Kareena's incestuous boyfriend). As Tony Jordan admitted, "It was like watching paint dry. 'Can I have your kidney?' 'No. Oh go on then.' It was dreadful." And yet the dreary saga dragged on for months in 2004, lasting longer than some soap marriages. It was to drama what Kryptonite is to Superman, with an unprecedented backlash from viewers and critics alike. Jordan acknowledged that the Ferreiras were "the least successful characters I created," in a later interview with the *Daily Mirror*. "Through no fault of the actors." The characters never recovered, and the Ferreira family was written out, leaving the Square in February 2005.

9) **Frank Butcher's 'funeral'.** In 2002, the great Frank Butcher faked his own funeral in Spain. The first time *EastEnders* went to the Costas, in the 1990s, it was terrific because it captured the genuine spirit of cockneys abroad. But, sadly, when the soap went back in January 2002 it left all sense of reality behind. I'm not sure who packed Peggy's luggage for the trip, but I suspect that it might have been Mary Poppins. She arrived with two cases, the smaller of which contained enough clothes to stock a medium-sized branch of Marks and Sparks. But this was just a minor quibble, when everything else about that week's shows was of award-winning quality ... if there'd been an award going for Worst Episode Ever.

Leaving aside such trivial mysteries as how Frank faked his own death, who signed the death certificate, whose body was in the coffin (reality went right down the gurgler there – how could any undertaker have fitted his ears into a box that flat?) and who invited Peggy over in the first place, there was a variety of reasons as to why the plot stank like the changing rooms on *Fat Club*:

- Peggy, stranded on the outskirts of Torremolinos, stumbled into a bar and met Alistair, who ran a golf club in faraway Marbella – the very same golf club that 'Fairdeal Frank' and Rula Lenska were trying to turn over.
- Coincidence? You ain't seen nothing yet. Peg learned that her daughter Sam was in Marbella and so she moved in with Alistair. Who should be living next door? That's right, Rula and Frank, who was now calling himself 'Neville'.
- Sam famously needed a nose job, but came back four inches taller with a completely reconstructed boat race.
- The golf club owned a splendid chunk of prime real estate between the course and the beach. They'd been turning down offers for it for years, yet they agreed to flog it to Rula in less time than it takes to neck a glass of sangria, without so much as discussing a price.
- Alistair had been in the CID for 21 years, but he didn't clock that Neville was in fact Frank ... even though his picture was splashed all over Torremolinos, disguised only by an astro-turf moustache and a Frankie Howerd wig. (In fairness, that was the only bit that I believed.) "Do you think we're some kind of pilchards?" I asked the BBC. This storyline was so farfetched it made *Footballers' Wives* seem like *cinema vérité*.

10) **Jane Beale, comedienne.** Ian Beale's wife Jane had never been a funny woman, yet suddenly, in October 2008, she became an overnight sensation as a stand-up comedienne (see also Tamwar Masood). Adopting the stage name of 'Mrs Beale', Jane went to a comedy club and performed an act consisting of a load of sub-Jo Brand, man-hating garbage. To wit: "Men are rubbish generally, some guy I went out with fell asleep while we were having sex." (Ever thought that you might be a lousy lay, love?) Naturally the main target for her humour was husband Ian. "Imagine a cross between Forrest Gump and Mr. Bean," she quipped. (Why? Ian's

not dim and neither is he childlike.) The writer threw in some stolen old jokes – "Why is it so hard to find a sensitive, good-looking man? I'll tell you why, because they've already got boyfriends!"; "Mr Beale thought a g-spot was an exhibition centre in Manchester." Be still, my aching sides! The storyline was half-inched from the US sitcom *Dream On* (a 1991 episode entitled 'So Funny I Forgot to Laugh'). Ian not too unreasonably objected to being ridiculed in front of all his neighbours, and Jane agreed to quit comedy in order to save their unlikely marriage. She has never been funny since, nor has she attempted to be.

11) **Nasty Nick and the Café of Doom.** June 2009 saw a shocking disaster – Bianca's new coat! (That naff pink and leopard print jacket would give Trinny and Susanah palpitations.) In contrast, Panto Nick's café lock-in was as scary as *Scooby Doo*, if not quite as realistic … Nick Cotton had come back to kill his ma, Dot (again), but his evil daughter Dotty doped his drink instead. Too drugged to drive, Nick still managed to hold four adults at bay with a chair leg, snarling, "siddown," repeatedly and smashing plates. It was a case of, "One false move and the crockery gets it." Scary! Outside, an angry Max, worried about his daughters, couldn't break through the flimsy café door that was 50 per cent glass. But still Dot wouldn't believe it. "My Nick wouldn't do that," she insisted. Eh? He's a convicted double murderer and he's tried to top her twice – he first poisoned her as long ago as 1990! The hostages finally escaped, leaving Nick overwhelmed by smoke. Brave Bradley Branning went in to save him, failed and stood staring at the gas, waiting for it to blow. Brad survived that huge explosion without a single burn, proving my theory that the red-faced bore is actually the Human Torch. The only one at risk from those flames was Nick, as he's solid wood.

(Incidentally, doped driver Nick careened into Mad Jean Slater's flower stall. By the time she was next seen onscreen the incident was forgotten and the stall had been miraculously repaired.)

12) Blossom Jackson, the Chinese-looking mother of Alan

Jackson, emigrated to Israel with Felix Kawalski, the barber, in 1997, a man she hadn't even kissed.

13) **Can you dig it? Sam Mitchell excavates Den's body.** After Dennis Watts had been killed for the second time, in February 2005, he was concreted under the floor of the Queen Vic cellar. Seven months later, Soppy Sam, a woman more renowned for her mascara than her muscles, dug up his moldering corpse with a pickaxe, reaching the body in as little time as it took Miss Piggy (Sharon) to marry her Kermit (doomed Dennis). We could only assume that either a) writer Sarah Phelps has never swung a pickaxe against concrete in her life, or b) the workmen who laid that floor are due a visit from *Rogue Traders*. But the strange case of the wedding-day stiff galvanised the Walford Old Bill into action. They spoke to Fat Pat, Stinky Miller, Plain Jane, Alfie, Ian, Martin, Mo ... the only person they didn't try to interview was Johnny Allen, the friendly neighbourhood gangster/killer who had vanished, but the plod didn't even enquire about his whereabouts. Soap police are never much cop, but this lot made Ian Blair look competent. They had Sam at the station as their chief suspect in a murder case, but didn't think to seal off her flat and search it. They talked to her for three whole days without realising she was too thick to mastermind a meringue, let alone a murder.

14) **He flies through the air with the greatest of ease.** The death of Joe Macer seemed to challenge the accepted rules of science. On 26 January 2007, lovable Walford grandad Jim Branning shoved Pauline's husband Joe with such force that he was propelled through a closed window, did a 90-degree turn and then shot sideways over the wall, and the pavement, to plummet to his death on a market stall. It was an incredible feat of strength and dexterity, the likes of which very few professional acrobats could have pulled off. But it gets better. This happened on the Friday. By Monday morning, the *Walford Gazette* was able to run the headline: 'Killer's Death, Verdict: Accident'. So over the weekend there had been a police investigation, a post-mortem *and* an

inquest. Who was running the operation, Jack Bauer? I'd hate to see the overtime bill for that little lot.

15) **Manhunt!** August 2007 saw the biggest Walford manhunt since Kat Slater's hen night. Poor Patrick Trueman had been brutally coshed in the Minute Mart. He was left with a fractured skull and a small blood clot (pronounced 'claat'). He would have been more badly hurt if the wads of cash he keeps in his hat hadn't softened the blow. Immediately, Sean 'Psycho' Slater went on the run. Despite his head-start and military training, Sean's idea of evading capture was to circle Albert Square without ever attempting to leave the area, spending most of his time lurking by walls. *Doh!* It was like the worst-ever episode of *The Fugitive*. Kevin crept up on him. Gus bumped into him. The only people who couldn't find him were the Walford plod, Keystone Division. The cops only stumbled onto him when Ronnie Mitchell realised that Sean was holed up in the Queen Vic cellar. (Well, it was either there, the allotment sheds or the swings. My tip at the time was that the best place to hide on BBC1 was *The One Show* – because nobody was watching that.)

The Best of *EastEnders*

In fairness, here is my list of the soap's all-time greatest scenes:

1) Den Watts serves Angie with her divorce papers, 1986.

2) The Sharongate tapes, 1994.

3) Arthur Fowler's breakdown, 1986

4) In a particularly dramatic scene, evil rapist Uncle Harry – secretly Zoe's father – asks her to go and work in his bar in Spain. A horrified Kat tells Zoe she can't go. They have a shouting match in the rain. Zoe: "You can't tell me what to do, you ain't my muvva!" Kat: "Yes I am." October 2001.

5) Carol Jackson discovers her lover Dan has also bedded her unfeasibly loud and ginger daughter Bianca, 1999. What a glutton for punishment!

6) Fat Pat and Peggy Mitchell's first face-slap exchange: "You *caaw!*" 1998.

7) Dot Cotton helps Ethel Skinner die, 2000.

8) Phil Mitchell is gunned down by girlfriend Lisa Shaw in the soap's moving homage to *Dallas*.

9) Lauren Branning wraps up a DVD showing her dad, Max, snogging Stacey – his son's fiancée. The family watch in horror. Christmas Day 2005.

10) Dirty Den shot by a bunch of daffs. 23 February 1989.

11) And then there's ... Nope, sorry. That's it.

The Eighties – The Glory Years

1985

19 February: the soap started as it meant to go on, with a corpse – in this case the murdered Reg Cox. The poor sod had a lucky escape. Incredibly, we were later to look back on this era of alcoholism, infidelity and drug abuse as 'the good old days'. In that glorious first year, Pauline Fowler found out she was pregnant (with Martin, not an incubus), and her schoolgirl daughter Michelle wasn't far behind her. She refused to reveal that Dirty Den, dad of her best mate Sharon, had knocked her up; 'Chelle had wanted a shoulder to cry on, Den had given her something harder – on the floor of the Queen Vic. Her brother Mark had a different head back then and hung about with Nick Cotton. On the day Panto Nick was taken in for questioning over poor Reg, Mark legged it to Southend.

Also this year: tragedy struck Turkish-Cypriot Ali Osman and wife Sue, when their baby perished in a cot death; single mum Mary Smith, aka Mary the Punk, became a stripper; a fresh-faced Ian Beale, bullied for his interest in cooking, briefly took up boxing, and Saeed Jeffery, original owner of the First Till Last grocery store, was visiting ladies of the night. (Maybe the shop name should have been Thirst For Lust.) The poor sod was desperate because his Bengali wife Naima wouldn't consummate their arranged marriage. When she did acquiesce, their happiness was short-lived. Dot Cotton grassed him up and their marriage went tits up. Which was exactly how he liked it, apparently. Spurned Saeed started making obscene phone calls to yuppie cutie Debbie Wilkins. Naima divorced him and he buggered off to Bangladesh.

1986

The year was dominated by Angie and Den's marital troubles. Den had Jan Hammond, his bit of posh; a distraught Angie was enjoying Gordon (or at least his gin) and Jack (Daniel's). As a cry for help, she downed a bottle of sleeping pills with a gin chaser (what Pete Doherty might consider a cheeky livener). She did shag male nurse, Andy the Yuppie, but she was always drawn back to the true love of her life, booze.

Ange did get her own back on Den by claiming she had only six months to live. Unfortunately she blabbed about this monumental porkie, Den overheard, and served the divorce papers on Christmas Day – arguably the soap's finest hour.

Elsewhere, Michelle hooked up with Lofty Holloway, the unemployable asthmatic, and gave birth to baby Vicki. She jilted Lofty at the altar but married him quietly a bit later. The cost of her first non-wedding proved the undoing of her dad, Arthur Fowler. He dipped into the Christmas club money and then faked a burglary to cover his tracks, but he cracked under pressure and began his descent into depression and mental illness. Bill Treacher's acting was riveting.

What else? Glaswegian nurse Andy O'Brien was knocked down and killed while pushing a child clear from the path of a lorry. And a dreadful new evil arrived in the Square: Fat Pat. Oh, and the gangsters of the Firm made their debut too...

Also this year, Sharon made a disastrous short-lived attempt at a pop career, fronting The Banned, and Lofty, the lanky streak of piss, started working as a kiss-ogram. And that wasn't the most far-fetched story of the year – in fact it was quite credible compared to Pauline Fowler winning a Glamorous Granny contest.

1987

The year that scandalised Fleet Street, because of the Gay Kiss between Colin Russell and Barry Clark. Actually it was more of a peck, but the papers went into overdrive. 'East-Benders!' screamed *The Sun*. I was more bothered by how unlikely they were as a couple. Barry was a barely legal barrow-boy, untidy, carefree and working class; Colin, who was nearly twice his age, was a rather anal graphic deigner. They were divided by age, class, attitude and manners, so how come they were ever a couple? It was the soap equivalent of Patsy from *Ab Fab* shacking up with Waynetta Slob.

The war of attrition between Den and Angie continued. She went to work for ex-army yuppie James Wilmott-Browne in the Dagmar wine bar, which became a huge success – at the Vic's expense.

The criminal 'Firm' decided the best way for Den to reimburse them for various favours was running errands to Morocco and a little light jury-nobbling. Elsewhere, Lofty and Michelle's marriage was falling apart, Arthur was 'horse-pitalised' with depression, Rod the Roadie joined the cast – a hapless hippy who always looked like a pile of dirty washing – and so did Donna, who was Kathy Beale's daughter by her terrible teenage rape ordeal, although we didn't know it yet.

1987 was also the year of the 'Walford Attacker'. He nearly killed Fat Pat. Better luck next time, mate!

1988

Not a great year for Kathy Beale – or anyone. Poor Kaff – of Kaff's caff – the nicest woman in Walford, had the worst time of all though. First she was sacked by Den Watts, then her daughter Donna revealed her true identity and found that she was as unwelcome as she'd been unwanted, and finally James Wilmott-Browne raped her – and the local bobby thought it was all her fault. Happy days…

Dirty Den burnt down the Dagmar in revenge for this shocking behaviour. Donna became a junkie whore and lived in the then fashionable Albert Square squat. Michelle aborted Lofty's baby; he found out and jogged on. Gay Colin got multiple sclerosis. Angie left for Spain and Den gave himself up to the Filth, when he realised the Firm were going to bump him off – so sparking the bizarre prison subplot that ran for months.

So much gloom, so much despondency ... but at least there was some happy news. The great Frank Butcher turned up, followed by his sprogs Fick Rick and Dismal Diane. Pretty soon he was running the Vic with *Patttttt* ...

1989

The end of an era as Den was 'killed' – apparently gunned down by a bunch of daffodils. The year's other big story was the love triangle involving Cindy the Slapper, Ian Beale and Simon Wicks; Cindy was dating Ian but had Wicksy's baby.

Elsewhere, the loathsome Willmott-Browne was tricked into confessing Kath's rape and was banged up, but Kath and Pete's marriage disintegrated. (Peter Beale wasn't a sensitive man or a bright one, often it was hard to tell where he stopped and the vegetables on his stall started.) Miss Piggy, a.k.a. Sharon '40' Watts, became a shop-o-holic. Appalling Pauline had a hysterectomy. And married Ali Osman was trying to bed every woman in the Square – he would have shagged a frog if it stopped hopping.

Also this year: Frank and *Patttt* had a big old cockney wedding, complete with a totter's horsedrawn carriage and a pearly king. Before long the Butchers had bought the B&B and Frank had opened the car lot, but it wasn't all good news. First, Fick Rick fell in with a racist gang and then Frank's five-year-old daughter Janine tuned up – a lying, bedwetting, sleepwalking, self-harming, lying thief. And, as the years progressed, these turned out to be her good points.

There was a sea-change in the show's mood this year, too. Old bosses Holland and Smith were replaced by Mike Gibbon, who tried to shoe-horn more laughs into it. Misguidedly, he went for slapstick rather than humour that grew organically out of the characters. This period notably included Arthur Fowler's appearance on fictional TV game show *Cat & Mouse*. For the previous four years, Arthur had shown all the mental agility of the cabbages on his allotment; now, suddenly, we were meant to believe he had enough general knowledge at his fingertips to make Bamber Gascoigne look like a turnip.

The new producer's other tricks were:

- To half-inch characters from other soaps – brassy Northerner Julie was a Bet Lynch clone; not-so-clever Trevor was Benny from *Crossroads*; an excess of kids – take a bow, *Neighbours*. I waited in vain for Texan oilman R. U. Joken to mosey into town and buy up the launderette.
- To recycle the soap's own past triumphs with Sharon and Wicksy rewritten as Angie and Den, right down to Wicksy getting another woman pregnant on the Queen Vic floor.

Mr Gibbon did not last long.

Criminal Records:
The Curse of Soap Pop

One of the earliest reasons to dislike *EastEnders* was the numerous pop spin-offs from the soap, some of which troubled the charts. (But not, it should be noted, Peter 'Pete Beale' Dean's overlooked 1986 classic 'Can't Get a Ticket for the World Cup'.) Wicksy actor Nick Berry notched up a Number One that same year with 'Every Loser Wins', and Martine 'Tiffany Mitchell' McCutcheon did the same in 1999, topping the charts with the dirge-like 'Perfect Moment'.

(She went on to dent the Top Ten twice more with 'I've Got You' and 'Talking in Your Sleep'. Her debut album, *You, Me and Us*, made Number Two in the UK Albums Chart. A follow-up album, *Wishing*, mercifully peaked at 25, while the third one bombed – it reached Number 55 – and her recording contract was duly axed.)

Other foul by-products of the soap-pop hybrid include:

- Anita Dobson's 'Anyone Can Fall in Love' (Number Four in 1986) – a wretched, ear-rotting, brain-curdling ditty sung to the *EastEnders* theme tune.
- Sid 'Ricky Butcher' Owen scoring with a karaoke cover of Sugar Minott's feel-good reggae hit 'Good Thing Going', which peaked at Number 14 in 1990. (A follow-up duet with Kele Le Roc flopped, and an album was recorded but thankfully never released.)
- Aidan 'Sean Maguire' Brosnan getting to Number 12 in

1996 with 'Good Day'. (It was a bloody good day when he stopped singing.)

- One later track by an *EastEnders* star that never saw the light of day was 'The Jacobs Song', recorded by Bobby Davro posing as Joe Pasquale. It was a song about testicles – 'Jacob's Crackers' being cockney rhyming slang for 'knackers'.

Tony Holland and Julia Smith were inadvertently responsible for the pox of poor pop caused by the cast's many dismal attempts to dent the charts. In 1986, they decided to create an Albert Square pop group to illustrate the perils of a career in the music business, but later acknowledged that the storyline had lacked all credibility.

Most of the soap's teenagers were roped in – Sharon Watts, Ian Beale, Kelvin Carpenter and Simon Wicks – and new characters were created, including the ludicrous Harry Reynolds, a humorless student-Marxist type who looked like Rik from *The Young Ones*' more obnoxious younger brother, and Wicksy's guitarist mate Eddie Hunter, a Butlin's Redcoat.

Wicksy and Eddie had started the band off-screen, but Simon's debt problems scuppered the project. When he'd got himself straight he reformed it as Dog Market with Eddie, Harry and the three Walford regulars; Wicksy played keyboards, Ian Beale drummed and the others sang. Dirty Den banned them from the Vic when their amps fused the electrics, and after that they changed their name to The Banned.

Scowling middleclass Harry owned all the instruments. He wanted the group to be a right-on agit-prop project, which would illustrate "decay in capitalist society". The song he wrote included the classic lines, "Are you slave or master, them or us? / Brick or alabaster, car or bus? / Have you blown your giro, us or them? / Fountain pen or biro, mice or men?" Tom Robinson, eat yer heart out!

Wicksy was more interested in chart success. When the band preferred his song 'Something Outa Nothing', a furious Harry denounced him as a closet Radio Two listener. In the row that followed, Wicksy told the rest of them they had to choose between him and Harry. As Harry owned the means of (noise) production, they sided with him and Wicksy quit. Unfortunately for The Banned, Harry, the poor man's Arthur Scargill, decide to sabotage their subsequent performance at a talent contest for reasons that are too obscure to bother repeating.

Wicksy's dire solo ballad, 'Every Loser Wins' (actually written by Simon May), became a genuine chart-topper; while The Banned's song 'Something Outa Nothing' was released by Letitia Dean and Paul Medford and peaked in the real world at Number 12. In 2004, it was voted the ninth worst record ever released by a soap star – begging the question, how bad do you have to be to be voted worst? *The Guardian* called it "an acne-scarred song of no merit whatsoever", which, on reflection, was putting it mildly.

Onscreen The Banned turned against Harry, who was last seen in October 1986; but the soap didn't kill off the pop storyline immediately. Sharon became interested in Mod, went to see a band called The Old Bill in Camden (probably based on real-life combo Makin' Time, who played secret gigs under that name) and started to wear a pork pie hat – not a good look with a perm.

EastEnders producers and writers used to frequent the Bush hotel at Shepherd's Bush, West London, where DJs Tony Class and Paul Hallam ran various Mod nights. The Bush was next door to the old BBC theatre; future Ender Phil Daniels used to drink in there too. Class recalls: "The writers were always in the Bush, they drank in the front bar regularly, that's where I got to meet them, Julia Smith and Tony Holland. We used to converse quite a lot about the storylines. The Mod storyline was stopped because they got hold of a copy of a Mod fanzine which was depicting violence and drug-taking and the scriptwriters didn't want their teenage characters to be associated with that sort of thing at the time."

Paul Hallam confirms this. "They were talking about The Banned continuing as a Mod band but the drugs and violence around the scene put them off; after they read that fanzine they lost all interest."

Tony Class adds: "The scriptwriters didn't see any violence at the Bush, but they did see some interesting video clips" – a reference to the porn films he used to show on a Monday.

(*Possibly the finest* EastEnders-*influenced song ever recorded was the punk anthem 'Grant Mitchell' by the Gonads, as featured on TV's* Top Ten Hardest Men *– but I would say that, I wrote it. See also 'Ska-Enders', featuring Francine Lewis impersonating all the most famous female soap stars over a cheeky retread of their theme tune.*)

All the Small Things

We'll get around soon enough to the big clangers and mysteries that have dogged the soap since before some of the cast started dogging. First though, let's consider some of the small questions of continuity, credibility and commonsense that make watching *EastEnders* such a chore.

Producers, writers, press officers and other toadying sycophants always maintain that the show 'reflects real life', but a number of simple issues conspire to undermine this conceit.

For starters, where do they all sleep?

At one stage eight Slaters were living in one three-bedroom house – or as they'd say, 'arhse – and not one of them shared a bedroom ... except when dirty Uncle Harry was about. In 2008 the same pokey hole housed Charlie, Big Mo, Stacey, Jean (Stacey's mad, drunk, lice-riddled muvva), Sean and Danielle, all of whom kipped alone.

The mystery of Walford's sleeping arrangements continues to bug me to this day. As I write, in 2009, Fat Pat's three-bedroom 'arhse is home to Pat, Bianca, Whitney, Fick Rick, Tiffany, Morgan and Liam. As Pat, Bianca and Whit all have their own rooms, you might assume that Rick and the two boys share the sofa – except they don't. So where do they kip? (There is no loft extension. I've looked. The only house in Albert Square with a converted loft is number 45.)

It's the same at the Queen Vic. There are currently seven occupants, none of whom share a room. Count them: Phil, Peggy, Roxy, Ronnie, Ben, Billy and Jay. Yet the pub has no more than three bedrooms. You're tempted to conclude that the Vic has been built using the same BBC technology that created Doctor Who's Tardis.

The only other explanation is that the walls of the buildings are elasticated – but once again, just for you, dear reader, I've been down to the set and checked. I can tell you that the exteriors of the houses are fibreglass.

And so the anomaly stands: the number of occupants exceeds the number of available beds by a factor of nearly two to one. If this was 'reality', then the whole of Albert Square would be Tent City … (as opposed to just the tentpole in Billy's bed every morning).

Where do they get their dosh?

At the start of 2007, I became intrigued by the mystery of Max Branning's stream of income. In the previous few months he'd bought cars, a £500 laptop, a beauty salon, endless bottles of champagne, expensive earrings and quality necklaces, MP3 players … He was also splashing out an awful lot of dough on five-star hotel rooms.

How could he afford it?

His every 'business meeting' at the time was a cover for shagging his son's fiancée, Stacey Slater. He even set her up in a love nest. The man is a walking cash machine!

We're told that Jimmy Somerville-lookalike Max is in insurance, but his actual job seems to involve looking at his laptop every now and then in the caff or the pub. Nice work if you can get it. In 2009, with the world's economy in meltdown, Moneybags Max is still splashing cash around like an MP on expenses. (I've long suspected that he is the secret owner of a magic beanstalk.)

The working arrangements of Bradley Branning, Max's permanently frowning and equally ginger son, are almost as puzzling. Early on, blushing Brad was said to have a 'high-powered' City job. He hardly ever went into the office, and took days off at will – once he stayed home just to mind a guinea pig – yet it never seemed to impede his progress. He was made employee of the month, got pay rises, promotion and the offer of a transfer to gay Paree.

He's fallen on hard times since and is now a property salesman. (Good luck with that!) But the commitments of the job hardly ever seem to intrude on his real occupation, which is to hang around the Square in a whistle all day long, getting humiliated by unsuitable women.

The realities of inner London prices never intrude much into E20. When Shirley Carter – a.k.a. the Terrahawk – first arrived she lived alone, paying for a two-bedroom flat on cleaner's wages, while still affording to drink like Shane MacGowan on a pub-crawl challenge. The credit crunch has yet to affect her boozing habits.

Money is of small concerns to Walfordians. Whopping cheques are routinely torn up if they have been written out by a 'wrong 'un' (e.g. Harry Slater, Max Branning or Archie Mitchell). Phil Mitchell once ludicrously sold his half share of the Queen Vic to Big Dan Sullivan for a fiver. (Yes, that's £5 sterling.)

In 2009, the Masoods were up to their eyes in debt and on the verge of bankruptcy one week, having sunk every penny they had into their business. (Mr M being the world's first postman-caterer.) Yet somehow, by April, his fragrant wife Zainab was urging her husband to invest £35,000 in property. Where he had suddenly acquired a spare £35 large was never explained – but then why get bogged down in reality, my friends?

Changing places

As with money, so with mortgages. No one has any trouble moving instantly in Walford. The actual business of conveyance and property chains troubles them not one jot. The funniest example was when the Ferreiras left; they just upped sticks and went – all five of them squashed into one tiny four-seater Toyota.

It was the tightest squeeze since Kylie Minogue's corset. They must have all been John Lennon fans too, because they had no possessions at all. Imagine ...

All of their worldly goods were packed up in just a couple of cases in the boot. Yep, two suitcases. My missus takes more than that on a weekend break, but Kareena had nothing at all. She hadn't been intending to go and left with just the clothes she was standing in. She didn't even take a change of drawers or anything.

Isn't that just like every woman you've ever met?

The Ferreiras had to go because of the mix-up over Johnny Allen's three stolen motors – he was so angry about it that, after they went, he never ever mentioned either the Ferreiras or the cars again.

The family and their dismal storylines were subject to much abuse from critics and soap fans alike, but, in all fairness, they were economic miracle workers. In May 2004 they were homeless and broke. They sold their red van and, with the takings, went out and bought a flat, a car lot, three taxis, which they taxed and insured, and bucket-loads of celebratory beer. Scoff if you must, but if these guys had been running the country the world recession would have passed Britain by.

It's the same when it comes to buying businesses. In February 2004 Ian Beale bought the caff overnight, without any apparent need of a contract. Isn't it amazing that, whenever anyone turns up looking for a place to live, someone will always pipe up with, "What about the flat over the salon/chip shop/Minute Mart etc?" that by some miracle just happens to be unoccupied, available and easily affordable.

* Stop press: in June 2009 it emerged that lesbian nurse Naomi Julien still owned a one-third share of the house Minty and Garry live in – 3a Albert Square – even though she'd moved out in May 2007. What a strange and magical world these writers live in, where low-paid nurses with no other source of income can retain part ownership of a Walford property while presumably paying either rent or a mortgage elsewhere.

(Don't be misled by the address either. 3a Albert Square may sound like a flat, but it's still got three bedrooms – remember, none of the residents share.)

Changing faces

Head transplants are an unavoidable part of soaps, often with rather plain children ruthlessly replaced by better looking teens. Peter Beale was the last kid so transformed in 2006, but the most extreme example is Janine Butcher, who, when young, was played for three years by a dark-skinned child (actress Alexia Demetriou) who was clearly as Mediterranean as Harry Enfield's Stavros.

The most famous transformation was Peggy Mitchell. Peggy first appeared in 1991, when she was played by a fierce-looking chunky actress called Jo Warne. She returned three years later, at least one foot shorter and five stone lighter, in the rather more agreeable shape of Barbara Windsor. Bar went on to become the matriarch of the Square. Poor Jo was last seen playing Mrs Bobbins in *Bodger & Badger*.

In April 2004, the soap entertained us with Fat Pat and Big Mo's past. You could tell it was April Fool's Day, because the young Pat looked like the blonde one out of Bananarama. There was no Robert de Niro waiting for her though, just Mo's brother Stan. He got out of the Scrubs and told today's Pat that she was "as lovely as ever", which just goes to show how 15 years of porridge can addle your brain. The young Mo was a foot taller than she is now and her eyes were a different colour.

Changing personalities

When Grandad Jim arrived in the Square, he was a small-minded racist bigot who hated the fact that his daughter Carol had married a black man, Alan Jackson. In his later incarnation, Jim became a cuddly Bob Marley fan whose best mate was ska-loving Patrick Trueman, from Trinidad.

A similar miraculous transformation happened to Minty Petersen – who went from being a ruthless slum landlord menacing Janine to a loveable but unworldly dimwit. In 2007, a mortgage inspector had to explain the concept of buying a house to him; in 2008, onetime hard-headed Rachman-ite Minty married the large and undesirable Heather Trott, not realising she would expect him to sleep with her on their wedding night.

Then there's the strange case of Alfie Moon. When he first hit the Square, Alfie was a silver-tongued wide-boy who could have charmed the drawers off a nun. He talked Martin Fowler into giving him free fruit and Fick Ricky Butcher into buying his breakfast. He had the presence of mind to convince Peggy he was the pub's agency manager and gave Martin advice on how to conduct his love life. Alfie was brilliant, an archetypal cheeky chappy with the gift of the gab, the Artful Dodger grown up.

It couldn't last.

Alfie ended up such a tongue-tied dunce that, within a couple of years, he couldn't even talk Little Moan into postponing a dinner date, leading to a 'hilarious' two-meal comedy moment. (It wasn't the first time Alfie had struggled with two puddings. He often got stuck talking to Pat and Mo.) When he first came to bed Kat, the formerly resourceful man of the world spent an entire episode trying to acquire a condom.

Why don't the women shop?

Unlike any woman you've ever met, Walford 'Richards' seem oddly averse to shopping expeditions. There is the occasional talk of going 'up west', but no self-respecting East London lady would waste her time in the tourist traps of Regent Street or Knightsbridge, or lug her purchases around on the tube, when she could be heading over to Lakeside shopping centre in West Thurrock, Essex, or down to Bluewater in Greenhithe, Kent, to fill her boots at Primark and TK Max. Both mega-malls are just a trouble-free 20/25-minute drive from the Blackwall Tunnel, close to where the soap is supposed to be set.

(Come to think of it, they never seem to do weekly shops at the supermarket either.)

Whither Walford Town FC?

Walford Town Football Club has been neglected for quite a while now. They only seem to play one game every 11 years, and have never regained the giddy heights of 1993, when talented young Irish footballer Aidan Brosnan (Sean Maguire) was tempted over as an apprentice. True to form, Aidan didn't go on to achieve success on the pitch, marry a WAG and party on Krystal; instead, like so many talented young footballers, he got dragged down into stories about homelessness, drug abuse and attempted suicide. (On Christmas Day, naturally. Cheers!)

To replace Walford Town, in 2008 the Queen Vic regulars launched their own pub team: Real Walford. They only ever played on a Thursday afternoon, only had three matches and then everyone forgot about them. And their best player was Roxy Mitchell! Still, it was nice to see her on her feet for 90 minutes...

Who uses a launderette in 2009?

Pretty much everyone in Walford, including relatively well-off types like the Brannings. Of course, the reason the show's bosses keep it on is that it provides an additional meeting point for the Square's wretched inhabitants, but it's hardly in keeping with the soap's watchword of 'reality'. Meanwhile, the DVD rental shop – with its extraordinary range of French film titles – has bitten the dust.

Gangsters

The tradition of local villainy stretches back to 'the Firm' – with Brad Williams as their man in the Square in the 1980s. Peggy dated local gangster George Palmer in the late 90s, and then Steve Owen became an unconvincing villain. The soap's obsession with gangsters of the plastic variety dominated the middle years of the Noughties. By 2005 it seemed that everyone in Walford who wasn't legitimately self-employed or signing on was either a gangster or a murderer, or they were working for gangsters or murderers. It was like Chicago in the 1930s. This was the era of Jack Dalton and Andy Hunter, when even airhead bimbo Sam Mitchell – played by Kim 'Daffy Duck' Medcalf –

turned into a kind of peroxide Ronnie Kray, ordering Billy to burn down Den's club. At the height of this nonsense Hunter started a protection racket and targeted Alfie's bric-a-brac stall (total value of stock: £9.99).

Jack Dalton was due to be played by the great Alan Ford of *Lock, Stock* fame. Instead, in 2003, the bosses decided that the fearsome head of the Firm should be portrayed by Hywel Bennett ... better known as Shelley, from the long-running ITV sitcom of the same name. A fine actor, no doubt, but for millions of viewers he would always be the witty but slothful James Shelley. (In his favour, Dalton did order Spencer Moon to be beaten up.)

The only thoroughly convincing gangster in recent years was Johnny Allen, played by Billy Murray. Johnny was half-gangster, half-Samaritan. St Johnny the Psychopath dispensed jobs, doormen and housework tips in between murders. Like the Krays of popular mythology, he could top a wrong 'un one week (he pushed Andy Hunter off a flyover) and be kind to old ladies the next. This led to criticism that the soap was glamorising crime, which is understandable when Walford has never had a decent, street-smart cop to represent the forces of law and order.

But no one should have worried. Inevitably, the writers nobbled Johnny with unconvincing storylines, a bizarre fascination with Fat Pat (the human space hopper) and, as detailed elsewhere, an insane timeline. His downfall was unintentionally farcical: not only did Johnny suddenly become a secret alcoholic, but the pink elephant he could see wobbling up his hallway turned out to be Phil Mitchell. As Johnny was safely holed up behind his steel-plated office door, with two hostile Mitchells outside, his drippy daughter Ruby ludicrously cut off the phone, their one link to the outside world, and started smashing vodka bottles. She then waltzed out, leaving the door open for Flabby Phil, while she settled down for scones with his pop-eyed bruv.

Billy Murray must have squirmed every time his character got rewritten. We had to believe that strict disciplinarian Johnny would be pushed around by his sulky, spoilt-brat daughter; that he'd give up liberty and lifestyle to keep Ruby (un)happy; that he'd employ a loopy loser like Danny Moon as his minder ... And don't get me started on that pink pullover.

The scripting was like bad kids' TV. Later, when a skip fell on Phil's car, I half-expected him to slide out of the vehicle completely flat, like a cartoon character, and shake himself back to normal. In 2009, the writers even had the hitherto respectable Peggy Mitchell demanding 'hits'.

More minor mysteries

- Why are there steps down to the Vic cellar, when its backdoor is on the same street level as the bar? And how many inner London pubs could have an unlocked cellar accessible from the street without being robbed on a daily basis?

- The allotments have moved. They used to be a bus ride away, now they are a short walk from the Square. How did that happen? Perhaps the area's been redesigned by the people behind the mobile island on *Lost*.

- Where's the church? Walfordians never seem to use the same church twice. The one where Alfie disrupted Kat's wedding to Andy, the plastic gangster, was not the same as the one where Frank married Peggy, which wasn't the same church as where baby Amy was christened this year ... they have more places of worship than the Vatican City, except, uniquely for East London, there's no visible mosque. And all the churches seem to be situated in leafy suburbia.

- Vicki Fowler's mutating accent: Michelle's brat-like daughter Victoria was played by three different actresses but, when she came back in 2003, Scarlett Johnson took over the role with a particularly unconvincing US accent – until Vicki went to Europe for a couple of weeks and came back speaking in middleclass English tones, going from Kelly Osbourne to Felicity Kendall overnight. I think the technical term for where she ended up is 'mid-Atlantic', which is where I hope they eventually find the body.

- Daytime nightclubs: what time did Angie's Den open, exactly? It was the only nightclub in London that was regularly banged out at teatime, and the E20 was just the same. The E stood for earache, 20 is the most punters they ever had at one time ... and also the minimum price of a round. (It was actually called the E20 because you'd need to take twenty Es to find it believable.)

- What's the deal with the Queen Vic's vanishing pool table? Is it collapsible? It disappears for months on end, just like Dr. Legg used to.

- Mrs Masood's now defunct post office is the only one I've ever seen in London with no security window, and yet by happy coincidence it was one of the few places in Walford that was never ever robbed.

- Where do they cook the food that's sold in the Vic? And who the heck prepares it?

- Remember Marge Green? She went on a world cruise in 1990 and never came back. Did she go by rowing boat? Who was the captain, John Darwin? No one ever mentioned Marjorie again, not even her dear friends Dot and Ethel Skinner or her pack of Brownies. (Marge was Brown Owl to the Walford Brownies, a storyline that ended up with the Beeb having to make a public apology for misrepresenting the movement.) In truth producers felt that Marge, played by the late great Patty Coombs, was a comic character and as such had no place in the BBC's grand homage to relentless misery. And I suppose 'Marge Green' does sound like something you'd find in Keith Miller's fridge.

- Toilet facilities: Ian Beale's café didn't have a khazi until 2008, when one mysteriously materialised just so Ian could get hilariously locked in it. (Laugh? You won't start!) In a clear breach of small business requirements, Phil Mitchell's garage hasn't got a bog either. We know this because, in 2009, Phil got locked in overnight and had to use a bucket. Shame he didn't dump the contents over the writers' heads. (Incidentally, when the café blew up in 2009, Nick escaped through a staff door that had never been seen before. Ally

Ross observed that it "popped up like the doorway to Narnia. More secret chambers than the Pyramids that café.")

- Nick Cotton's neck tattoo – never in the same place twice. When he came back in 2009 it was clearly visible but, after a couple of weeks, it turned into a smudge.

- Clown Court: Walford's court is the only one in the land to have night sessions, allowing minors into hearings and the victim to visit the alleged perpetrator at will. Even the colour of the judges' robes is wrong.

- Intercontinental travel: Sharon dropped by, as you do, on a two-minute visit from America (round-trip flying time: 16 hours) to see the three witches of Walford – Sam, Mrs Watts and Zoë – confront Den in the Vic. Then she left. Then there was Phil, turning a journey to Rio de Janiero, Brazil, into a daytrip. Going by the time he was back in the Square, he would only have had time to wave to Grant from immigration before checking in for the return flight.

- I spotted one of the show's most puzzling minor mysteries at Peggy's ill-fated wedding early in 2009: it took place at the Vic, a proudly West Ham establishment, so why was there clearly a Millwall FC team photo on display?

Big Swinging Cobblers

That's the small stuff taken care of; now let's address the truly monumental mistakes that the soap has made over the years, starting with the three abominable escapades that they'd all rather we forgot.

Ireland

In September 1997, the soap went to Ireland for three episodes and caused an international storm by portraying the Paddies as pig-thick drunks. The Irish Embassy made an official complaint, viewers were up in arms and shaken BBC executives were forced to issue an official apology. (To date, there's been no apology for the endless insults inflicted on Londoners over the years.)

The Fowlers went to the Emerald Isle to meet Appalling Pauline Fowler's long-lost and never-mentioned relatives, including a sister, Maggie Flaherty, who'd been given up for adoption by old Lou Beale. Pauline, Mark, Martin, Ruth, Ian and Lucy made the journey, only to find an Eire lost in some mythical 1950s time-warp. The place was full of rude, sloshed and ignorant dirt-poor Micks whose farm animals cheerfully wandered the streets.

Naturally, the backlash this shocking portrayal sparked off was far more entertaining than the actual show. Irate viewers bombarded radio stations here and in Southern Ireland, branding the episodes an insult to Irish people everywhere. Callers demanded that the scriptwriters be sacked. Broadcaster Mike

Philpott described the show as "the worst case of stage 'Oirish' seen for a long time", and "one of the most shameful half-hour episodes in the history of British television".

The Irish Embassy in London concurred. They dubbed the shows "prejudiced and stereotyped", and said that the soap had "caused a great deal of upset and annoyance in the country of Ireland and with Irish people in Britain". Ted Barrington, the Irish ambassador, described the portrayal as an "unrepresentative caricature", adding, "Irish people can laugh at themselves but, the point is, this is one of the most popular programmes on British television, and it decided to present an image of Ireland that conforms to old-fashioned negative stereotypes."

On it went. Broadcaster Gerry Kelly called the episodes racist, "an unmitigated disaster". Dublin-based comedian Brendan O'Carroll noted that whoever wrote the script had "obviously never been to Ireland". And the chairman of Ireland's national tourism development got stuck in too, adding succinctly: "the single biggest television audience in Britain was shown a negative image of Irish hospitality. It has the potential to be enormously damaging."

The toothless Broadcasting Standards Commission upheld the complaints, concluding that, although the soap's intention had been positive rather than negative, "the result was clumsy and irritating". The BBC admitted that the episodes were "ill-judged" and Beeb telly bigwig Jana Bennett apologised, saying, "It is clear that a significant number of viewers have been upset by the recent episodes of *EastEnders*, and we are very sorry, because the production team and programme makers did not mean to cause any offence."

George Michael: I knew you were weighty for me...

February 2009. A new toe-curling low in the show's long history came when 15-stone Hefty Heather Trott decided to stalk the rather sleazy pop star George Michael – an episode so bad it caused major internal rows at the BBC, with former *Enders* executive and current Controller of Drama John Yorke going ballistic.

The story was lamer than Don Brennan in size five boots. It was

Hefty's turn to play victim – poor tubby bird can't get a date, aren't men bastards etc – so she set off to find and meet her perfect man, former Wham singer George … who is famously homosexual.

The resulting episodes were neither credible nor funny, just an ill-conceived embarrassment in dubious taste – not least because Geo was once the victim of an insane real-life stalker who broke into his house and hid under his floorboards for the best part of a week. It's hard to see who they thought this badly-written storyline would appeal to, unless they had a load of chubby, frustrated, obsessive women in mind.

Hev was upset after finding out that men don't fancy her. (Was this really news to her? Has she got no mirrors in her house? The woman is so rough she could turn Barry White into Reverend Al Green.) Her drunken pal, Shirley the Terrahawk, roughed up former hard-man Minty Peterson, calling him an "impotent little weasel" (for not fancying Ten-Ton Tess!) and the duo set off on an insane mission to find Geo's North London mansion. Cue lame Humpty-Dumpty comedy as Hev fell off his wall, a cringe-worthy scene where she recited the lyrics to his first solo album (!) and a ludicrous pay-off where she finds true happiness with the lid to a discarded Greek yoghurt pot (I'm not making this up).

The week ended up with surly Shirl hiring a male escort to bed Hev, but what do you know, she pulled anyway, 'cos the magic yoghurt pot lid had made her confident … Or maybe because the bloke she met in the R&R club was a) half blind b) blind drunk or c) attracted to her 36-24-38 figure. (The other arm is just the same size.)

Did you feel for Heather? Or did you feel like shaking her and saying, "Lose some weight, you fat, lazy, greedy cow!"? Or at least, "Get thee to a chubby-chasers website …"

Stop press: in May 2009, it emerged that Heather had become pregnant as a result of that week's adventures. The soap tried to recreate a Who-Shot-Phil moment (Who Upped Tubs?): was the father-to-be nightclub encounter Billy Mitchell, who she snogged, Minty, who had never consummated their marriage, Shirley, with a turkey-baster, or even George himself?

For all we know, that pot may have contained natural Greek yoghurt of a very different kind. But if you really wanted to meet George Michael, wouldn't it be easier just to dress as a bloke and hang about on Hampstead Heath with a spliff on for a night?

(This was the second time George Michael was associated with *EastEnders*. The soap had talks about him actually appearing back in the late 90s, and it was Geo who suggested that they sign Martin Kemp as Steve Owen.)

The strange case of the schoolboy vice king

July 2005. There were moving scenes as, out of the blue, Pauline Fowler decided to throw a 21st 'birf-dee' party for Fat Pat – even though she was 62 and it wasn't her birthday until December.

Pat had missed her real 21st back in 1963, you see. It was a touching back-story: on the night of her big do, she'd had to take one of local villain Johnny Allen's hookers for a backstreet abortion. Afterwards, he was so chuffed that he made her his brothel madam. (All together: "She's got the key to the whores, never been 21 before ...")

But hold on a minute – there was a hole in this plot you couldn't fill with Shane Richie's head. How old was Johnny in 1963? It had only been a month before that we'd seen him and Dot poring over pictures showing him as a small kid at the Coronation. And if he was three in the summer of '52 he would have been 14 when Pat was 21, leading us to conclude that he was running brasses at playtime.

Picture the scene: Johnny bunks off school with a catapult in one pocket and a supply of Fisher Price condoms in the other. "Where are you going, boy?" asks a teacher. "Sex education, sir," he squeaks.

"But it's long jump this afternoon.

"That'll cost you 3/6d an hour."

Other lads got the cane, Johnny supplied one – with handcuffs for ten bob extra. You can see him now, scaring off rivals by snarling, "Legs will break ... when my voice does." (His minder was his imaginary friend.)

To add to the absurdity, Johnny revealed he'd had a crush on Pat and often pondered how different his life would have been if they'd got together.

Surely, if he had fancied her back then, he'd look at her now and thank his lucky stars that they *hadn't*?

Top *EastEnders* Look-alikes

1) Gianni Di Marco and Captain Scarlet
2) Pauline and Dr Zaius from *Planet of the Apes*
3) Kat Slater and Terry Scott
4) Sharon Watts and Miss Piggy
5) Ronnie Mitchell and a preying mantis
6) Dot Branning and Gary Neville
7) Fat Barry and Chairman Mao
8) Pat Butcher and Shane Warne
9) Phil Mitchell and an uncooked sausage in a shirt
10) Jeff (Leslie Schofield) and the lion from *The Wizard of Oz*

Minor Irritants – Characters Who Drove You Nuts

- Mad Jean Slater, with her voice like a cat clawing its way down a blackboard.
- Huw Edwards and Lenny Wallace – a pointless pair of time-wasting squatters who ran a pirate radio station, played crap music loudly and bored the hell out of everyone between 1996 and 1999.
- Hell's Nell – Auntie Nell, so insignificant that most viewers have forgotten her, with an accent unheard in any authentic corner of East London. It's no coincidence that 'Aunt Nell' is rhyming slang for smell.
- Mad Joe Wicks – the Square's first poster-boy for schizophrenia, mostly remembered for his imaginative tin-foil makeovers; he covered the telly with Baco-Foil non-stick and wore a tin-foil hat for 'protection'. He was the son of soap love rat David Wicks and dreary perm-blitzed Bolton barmaid Lorraine, who was cruelly but accurately renamed 'That Bitch Lorraine' by TV critic Tapehead in *The Guardian*. Mother and son left for good in 1997. And I do mean good.
- The Di Marco clan, cruelly nicknamed 'the Dim Arseholes' by *The Sun*. They included wooden 'heartthrob' Beppe and his git of a brother Gianni. Poor Rosa Di Marco – not only did she raise a family of liars and psychopaths, but her hairstyle made it look like a skunk was constantly trying to mate with her head.

EastEnders & Me – My Soap Shame

My love-hate relationship with *EastEnders* began when the show did, in the 1980s. The early years were clearly the soap's first golden era (the second being the Mitchell era, the third and last symbolised by Kat and Alfie Moon). At the start, I loved its pace and grit. It was bold, earthy and refreshing. But before long the wet liberal agenda of the *Guardian*-reading writers began to rub me up the wrong way. Some of the more reprehensible female characters were put on pedestals by these middleclass muppets. One was particularly vile, a poisonous specimen of womanhood, and I said so in print. Unfortunately, my Bernard Manning-style putdown of her fictional character (actually a line suggested by one of her co-stars) incurred a libel writ and *The Sun* ended up having to give her five grand to go away.

I was taken to the court steps a decade later, when I compared one of the di Marco brothers to a plank of wood and invited my readers to vote as to which was the better actor. (The plank won.) The actor in question broke down in tears before the action began and said that he "just wanted to be loved".

Understandably, I became a hate figure for the cast, who put my photograph on their green room dartboard. Many years later, one star laughed till the tears came, recalling the collective horror that would grip the others on a Wednesday when my column appeared and they would scour it for references to themselves. When June (Dot Cotton) Brown saw me wandering around their

Borehamwood studio the poor old stick alerted security – I was there legitimately to interview a leading cast member, but the look of panic on her face was a picture. The thought of June – a terrific actress herself – getting all hot and bothered about a possible tabloid invasion tickles me to this day. *Oh I say …*

Unknown to the show's producers, more than a few cast members privately agreed with my analysis, and cheerfully suggested their own criticisms, jokes and insults for possible inclusion. (Others were profitably engaged with leaking plot developments and scurrilous gossip to various news desks.) A few took it all personally. More than one soap star has sidled up to me at functions wearing a pained expression and asked, almost tearfully, "Why do you hate me?" Others appreciated that most of my barbs were powered by logic and/or a genuine affection for cockney culture. The more down-to-earth ones took it all in good spirit. Back in 1998, Ross Kemp and Steve McFadden came across me waiting innocently on the Queen Vic set for an interview. "Oi, Bushell!" Kemp roared. "You can't do that in 'ere!"

"Do what?" I asked innocently.

"SMILE!" they both shouted as one, and then doubled up with laughter.

I didn't have it all my own way, of course. As well as the writs, I was pied on stage in front of a thousand people at a charity function in Canterbury by Nasty Nick actor John Altman. Mike 'Frank Butcher' Reid also got me back in the most spectacular fashion. He got his agent, Tony Lewis, to invite me along to watch him record his first ever comedy video at the Beck theatre in Middlesex, in the early 1990s. He then proceeded to make me the 'star' of his brilliant but hurtful clock joke (a gag supplied to him by the great cockney comic Mickey Pugh). It still makes me chuckle: St Peter is showing a new arrival around heaven where everyone on earth's life is represented by a clock. The chap notices that every so often one of the clocks would leap forward an hour. He asks why and is told that, whenever the person delights in self-abuse, they lose 60 minutes of their life. "Where's Garry Bushell's clock?" he asks. "Oh," says St Peter, "that's in the kitchen. We use it as a fan."

The Beck was packed out with Mike's fellow Enders, including Sid Owen, Barbara Windsor and Fat Pat actress Pam St Clement, who hated/hates my guts. My, how they laughed!

To show I could take it, I gave the vid a huge plug in *The Sun* and it sold shed-loads. Reidy became friendlier; I went round his house a couple of times and he invited me to watch his live club act – at an Indian restaurant in Essex called the Thundersley Tandoori. It started with him introducing me as "the man who calls me Frank the Plank, my son Thick Rick and my wife Fat Pat." I thought I was going to get another roasting, but instead Mike turned his attack on to the soap itself, saying, "I must be a great actor, I have to pretend to fancy Pat! What a beast that is! I have to kiss it! And half an hour before we film the kissing scene she'd been going down on her girlfriend ..."

It was clearly a joke and not meant to be taken literally – Mike never seriously suggested that his co-star was engaging in oral sex in her dressing room (and in truth he'd done far worse in his), but the punters found it hilarious.

I saw Reidy live quite a few times, but unfortunately I fell out with him over the jokes I wrote about his ears – I said they were the size of satellite dishes and that he should get done for receiving.

Mike took jokes about himself very badly; at one stage, his agent David Hahn – an engaging character and a real-life wheeler-dealer – asked to meet me in my local. He had big news for me: Frank Butcher was to make another return (his last) to Walford. Hahn and Reidy had agreed terms with the producer, but Mike had one final condition – before he would commit to coming back to the show, he needed a guarantee from *me* that I would not write any more ear gags. A tough call, but in the end I decided having Frank back in the Square outweighed the small joy of joking about his lugholes. We shook on it, and Reid duly returned.

Mike was extremely paranoid – a by-product of the immense quantities of dope that he smoked. Once he kipped in his BBC dressing room overnight, had a 2am spliff and got the munchies. He mooched down to the Minute Mart and helped himself to all the chocolate he could fit into his pockets – this caused chaos the next day when the confectionary was due to be used in a scene.

I was also a victim of Mike Reid's paranoia. In his autobiography he devoted several pages to savaging me, saying that I was a 'wannabe' (a wannabe *what* he never said). He didn't realise I was one of his biggest fans. He was a terrific comedian and one of the best things about *EastEnders*.

The soap is now so bad that, if Mike were alive today, he'd turn in his grave ...

In 1994 I appeared in pantomime at Southend on Sea with Ross 'Grant Mitchell' Kemp, which gave a fascinating insight into the madness of some soap fans. I was sitting in the bar on the opening night having a beer with a friend, when this woman came up to me – an attractive lady, she looked like Heather Trott's heavier sister – and said, "You know Grant, don'tcha?" I said, "Well, I know Ross, who plays Grant." She launched into a rant about his screen wife, Sharon, as played by Miss Piggy – sorry, Letitia Dean. "What that Sharon's done to him!" she raved. "That bitch, that cow, I'd ****in' strangle her!"

She was screaming. The woman was so over the top, I was looking around for a camera crew from *Beadle's About*. But she was for real. And so was the woman who sent Ross a bouquet of flowers every afternoon. And the two girls who came up to him in a nightclub and said, "She's black, I'm white, let's spend the night ..."

"That's nothing," Ross told me later. "In 1993, a woman waited for hours outside of the *EastEnders* studio to propose to me. She had bought a ring and everything. I get the most blatant propositions everywhere I go."

This was true. I once went with him to a personal appearance he made at a nightclub in Croydon, South London, called Joey Bananas. The capacity was about 300, and 299 of them were women trying to get off with Ross. I finally ended up back in one of their flats, chatting to an attractive amputee while Kemp, who was then unattached, gave her mate a 40-minute seeing to. He later married *Sun* editor Rebekah Wade, started hanging out with Tony Blair and we lost touch, but knowing Ross and socialising with him gave me an insight into the celebrity status that the soap gave its stars.

It wasn't only the good-looking ones either. Spotty Dean Gaffney couldn't go out in Essex without having to beat babes off with a stick, and it was the same story for Fat Barry, a.k.a. Shaun Williamson – even before *Extras* made him hip.

The downside of the fame was having to put up with the shockingly poor plots, some writers' obvious ignorance of their characters, and increasingly last-minute rewrites of the scripts, as the soap struggled to keep up with the manic pace forced upon it by the demands of going to four episodes a week, while budgets were cut ...

Other Walford Irritations

- The middleclass actors can't keep a hold on their accents during emotional scenes. Every time Fat Pat has to cry you can hear her posh voice coming through. And Mad Jean Slater loses her irritating bleat whenever she has a serious scene, although granted, this is an improvement on six cats sliding down a ten-foot chalkboard.

- The magic jukebox in the Queen Vic automatically turns itself off when any arguments or fights break out.

- Sean Slater doing a runner every other day. They should have played the 'skedaddle' cartoon sound effect every time he legged it; *Corrie* added a *Popeye*-style punching sound when misery-guts Michelle decked Steve and cheered up a bad scene no end. Now Sean's gone the Square's chief offender is Ronnie Mitchell, who stomps off at the drop of a hat.

- Stag nights: why does every Albert Square stag night have to be in the poxy Queen Vic? Why can't they go up west for a change, or to a lap-dancing club?

- Pub merchandise: throughout the 90s, all you could get in the Queen Vic was beer, spirits, wine and crisps. The last time I went to a pub in Shadwell, you could buy tellies, i-pods, mobile phones ... at least Big Mo Harris has revived the black market

- Clichéd set-ups: if the character is upset, they always sit on a bench. In more extreme cases they sit on swings.

OTHER WALFORD IRRITATIONS

- Registry offices and public buildings are always open on Bank Holiday Mondays: Sharon Watts married her brother on August Bank Holiday 2005.

- In January 2008 they had a scene in Urdu with no subtitles. But no one ever speaks in cockney rhyming slang. (If they did, would they use 'Patsy's' for piles – Patsy Palmer's = Farmer's/Farmer Giles = piles?)

- Vanishing vehicles: like Garry's motorbike (left to him in Mark Fowler's will), Barry's Merc and Sonia's Metro. Characters just seem to forget about them. At time of writing, Grandad Jim's Morris Traveller is still parked in the Square, but we've never seen Dot pay road tax on it.

- Plot and character recycling: Brad was naked save for a bowtie in 2007 – just like Frank Butcher; Billy Mitchell was made to wear ridiculous fancy dress – just like Fat Barry. The soap falls back on the rather tired 'Who shot JR?' formula far too often too. It's been used a fair few times since 'Who shot Phil?', the latest example being 'Who ran over Max?', with the added twist of Tanya's false confession. At the time, I asked, "Who ran over Max? Who gives a s***? All I want to know is why didn't they do a better job, and reverse over him just to make sure the job was properly done?" Writing in *Broadcast* magazine, soap fan Ruby Gordon was moved to state, "the *EastEnders* writers are no match for Agatha Christie's murderous mind and should leave whodunits alone. The Max/Tanya/Jack saga has dragged on for so long that I no longer care who's guilty." The answer, in case you missed it, is Max's 14-year-old daughter, who couldn't drive. Ho hum …

- Animals hilariously on the loose: a long, dull staple of the soap that has included snakes, dogs, turkeys, donkeys, budgies, rats, Marge the guinea pig, Tiff's caterpillar, Chops the pig, parrots and that other mad squawking bird, Jean. (But I do miss that old goat Ethel Skinner.)

The Nineties –
The Mitchell Era

The 1990s were defined and overshadowed by the Mitchell clan, as the soap turned back to pre-Gibbon grittiness under new exec producer Mike Ferguson who managed to make the sinking show watchable again.

Taking over at the end of 1989, this former producer of ITV's *The Bill* took the soap away from lame slapstick and back to reality; he also introduced more location shoots. Comic characters were axed, including Marge Green and dimbo Trevor, who was so far down the food chain it was a miracle he didn't take root; out too were redundant space-wasters like Rod the Roadie. And in February two strong new faces joined the show: tough guys Grant and Phil Mitchell.

Although known on the set as 'Bill and Ben', the Mitchell Bruvvas were taken seriously by viewers and went on to stamp their size-11 boots all over the coming decade.

1990

Dismal Diane Butcher did a runner in January, sending Frank frantic. He went up to Leeds a few times, thinking she'd be with her occasional boyfriend Paul. A young girl's corpse was discovered, but it wasn't her. Frank celebrated by slapping Ricky about. What a pilchard!

Di eventually got in contact a couple of months later and Frank picked her up from King's Cross. In a flashback story we learned that she'd fallen in with a bad bunch, including Disa O'Brien – who tried to persuade her to go on the game and would later dump a baby on her doorstep – and a dodge-pot artist called Matthew who talked her into some nude modelling. After Di returned to Walford, he erected a nude statue of her in the Square, which was certainly easier on the eye than the murals she started vandalising walls with, or the crusty bag-ladies who she brought back to the B&B.

Cindy, Ian and Wicksy's lurv triangle was the year's best storyline. Cindy – a.k.a. the Big Easy – had tried to end it with Simon Wicks after having his kid, and wanted to make a go of it with Ian; but Wicksy wanted the sexy minx back badly, and dumped Miss Piggy to show he was serious. Ian's mum, Kathy, overheard them via baby Steven's baby alarm – a scene so memorable that the soap has recycled it several times since.

Cindy eventually told Ian he wasn't Steven's father. The wretched Beale tried to top himself by crashing his van, but couldn't even manage that. (Actor Adam Woodyatt really made his mark though; as a coma victim he was a natural.)

Cindy and Wicksy high-tailed it to her parents' house in Devon, but Ian traced them and lobbed his crutch through the window. He ended up returning to Walford with Cindy's father's shooter. It was gripping stuff. Viewers hissed heartless Cindy and, for the last and possibly the only time, felt sorry for Ian Beale. But he bottled out of his planned revenge at the end of September. Wicksy was coming up the stairs to sort Ian out; Ian reached inside the cupboard for the gun. Wicksy was out in the corridor; Ian clutched his weapon, eyes blazing with hatred. Then he … put it back in the cupboard.

It was, I noted, the biggest washout since Noah went into the ferry trade.

Ian dumped the shooter in the canal. Instead of getting even, he just got drunk. Blood tests confirmed he wasn't Baby Steven's dad, and he settled for trying to frame Wicksy for a series of pub thefts. When that didn't work he drained all of the brake fluid out of his van – although, this being *Enders*, the brakes still worked. Eventually, Simon and Cindy had enough of it and left Walford for a new life on Steven's first birthday.

Part-men, part-monkeys, the Mitchell Brothers arrived in February, turning up in a white Porsche looking like they'd wandered in from a lager ad. Car mechanics and petty hoods, they set up the garage in the Arches and persecuted their gormless mechanic, Fick Rick, endlessly. Ricky fell for their fit sister, Sam; Grant started dating Sharon '40' Watts.

That summer, Panto Nick tried to poison ma Dot for the first time.

And in July a new black family joined the cast. But the Taverniers were handicapped from the start by paranoid BBC bosses decreeing that Celestine and Etta should stay happily married, work hard and be scandal-free. Scriptwriters were told that the family could do nothing that might be conceived as negative – in other words, they were to be completely unlike every other family in Albert Square. It was positive discrimination built into a soap script. As I wrote at the time, "wouldn't it be braver and more honest if the Beeb made them as flawed and miserable as everyone else?"

The Taveniers' naff granddad, Jules, was such a cliché you half expected him to break into a chorus of 'Ol' Man River'. He was like the Uncle Remus of Trinidad. In August Jules got drinking with a wizened IRA supporter reminiscing about the Easter Rising – just what you wanted on British telly after a summer of shocking terrorist attacks which included bombs at the London Carlton Club and the Stock Exchange, and the assassination of MP Ian Gow.

Of course, you did get blokes like that in London pubs – but you also got quite a few more who would have told him to put a sock in it. That's if he was lucky …

November saw a second bed and breakfast open up in Walford. "What next," I asked, "seagulls? A boot-faced Les Dawson landlady? Why don't these silly sods have a look round the real East End? They'd find more mosques than B&Bs. Boarding houses? They ought to board 'em up."

Also this year: a body found in the canal was assumed to be Den's and given a proper East End funeral; Mark Fowler came back with a new head and the Vic had a new guv'nor, Eddie Royle, a man so wooden many viewers assumed he was permanently wearing a mask.

Dr Legg started disappearing, too. His surgery was once the hub of Walford life. Now it was as forgotten as the Chinese takeaway, seen only once back in 1988. Legg became Dr Doolittle, turning up just once all summer to diagnose Mo Butcher's dementia (a storyline still dragging on in December, months after the poor old dear would have been put in a home).

1991

The year the soap went positively nuts ...

The HIV virus hung over Mark Fowler like a curse all year. He'd always been as miserable as a boil, but even Appalling Pauline realised something was amiss with her wayward son. He was secretive and became almost as glum and moody as she was herself. The soap had made him HIV positive in a bid to 'prove' how heterosexuals – he'd caught it from Geordie girlfriend Gill – were just as at risk as needle-sharing junkies and gay men who had unprotected sex. It was propaganda plain and simple, and it boiled away all year – Mark didn't come clean to his family until Boxing Day, although he'd confessed all to Diane Butcher.

The arrival of Joe the Jonah in the Square, and the prejudice he faced, helped convince Mark to end his silence. Gay, HIV-positive Joe trailed Mark around like a lost tripe-hound; he got a job at Ian Beale's Meal Machine but, when Ian found out about his condition, he gave him the tin-tack and went potty with a bottle of bleach. Although they did become supportive, the Fowlers' first reactions to Mark's bad news were fear, anger and open hostility.

To lighten the mood, Eddie Royle was murdered. The publican's lifeless carcass had often been seen behind the pumps at the Vic, and eventually he was fatally stabbed too. The soap tried to get us going with a Who-Killed-Eddie? mystery, to which the *Daily Star*'s critic retorted: who gives a tuppenny damn?

Grant Mitchell was in the frame, as was young boxer Clyde Tavernier, who'd been seen bending over the body holding a bloody knife in his hand. Instead of telling the cops the truth – that he'd come across the corpse and panicked – Clyde sensibly did a runner.

He was entirely innocent though, as the real killer was Panto Nick.

Elsewhere, romance was in the air. Fick Rick and Fit Sam Mitchell eloped to Gretna Green and got married, staying happy together for several weeks. Sharon married Grant on Boxing Day, having realised it was true love back when she saw him batter the granny out of the late Eddie Royle. Michelle and Clyde got it on too, although she seemed to get bored with him when he wasn't a murder suspect.

At the start of the year Mark rowed with his cousin Ian Beale, establishing a pattern that remains in the soap to this day: Ian, who has the gumption to graft and try to build a business, was portrayed as a wrong'un; Mark, unemployed and unemployable, was the good guy. This was the BBC's message then and it remains so now: better to be apathetic, diseased and morose than embrace those dreaded 'Thatcherite' values of enterprise and self-improvement.

Racism reared its ugly head this year, but strangely it was all one-way. The white folks were racially abused as 'pork-heads' and 'honkies', while any unease felt about Michelle's dull relationship with Clyde was expressed only by black characters. It was an odd state of affairs. Were the writers trying to tell us that racist feelings no longer exist among white East Enders? The BBC still claim to confront the realities that *Corrie* ignores, but they actually run away from them for fear of glamorising attitudes they don't like. (See also the lack of casual homophobia.) You wonder why they bother...

Also this year: Clyde turned out to be the Nigel Benn of Walford; Grant was given a past in the Paras; Nick Cotton became a junkie, and Fat Pat – who'd wobbled into the Square like a toxic dump on legs, poisoning all she touched – was rewritten as a cuddly earth mother. There was still no sign of Dr Legg, the Lord Lucan of soapland, but the writers were too busy trying to 'educate' us to pay any attention to anything as trivial as consistency.

> *Bores of the Year:* emotional Etta Tavernier, constantly rowing with husband Celestine, and posh Rachel, the right-on polytechnic lecturer.

> *Mystery of the Year:* Walford bookies showing Pat Eddery riding in a flat race at Newbury in January. There was no flat-racing at Newbury at this time of year.

1992

Oi, Grant, NO! 1992 belonged to the pop-eyed, pin-headed Mitchells. It was also the year of Sharon's great betrayal and Arthur Fowler's rebirth as a Love Machine.

A raging Grant drove his marriage onto the rocks with the efficiency of a Force 9 gale, and then managed to torch the Vic with his bride inside. In short, the big lunkhead did everything he could to drive Miss Piggy into his brother's bed without even meaning to.

Their marital problems started because Grunt wanted a baby and Sharon didn't. She lied to him, saying that she'd stopped taking the pill. Big mistake – but maybe not as big as Grant's decision to get involved in a raid on the betting shop. Distraught, Sharon turned more and more to Phil for a sympathetic ear.

Grant bullied her, snarled at her mates and 'went Garrity'– as Londoners say – when he discovered she was lying about coming off the pill, smashing up the Vic. If he was scary when he was angry, he was even more disturbing in the mood for love. Grant appeared to have learnt his romantic techniques from watching *Wildlife on One.*

Before long he decided to set the pub alight for the insurance money, not realising Shazza was still upstairs. Finally the penny dropped for her, and she realised she'd married a psycho. Then Grant got careless about his appearance – he didn't show up for days on end. So Shuddering Sharon turned to Phil to fill the 'gap' – great thinking, love! You're married to a scary nutter so the way to go is to start shagging his brother?

The seeds of disaster were neatly sown.

Elsewhere, there was a tragic death that moved us all to tears – yes, Ethel's pug dog, Little Willie, barked no more. Oh, and

Mark's girlfriend, Joyless Gill, came back to croak as well...

Mark hadn't been having much of a time at home, not with Arthur bleaching his cutlery after every meal and tearing up his leaflets. So he got back together with Gill, who was rapidly deteriorating, they wed in June and had one honeymoon night together before she went off back to her hospice to pop her clogs.

But it wasn't all hell for the Fowlers. For starters, Pauline buggered off to New Zealand for months to care for her brother Kenny, who had been in a car crash. Arthur, meanwhile, started his own gardening business and was employed by the fragrant divorcee Mrs Hewitt, a.k.a. 'Hot-Lips'.

Christine Hewitt was different from Appalling Pauline in so many ways. Happy and softly-spoken, the love-starved divorcee didn't nag or moan and her wardrobe extended beyond a few rotten old cardies. With Pauline away, her friendship with Arthur blossomed into something stronger. Before long she was staying over and they were forever snogging in alleyways like lovesick kids.

Nothing actually happened, but Jules Tavernier did video them together and whispers of their affair were the talk of the Square.

Eventually, Hot-Lips sent him a letter telling him she loved him, along with a nice picture which Arthur dumbly pinned up at his allotment shed.

And that would have been the end of it, except that when Appalling finally came back she was more delightfully unpleasant than ever, bossing Arthur about and having stand-up rows with all and sundry. It drove him straight back into Hot-Lips' arms.

Pauline got wind of it and turned up to confront Christine, who told her straight that nothing was going on and that Arthur had just shown kindness to a lonely widow. Incredibly, Pauline believed her.

And that was it. It was the biggest washout this side of the launderette.

Unfortunately, the damage had been done. Arthur and Christine fell into bed on Christmas Eve and started the full-on affair so many had suspected them of. It seemed that 'prick out every six inches' was no longer just a seed-pack gardening instruction.

Go on, my son, get in there! With his green fingers, red face and (if you can imagine it!) his little pink bum going like the clappers, Arthur emerged as the Rainbow Rogerer of Walford.

Also this year: Pat Butcher opened Pat Cabs, but was jailed after knocking down teenage Stephanie while drunk-driving on Christmas Eve; the following week the girl died. Market manager Tricky Dicky bedded Rachel and Kathy. A distraught Ian Beale started hiring Cindy look-alike hookers. And malignant Mandy Salter arrived.

What a piece of work she was. Mandy the Minx stole from Peter Beale's stall, tried to blackmail Ian over his 'vice girl shame', snogged Ricky and then told Sam he'd started it. She nicked dead Gill's diary too. She was a right old laugh! Strangely, Mandy ended the year homeless ...

1992 also saw the soap tackle the growing menace of street robbery. In August the spectre of mugging finally reached Albert Square when Jules, an elderly black man, was brutally robbed by two teenage white girls. There's reality for you.

Worst attempt at humour: the saga of Arthur's stolen garden gnome.

Funniest unintentional humour: Jason, the new hard-man; every time he rolled his eyes he looked like Marty Feldman.

Mystery of the Year: Appalling Pauline went to New Zealand for three months, so how come she came back with no suitcases? Maybe her cardie was self-cleaning.

1993

Sharon tried to take over the Queen Vic this year, putting her on a collision course with the Gruntster. She'd been staying in Spain with mum Angie, recuperating from the strain of being married to Grant while banging Phil. Grant's response wasn't pretty – he treated her to a slap-up meal, only without the meal and with extra slaps.

It got worse; he hit her some more, called her a tart in public (at least that was accurate) and chucked money at her. Eventually she called in the Old Bill, who overpowered him and charged him with assault and battery. With the gorilla away, the pouting Shazza felt free to flash her thunder-thighs at Phil again and wheel him back into her bed. They were going to run away together, but instead Grant came back a (temporarily) broken man. Sharon's heart melted for him all over again and Phil was duly chucked. The discarded bruv reacted by marrying Nadia, a Romanian bag-lady, before giving Kathy an Eiffel in gay Paree.

I dubbed it the soap wedding of the decade – Phil Mitchell and Rasputin's daughter. If Nutty Nadia had been Miss Romania you could have just about swallowed Phil's interest in her, but the girl looked like she slept hanging upside down from the rafters in Castle Dracula.

He spotted her in a wine bar after taking a day off to ferry Hattie Tavernier (Michelle Gayle) to Southampton. Honestly, she would have lowered the tone in a parade of tramps; she seemed to be wearing the entire contents of an Oxfam shop and was clearly not the full exchange rate. But Phil chatted her up, took her round some ruins and, before you knew, it he'd decided to marry her so she could stay in the country.

Credit where credit's due: the *EastEnders* writers had long led the field in crackpot plot twists, but this time they'd played their joker. Phil was supposed to be a streetwise wide-boy, not a soft touch for any passing waif and stray. Then, two months later, the Brothers Dim went to France where he fell for Kath of Kaff's caff – all those beautiful Parisians birds and he went for someone from his own ghetto…

It was a Mitchell year all the way, although grubby gardener Arthur gave them a run for their money. As the months went on, Hot-Lips Hewitt got fed up being his bit on the side. She wanted more and, when Arthur wouldn't leave home, she got a job in Kath's caff to stay close to him. Although quite why he excited her so was never clear – Arthur lived such a dull life he made the average battery chicken look like Peter Stringfellow. (Hot-Lips was played by Liz Power, the wife of TV's Michael Aspel. When she dragged Arthur down an alley, Mike must have wished the bags were growing *over* his eyes and not under them…)

Inevitably, Kathy caught them kissing and made a tearful Hot-Lips tell all. Arthur lost his bottle and went cool on her. In return, Christine hit the bottle and threatened to tell Pauline everything.

In the end Arthur confessed instead and his wife responded as only she could – smacking him in the kisser with a frying pan. (If she'd really wanted to make him suffer, she might have left her cooking in there.) Pauline also biffed Hot-Lips in the bistro. (Painful!) The only thing that jarred was Michelle lecturing her dad on morality – that's the same Michelle who was happily knocked up by a man she knew was married, at the tender age of 16 ...

The Fowlers were eventually reconciled after Arthur helped Pauline deal with the death of her brother Pete. But she never ever forgot his betrayal.

Also this year: Pauline was hit on by old flame Danny Taurus, but the Growler gave him the bum's rush. Ian and Sinful Cindy tried to make a go of things and, despite the ardent interests of slimeball Tricky Dicky, she managed to give birth to his twins – Peter and Lucy. The craze for raves and Es finally hit Walford – two years after it peaked in the real East End, and nearly four years after it started. Dr Legg came back, but no one ever noticed that he'd been gone, and the original Pete Beale got himself a new bird, Rose – unfortunately, she was married to jailed psychopath Alfie Chapman and so Pete's days were now numbered ...

Meanwhile, Kaff's caff became a bistro, despite not having either a toilet or a drinks licence. This was also the year Michelle got a stalker, the Jackson family arrived, as did Sanjay and Gita, and Fat Pat did six months for manslaughter after killing a young girl while driving drunk. It was either unfortunate or slyly clever that, in January, Frank Butcher told Pat he was late because "the traffic was murder". Ouch! (Pat got six months but viewers had already had her for six years – we were serving life!)

> *Irritation of the Year:* Fick Rick's eating habits. He slurped his food and held his cutlery as if he were digging up Arthur's allotment; Roly the poodle had better table manners.

Romantic of the Year: Hattie's boyfriend Steve Elliott, saying that going to bed with her was "our way of saying goodbye." Imagine how he says hello!

Horror of the Year: Dot Cotton bursting in on Mandy and Aidan looking like something that had just blown in from the Twilight Zone via a medium. She proceeded to lecture them about a cup of tea being safer than sex – which is what Boy George thought, until he woke up with Earl Grey.

(Aidan, if you've forgotten, was the promising Irish footballer who Arthur virtually adopted in between leg-overs. It took Mandy a matter of months to wreck his career and turn him into a drugged-up, suicidal mess.)

Mystery of the Year: Panto Nick introducing Dot to his nine-year-old son. It was only two years before that he'd invented a son to con her dosh out of her. Why bother if he'd had a real one all along?

Saddest Death of the Year: 1) Roly 2) Big Ron, the market man extra.

1994

The year peaked with the towering magnificence of the Sharongate tape in October. Sharon coughed about her affair with Philthy Phil, her bruvva-in-law, to Michelle – who, as luck would have it, had recorded the whole thing on a tape which ended up in Grant's car stereo. He thought it was a compilation of hits he could take to Phil and Kathy's engagement do in the Vic, to get the party started. It certainly got everyone on their feet…

Contrived as this sounds, it worked wonderfully. Everyone was crammed into the Vic and, in a soap first, they were all smiling. It took seconds for Grant to poop the party, stopping the music to play the tape of his wife admitting her affair with his own dear bruv. Grant had played it again and again as the extent of their betrayal sank in; the hard-man with the granite exterior had turned to slush inside. Suddenly, the whole Square could hear the casual confession that had wrung out Grant's heart. One question was on the lips of 19 million viewers: what next? Even Sharon couldn't pout her way out of this one...

Tears trickled down Grant's face, a mask of hurt and hate. He stormed out, leaving Kaff to throw the first blow. "You slut!" she roared, slapping Miss Piggy around the chops. "You dirty cow!"

Everyone had an opinion. "She wants her head testing," snorted Pauline. "Sleeping with one of them is bad enough."

"He wants locking up," said Nell.

Kaff broke down on the caff floor like an old banger. Nigel, who was part of the Mitchell family scenery back then – and acted like it – went looking for Grant, but Phil found him first.

"Why, Phil?" he asked, hurting like a wounded animal. "I can feel every stroke. You might as well have put a knife in your hand." It was Ross Kemp's finest hour.

Phil had to beg his bruv for the spanking he so richly deserved. Grant left him near-dead in the inspection pit of the Arches. Job done...

Some good came of it all, though. Mum Peggy Mitchell came back *to sort it all aht*. Grant was so cut-up he didn't notice she had a new head – it was Barbara Windsor's debut. But Grunt still hated Phil and was intent on divorcing Sharon. He decided to break it to her gently on Christmas Day. And what fine festive spirit he was in, announcing the season of "good will to all sluts" before smashing plates to the tune of 'Jingle Bells'.

"I don't love you," he snarled at her. "We're not getting back together and there's no such thing as Father Christmas." He also told her she was "drunk and begging for it, just like your muvva!"

Harsh but fair. What a story. From holy wedlock to unholy deadlock...

It had been a funny old year for Grunt. His ex-army mate Dougie Briggs turned up in January and tried to persuade him to join in a little light armed robbery. Why is it that every ex-squaddie in the soap has to be portrayed as a certifiable nutcase?

Grant found out his pal was a convicted rapist and murderer just in time to save Sharon from a frontal assault. But, in the resulting fracas, Doug KO'ed Grant with a vase, hitting him round the head (presumably to avoid permanent damage); in the ensuing shootout Doug fired directly at the bar twice and somehow managed to hit Michelle, who was running off at a 90-degree angle. (The last time she laid groaning in agony on the Queen Vic carpet in a pool of blood, Vicki was born nine months later. This time round she gave birth to the new third *EastEnders* weekly episode ...)

Mercifully, 'Doug the Mug' got nicked before he could do any more damage.

Phil had a rough year too. He torched Frank's car lot, accidentally barbecuing a dosser, and confessed to Kathy who promptly dumped him. Phil hit the bottle but eventually they made it up and he proposed. Then he paid off Nadia, who came back like a bad smell, and nearly fell back into bed with a jealous Miss Piggy. All of which was overshadowed by their engagement party, of course ...

Elsewhere, Frank Butcher sloped off after Pat unintentionally ruined his insurance scam. I missed him immediately. Mike Reid was one of the best things about the soap, even if Frank was the unluckiest man in the Square (until Billy turned up). His mum went mad, he was lumbered with a peroxide Sphinx of a missus and he flopped as a publican, a cafe owner and a landlord. He ran a guest house with no guests, a minicab firm with no drivers, and when he needed an insurance scam he turned to Phil who, frankly, couldn't be trusted to light a birthday cake. It makes you wonder why he stayed for so long.

Meanwhile, Frank's son Ricky hooked up with Bianca – I didn't think much of her thin white pins, they looked like straws, but legs apart she was great – apparently ... (Before playing Bianca Jackson, Patsy Palmer was in the Clearasil ads. When I first saw her, I assumed she'd come to sign up Michelle for a new campaign.)

And a bored Cindy got jiggy with Matt the lifeguard.

Also this year: David Wicks turned up, Gita caught Sanjay in bed with her sister and Pauline's auntie (aka Hell's Nell) moved in with the Fowlers. Nell, more commonly known as the Auntie Christ, was a migraine in human form who made Arthur's life even more hellish when she found out about his fling with Hot-Lips. After she'd stuck her oar in, he had more chance of bedding Madonna than clambering back in with his wronged wife. Auntie Nell was Irritant of the Year, being marginally more annoying than Griping Gita, who was such a prize nag it was a wonder no one called her Pegasus.

Scandal of the Year: Gillian Taylforth suing *The Sun* over the story of her giving her fella a blow job in public. What a shame no one put a poster in the window of Kaff's caff: 'Best nosh in town.'

Insult of the Year: Fat Pat telling Carol Jackson, "You lying little slapper, you've had more traffic through you than the Blackwall Tunnel!" What was that about a pot and a kettle?

Ishoo of the Year: lesbians – Della and Binny, a.k.a. Dulla and Lusty Bin.

Irritation of the Year: the Jackson family's kitchen; it had purple walls, green window frames and a pink clock ... I reckon their decorator had been sniffing Windolene.

Mysteries of the Year: Alan's gran, Blossom – she was supposed to be West Indian, so why did she look Chinese? Why did Ethel come back for Nigel and Debbie's wedding? She never knew them! And Dr Legg came back in July, but where was he for the rest of the year? No one asked and he never said – I was the only one who ever cared (apart from Leonard Fenton's agent) ...

1995

Quite a lot happened in 1995, but none of it was as memorable as Ian Beale's moustache. He appeared with a vile growth on his top lip in December which provoked a national debate. What was it, we asked? A mutant whelk? A small black hole? Or maybe one of the errant Dr Legg's eyebrows. (After all, they'd never been seen on screen together ...)

It was just a 'tache of course. He'd probably grown it to look like his gran, but what a faux-pas. It made Ian look like George Roper's love child.

The big drama was still dominated by Grant Mitchell and Arthur Fowler: before emigrating to Birmingham, Alabama, Michelle Fowler made it her mission to tell Grunt exactly what she thought of him. She called him 'the Missing Link', fully expecting an irate backlash. Instead, he opened up and started talking. Alone in the Queen Vic, sharing a heady cocktail of booze and openness, both of them had a romantic history that involved the pub carpet so it was really no surprise that they should end up rutting on it. It was like a scene off of the Discovery Channel. It was hardly surprising that Michelle left the Square without bothering to tell the big ape that she was carrying his child.

The BBC talked up the Michelle Fowler character, saying she was a "role-model for single mums". But was she? She'd ballsed up her life, getting pregnant by two psychotic pub governors and ending up blaming everyone else for her misfortunes. Every big decision she ever made was wrong. But, like a leopard, she had far too many spots to change ...

Arthur Fowler had it worse than anyone else this year though. He really must have done something to piss off the writers. In 1995 he was nicked for the disappearance of the Flowering Wilderness Fund. He was innocent – he'd been duped by a slippery customer called Wily Roper (no relation to George), who'd legged it with a cool £20K. But after the Christmas club money affair, nobody believed him.

Arthur faced a Kafka-esque ordeal. Grilled by cops, he was then slung in a dock more suited for the trial of Klaus Barbie, as well as being hounded by the gutter press over his affair with Hot-Lips. ('I Didn't Do It, Mrs Hewitt' was the inspired *Walford Gazette* headline.) He ended up behind bars, a broken man.

Meanwhile: Grant had a tiff with Tiff, and then he had Tiff

herself. Cindy Beale and David Wicks got it together. It was the real thing; he'd regularly pop round to the fish shop for a portion, but never of cod. It was unsavoury even by this soap's standards: David was the half-brother of Simon, in turn the father of Cindy's eldest son and half-brother of Ian. (Who was writing this stuff? Hillbillies?)

The soap celebrated its tenth anniversary in February. I wrote in *The Sun*: "I'd like to wish *EastEnders* a happy birthday but the shock of a happy anything would probably send the cast into a coma. If you got the bumps in Albert Square it would turn out to be an outbreak of boils." I suggested that the BBC should open a theme park in the soap's honour called Walford World: attractions to include the Dirty Den Canal Corpse Ride, the Pete Beale Bumper Cars, the Willmott-Brown Lucky Dip and junkie Sue Osman's Needles of Death. But they never took me up on it.

Also this year: Tiffany Raymond turned up; Phil and Kathy were reconciled and got married; Fat Pat's new fella, Roy Evans, turned out to be impotent. To her surprise he turned her down, but there were no hard feelings! (His favourite ice cream was Mr Softy.) Roy frequently got Pat's back up but, in fairness, it was the only thing he *could* get up.

The peroxide bulldog was also left quite distraught when she received a letter from Frank via a psychiatric nurse – I knew you'd have to be mad to marry her! He returned on Christmas Day, only to discover there was another rooster in the hen-house. Suddenly, there were three of them in the relationship...

Mystery of the Year: Sharon spent June scheming to get her revenge on Grant. She said she wanted to make him sorry that he'd ever been born, and planned to get him to propose again so she could turn him down in front of his family and friends. Uh, why? Sharon slept with Phil, broke Grant's heart and now she wanted to hurt him some more – it's the kind of logic only a woman could follow. The soap strung it out for seven long weeks of secret meetings and vows of vengeance, and in the end she bottled it and upped sticks for the States. Like you do.

Other mysteries: why did ex-prostitute Pat need a chaperone to date amiable old Roy of the Range Rovers? And when Robbie Williams turned up in the Vic in September, what was he asking on the phone? (My bet: "Why is Frank's daughter Greek, and is Gita really playing in goal for Colombia?")

Irritation of the Year: Ruth's fire-and-brimstone Scottish dad, the Reverend Aitken, being painted as a bible-bashing bigot – like Christians always are. But was it that unreasonable for him to object to her marrying Mark 'Philadelphia' Fowler?

Row of the Year: Peggy finding out about Phil's fling with Sharon. She whacked him, saying, "One ping of knicker elastic and the blood leaves yer brain and heads south!" Then she slapped Sharon, calling her a "two-faced lying whore ... I'll do time for yer!" The *Carry On*s were never like this.

Episodes of the Year: the Walford Jolly Boys' beano to Torremolinos – the reallest the soap has ever felt. Scripted by Tony Jordan, this was *EastEnders* at its most believable, full of birds, boozing and gutbuster breakfasts.

1996

The Hitman and Her: this was the year that cheating Cindy Beale nearly got shot of her husband. In October, she paid £1500 to John Valecue to have chip-shop magnate Ian gunned down like an LA rapper. Battering him to death with a frozen jumbo skate would have been more poetic – especially if the act had been finished off with a strategically placed gherkin. And thrusting him face first into his deep fat fryer would have been more effective as the hit-man's bullet went through the small of his back ...

Under pressure from the cops, and realising that David had let her down like a ruptured parachute, Sinful Cindy snatched her sons and caught the Eurostar to Paris. I'd miss her, but not half as much as Walford's mascara and condom suppliers.

Meanwhile, Phil became an alcoholic; Kathy gave birth to his son, Ben; Alan Jackson started cheating on new wife Carol with sexy singer Frankie. Luckily her ex, David Wicks, was there to offer her comfort.

Also this year: Mad Joe turned up; Grant hit it off with Tiff; Arfur Fowler popped his clogs. Newly freed from chokey, the Walford One collapsed up the allotment with his little dibber in his hand. He never regained consciousness. Cause of death? Acute cranial pain, possibly triggered by the voices in his head. (If they sounded anything like Hell's Nell, it's no surprise.)

Appalling Pauline now faced months of anguish and mourning. How different from her usual air of devil-may-care gaiety ...

In June we discovered that Arthur's death was caused by a brain haemorrhage. (A big shock – who knew he had a brain?) Pauline remembered him as being "like a young Frank Sinatra". (Frank Spencer, surely?) Mark called him a good man who had taught him the difference between right and wrong – yeah, by stealing the Xmas club money and signing on while he was working, defrauding the honest taxpayer ...

Elsewhere, Pat and Roy married and Phil nearly died when the car lot was torched. (Again.) In September, Tiff told Grant he was the real father of her baby (but only after catching her boyfriend, Tony, snogging her brother, Soppy Simon). He said he'd stand by her. "Grant," she said, "this is the 20th century, men don't have to stand by women anymore." 'Course not. These days, Mr Mug Tax Payer is only too happy to bankroll the careless trollop ...

And in November Peggy was worried about suspicious lumps – not Grant and Phil, this was the start of the breast cancer story that ended with her mastectomy. Also that month: Mad Joe was going to kill himself, but didn't. Shame. At the time I advised him to be more like a jockey and get straight back out on that window ledge (and take boring Felix the barber and demonic Aunt Nell with him).

On Christmas Day, Joe saw mummy kissing not Santa but Grant – the man he called the Devil. If he'd lingered a bit longer he'd have seen her sampling Satan's sausage. Nigel later asked Lorraine if things had been getting on top of her – no mate, just 'the Thing'.

The worst awayday was to Blackpool: Kathy's niece, poor Sarah Hills, had her orange juice spiked by her brother's pal Dan Zappieri, a.k.a. Dan Dan the Ecstasy Man. (All together: "Oh I do like an E beside the seaside …") Mad Joe went loopy in the Hall of Mirrors. And Gay Tone 'did a Barrymore', coming out in various Boys R Us gay haunts.

> *Small Joy of the Year:* Patsy Palmer. She brought a unique thespian style to Bianca Jackson – sort of bungee acting. She could go from outward calm to wild extremes of emotion in seconds flat.

> *Thought of the Year:* if it was £1500 to shoot Ian, how about negotiating a group discount? I'd have put up £5K if it meant taking out soppy Robbie Jackson and the entire Hills clan.

1997

This year saw the worst ever *Enders* away trip, to Ireland (see '15 of the Most Ridiculous Storylines Ever'). It also witnessed the birth of baby Courtney, Phil hitting the bottle even harder and Ricky and Bianca tying the noose.

But the most memorable and miserable scenes were saved for Boxing Day, with Grant kicking in his bedroom door to yell, "I'm gonna kill yer! SLAG!" at trembling Tiff. Then he threw her to the floor and cut her head open. (Tsk. You're supposed to deck the halls, mate, not the missus!)

Elsewhere, Sarah Hills lost her virginity to Robbie Jackson, a spotty youth barely able to control his own saliva. It was a result for Robbie, whose previous girlfriends had been inflatable, but a big shock for Sarah. When she realised what she'd done, she immediately went potty and did a runner. Her dad Ted, thinking she'd been raped, threw Robbie down the stairs, knocking him unconscious. (Although it was hard to tell.) Irene Hills, Sarah's mother, later hit it off with Tiff's dad, Terry Raymond.

Ricky and Bianca's April marriage didn't get off to a great start.

He'd already cheated with the bride's best mate, while Bee spent a night getting a full 12-inch mix from a pirate radio DJ. The highlight of the day was Fat Pat's wedding hat. How many emus had to die to make that? It looked like two crows locked in post-coital paralysis.

Also this year: Fat Barry got stung by a con-woman for £140K; Frank came back and fancied Peggy; Peggy's unlikely and unlikeable sister Sal turned up, and the Mitchell boys snatched Cindy's kids back from Italy.

New girl Frankie quickly split the nation. She was an even bigger slapper than Cindy, so women viewers hated her. Men tended to be more understanding. OK, she wasn't exactly Iman Bowie; she looked more like the little green men who worship the Claw in *Toy Story*. But the way Frankie puts it about you'd think the species was endangered. She seduced Alan Jackson and 'turned' Gay Tony with ease.

In January an Arthur Fowler memorial bench was erected in the square. To date no one has had the gumption to carve 'Hot Lips Hewitt woz 'ere on it, and there is still no sign of a Cindy Beale memorial mattress.

In May Gay Tony became a journalist. "Start at the bottom and work your way up," advised the *Walford Gazette*'s editor. If he had a quid for every time he'd heard those words …

Tony had set his heart on a big splash, although if pushed he'd have settled for a single column up the back. Tone seemed immediately drawn to fellow journo Polly, and it was easy to see why – she could have been separated at birth from Simon. They were identical.

Mystery of the Year: how did Billy Jackson witness a robbery? With his fringe he'd be hard-pushed to witness his own breakfast.

Other mysteries:
- Kathy lent her brother, Ted Hills, the money to emigrate to Dubai. So how come he ended up in South Africa? Did the writers think Africa was the size of Kent?
- After lending him her life savings, Kathy went to Paris

and then Florida. How come she was so flush? Where was she getting so much dosh?

- What became of Fruity Frankie? She vanished for so long that I suspected she was working as Dr Legg's receptionist. Then, when she did turn up, Alan just said, "Goodbye, Frankie, may you rot in hell." And we never saw her again. No one ever mentioned her, either.

Irritation of the year: the Mad Joe storyline. The BBC said they wanted to "tell it like it is" about schizophrenia. They should have made a documentary then, because their good intentions translated into a tedious storyline that went on longer than a queue outside Northern Rock when it went belly up. By June Joe was having electric shock treatment, but there wasn't enough voltage in the world to bring his whingeing mum Lorraine back to her senses.

Small joy of 1997: Ian Beale recruiting Clare Grogan from Altered Images to hunt down Cindy, his morally challenged missus. If only this had started a trend: Lemmy from Motorhead to restock the jukebox; the Prodigy's 'Firestarter' to take care of the car lot's recurring arson requirements. (And possibly smack up a bitch or two ...)

My personal contribution to the soap? In January I shaved off Ian Beale's moustache live on ITV's *This Morning*.

1998

It was a rotten year for Tiff, who got stiffed. As well as battling with the moustache on her top lip, the brunette beauty survived falling down the stairs during a row with Grant only to perish under Frank Butcher's wheels. Poor cow. The nearest Tiff ever got to her own nuclear family was Grant blowing his top.

There was plenty of agony along the way too. In one sensational hour-long special, Grant bedded Louise, his mother-in-law, and Tiff put on cuffs to snog Beppe Di Marco. Who was writing this stuff, Jerry Springer? It built up to Tiff and Grant both crying in the rain – two lost souls caught in life's great downpour without a brolly. Wonderful!

October saw a great punch-up between Pat Butcher and Peggy Mitchell, a catch-weight contest obviously. The pair were at each other's throats (and this is where you had to suspend belief) over the love of serial loser Frank Butcher. "No one wants you, Pat," sneered Peggy. "Fwank left you, yer boys left yer and now Woy's left yer."

Pat turned ugly. Not for the first time. "You fink Frank wants you?" she sneered back. "Mutton dressed as lamb?"

"You *cawww*!" Peg yelled and slapped her face. "You cow!" Pat roared back, returning the favour. Then the door bell went. Brilliantly acted and beautifully written (by Tony Jordan), there was even a decent impotency joke: "The physical side," mused Peggy. "That must have been har … difficult."

Sadly, the soap's usual agenda bubbled along, with complaints about the newsagents selling girlie mags. Outside of student unions does anyone care? Especially when there are bigger issues at stake – like how come Terry was the only white newsagent left in East London? And when would Pat pick on someone her own size … like Godzilla?

At the beginning of the year, Kathy fell for the local reverend – who proved you can't shag quicker than a quick fit vicar. And Gita the malignant midget went missing.

In April, Grant hit Peggy. OK, it was more of an accidental tap, but it sent her flying. By the summer she was hooking up with Frank Butcher, which was just as terrifying. He's six foot, Peggy is four foot two – when they finally slept together she had nobody to talk to.

In November Cindy Beale died. The soap's top slapper expired as she had lived – on her back with her legs apart. Shame it all happened off-screen.

In December Spandau Ballet's Martin Kemp joined the cast, as club owner Steve Owen. Yes, to cut a long story short, the exec producer lost his mind. Sadly, in his three-and-a-bit years in the soap, Kemp never said the immortal line, "I don't need this pressure on."

Also this year: Gita and Sanjay went after he was suspected of murdering her (see '15 of the Most Ridiculous Storylines Ever'); Jamie Mitchell arrived; Kathy's randy reverend boyfriend, Alex, chucked her. Kaff had offers from both of the brothers Dim, but instead decided to emigrate to South Africa where Ted now lived (his plane having overshot Dubai by several thousand miles).

Washout of the Year: the Di Marcos. But I did like mum Rosa, who was once Doctor Who's sexy sidekick Leela. She didn't find any docs in Albert Square, but if she'd cornered Nigel she might have got Tom Baker's clothes back.

Mysteries of the Year: Alex the vicar's dad, Jeff, once played Wicksy's father. Why didn't Pat recognise her ex-husband? Why did Beppe the detective never go to work? How did Robbie Jackson work in the caff without someone mistaking his face for a pepperoni pizza? Why did Bianca forget her 21st birthday? And why, in August, did Peggy start investing in Frank Butcher? Every business he ever had has gone belly up – the car lot, that poxy Marie Celeste of a guest house … Peggy is supposed to be a tough cockney landlady, not a mug punter.

1999

A bit of a crap year. After the excitement of Grant and Tiff, we had to make do with the farfetched yarn of flaky nightclub boss Steve Owen murdering Saskia with an ashtray, with Matthew Rose as the only witness.

She was his loopy ex. She'd aborted his child when he'd dumped her and come to Walford seeking revenge. Saskia tricked Steve back into her bed (not hard), then found out his new girlfriend, Melanie Healy, the vicar's sister, knew all about it. On Valentine's Night, she turned up at the E20 nightclub, told Steve she was going to muck up his life and started belting him. Things came to a head – sorry! – when Steve grabbed an ashtray and bashed her round the canister with it. The whole thing had been recorded on the club's CCTV system. Instead of calling the cops, Steve decided to bury her body in faraway Epping Forest. (The Thames was much nearer.) By summer they were both banged up for it. But not before Steve Owen had showed Grant Mitchell up.

Because Ross Kemp was leaving, the soap seemed intent on watering down Grant. He was pushed about by Owen, he was doing tai chi classes, he gave himself up to a single, soft community plod … *leave it aht*. Why ruin a great character?

The soap finally heated up in September, as it came on top for Bianca who was having a fling with her mum's fella, Dirty Dan Sullivan. They'd started to get it on in July. Let's hope for his sake he wore ear plugs.

Bianca was supposed to be house-hunting when Dan tricked her round to his mate's place for a bit of one-up, two-down. The only things semi-detached were her clothes. A week later, Carol told him she was pregnant with his baby. Dan and Bianca got away with it for weeks; Carol caught them out just months before Sonia was old enough to join the fun as well.

Hurt and betrayed, Carol called Bee "a lying little slag" and Ricky branded her "a selfish slut", shoving her on her back. Grant was gloating; Carol tried to top herself and decided she wanted an abortion. Happy families! But Lyndsey Coulson was sensational as the betrayed mum.

In April, Fat Pat turned Roy down for a shag. Eh? Why? Roy was charged up on black-market Viagra and busting to consummate their marriage. So Pat has been up for it all her life and suddenly the woman has a headache? With no explanation, the former hooker was now horrified by the thought of making love to her own husband. Roy was so frustrated he kipped on the couch. It was a wonder he didn't pole-vault out the window.

In May, Carol Jackson returned but she left son Billy behind. Had she abandoned him or did he try to follow and couldn't see through his fringe? (They never said.)

In August, Roy and Pat finally consummated their marriage. And there was a dummy outside the caff – it was as if Peter Beale had never died.

In October, Kathy came back with a new hair-do. One of her

first tasks was to have it off with Grant – this was a revenge shag I'd been advocating for years, but the writers chucked the potentially explosive twist away by making them agree to forget it happened the next morning.

By the way, why was Grant the bad guy for dropping his girlfriend, Nina, when he found out she was a hooker and why would Peggy tell him he was out of order? Typically, no one in the Vic made a single joke about Nina's past. Also this month: Steve Owen's trial started. Why didn't he just tell the truth, that Saskia was nuts and she had it coming?

In November, Dr Thong-sucker (Fonseca) admitted he had been leading a secret gay life. Apparently he discovered he was gay when playing Doctors & Doctors at school. And Irene was bedding Troy, her toy boy. A young fella can fall for an older woman, of course, but it's usual for her to be a seductive Mrs Robinson type, not a menopausal Mrs Munster ...

Mysteries of the year: Why was Irene Hills so miserable? Was it because her house had mirrors? Comedian Dave Lee said, "Irene had women's problems – she didn't look like one." And what on earth did Nat'lee see in Fat Barry? Every woman kisses a frog before she finds her prince but he was fat, broke and a financial disaster. But in April they started running a dating agency together – it was like Saddam and Mugabe opening a branch of Amnesty International.

At least we found out why Gianni Di Marco couldn't keep a woman: timing. The Italian Stallion started making love to Louise as Alex began reciting the vows at Peggy's wedding. He was dressed and kissing her goodbye before they'd been pronounced man and wife. Mussolini's army had more staying power.

Irritant of the year: feng shui-crazy Irene Hills, the New Age freak. What colour was Irene's aura? Beige ...

Random *EastEnders* Irritations

1) *Sexual Desire*

As soaps are written from a feminist perspective, female sexuality is always painted as liberating. Women on Walford hen-nights who ogle male strippers are portrayed as enjoying a wholesome, life-affirming experience. Male sexual desire, on the other hand, is seedy and perverted. Poor old Grandad Jim Branning was depicted as a dirty old man for wanting sex with his wife on their wedding night; Big Mo Harris, who is in her 70s, is seen as a right old laugh for lusting after fellas, holding riotous Ann Summers parties and leaping into bed with Bert the Berk or her on-call lover, Fat Elvis. Female desire is good; male desire is sexist and unsavoury. (See also inter-sexual violence: man hits woman = bad; woman hits man = funny or deserved.)

2) *Not tonight, Josephine*

This is another strange only-in-Walford phenomenon we have seen emerge over the years: men turning down sex. This applies both to single men – like Jack and Bradley Branning – and married love cheats like Max 'the Mekon' Branning. They've all said no when they've been offered a no-strings shag on a plate.

Believe me girls, this *doesn't* happen. Most men are as faithful as their options, and erections are devoid of conscience.

3) *Stacey Slater calling Big Mo 'Nan'*

Why does she do it? Big Mo Harris was the Slater sisters' nan – she was their mum's mother – but she is no blood relation to Stacey, who is the girls' cousin and Charlie's great-niece. A young cockney girl might call an old dear she doesn't know 'Nan' as an affectionate term of address – like 'love' or 'mate' or 'Grandad' or 'darling' – but Mo isn't a stranger. It wouldn't happen.

4) *St George's Day*
English people have long celebrated their patron saint's day, especially in the East End of London, but it took the self-loathing BBC decades to acknowledge it. For years the Vic gave St George a blank while gleefully celebrating Diwali (the Hindu festival of lights), US Independence Day, St Patrick's Day and once even Bastille Day. Finally, Alfie Moon was allowed to have a St Geo knees-up, but it was a scam and the only one who really seemed into it was some old extra. It wasn't until 2009 that the pub was properly decked out with England flags for the day – but only as background decorations and no one commented on them.

5) *Nigel Bates' shirts*
Talk about what not to wear! Nigel's dicky-dirts should only have been worn by a man in a grass skirt dancing around a volcano. These psychedelic fashion disasters induced migraines for six years in the 90s. Apparently, he had them on a timeshare with Fat Pat.

6) *Christmas misery*
Yuletide in Walford is traditionally a combat zone with crackers, but they really excelled themselves in 2000: Phil and Mel skipped the turkey and went straight for the stuffing, and Peggy Mitchell took a baseball bat to the Queen Vic. *Oi, Peg, no!* You're supposed to deck the halls, not wreck the walls! So much for tidings of comfort and joy; even *The Telegraph* was moved to reflect on the effect such relentless misery might have on the national psyche. For gawd's sake, give us a day off...

7) *Penny-pinching*
The show's miserly budgets are surely self-defeating. If *Enders* is

the BBC's flagship show, why do they use cheap unproven writers on it and why are the cast's wages so poor? Most of the newer stars are on short-term contracts and aren't paid much in comparison with more established faces, some of whom aren't anywhere near as good or as popular. Rob Kalinsky was their biggest star of the noughties, attracting fan mail by the sack-load, but, according to one insider, exec producer Diederick Santer "didn't realise what he had with Rob and refused to negotiate a pay rise to keep him." Kalinsky promptly quit and is about to star in the new George Lucas movie. Never mind – they've still got Charlie Slater …

8) *Murder they write*

The soap's increasingly casual attitude to killing is a growing source of annoyance. In 2009, Peggy demanded that Phil murder Archie and Phil gave Billy the opportunity to top Nick Cotton. The previous year, Tanya buried her husband alive … and there have been no repercussions for any of them. Max wanted Tanya back. Peggy forgets that Phil let her down. The show has lost whatever moral core it once had.

9) *Doctors*

A 'dishy' new doctor arrived on screen in 2009. Most overworked GPs are lucky to see sunlight; Dr Alexander 'call me Al' Jenkins spends most of his time jogging around the Square or drinking in the Vic. At time of writing we have never seen him in his surgery, but he has given a couple of consultations in the launderette. A small surgical procedure on the swings can only be a few weeks away, ditto his first affair with a patient. (Dr Trueman should have been struck off for the way he carried on – or at least struck often.)

Al Jenkins replaced Poppy Merritt, who lasted just seven months. She succeeded Mad Dr May Wright, the deranged child snatcher who had taken over from the entirely forgettable shop-window dummy Dr Oliver Cousins (who managed to last a miserable five months). Before that we had Tom Jones (Dr Leroy), Anthony Trueman, secret gay Dr Thong-sucker, the Sikh Jaggat Singh and Dr

Legg's so-what nephew, David Samuels. None of them were as believable as good old reliable Harold Legg, played by Leonard Fenton. Dr Legg was a traditional community GP with roots in the East End; he had a genuine concern for his patients, who trusted him and treated him with respect. Fenton was cast because he looked and sounded like a credible doctor, not a male model with occasional recourse to a stethoscope.

10) *The Park*
It's the size of a postage stamp; if more than two families turned up and tried to have a picnic on the grass at the same time, they'd have to sit on each other's laps. You feel sorry for the kids – where can they play? There are only two swings and no child can get near them, because of the queue of adults waiting to sit on them for their heart-to-hearts.

11) *Coppers*
Clueless, incompetent, unconvincing (even by soap standards), the Walford cops are as much use as paper handcuffs. Crimes are rarely solved. Crime scenes aren't sealed off. They don't appear to have a forensics team – never once have the experts been called to a crime scene to look for tell-tale evidence. Even when Johnny Allen confessed they didn't believe him.

12) *Short-lived crazes*
Alternative French cinema briefly excited Kevin and Denise in 2006. The pub football team lasted just as long. I can't imagine the Walford Book Club having a Christmas do. (See also overnight alcoholism and one-sniff drug addiction.)

13) *Decor*
Hardly anyone in Walford ever decorates. Some of the kitchens look unchanged from the 1960s, but the worst one ever belonged to Alan and Carol Jackson. The colour scheme could have induced migraines: purple walls, green window frames, pink clock. Was it based on Nigel's psychedelic shirts?

14) *Rotten continuity*

Ronnie first said that when she had Danielle she was in a damp, dark room with a skylight. At her graveside, she told Stacey that she'd had her in hospital.

15) *Phones*

People chuck their mobiles into bins in public places with the Sim card still in them. They don't even cancel their contracts.

16) *Sexual horrors*

Was there anyone who saw Fat Pat flashing – all fur coat and no knickers – at Patrick able to keep their tea down? And does anyone want to picture her *at it*? (Or Big Mo for that matter.) Pat ripping off her corset must be like pulling the ripcord on a dinghy. It was the same with Martin and Sonia and their mating honks. For one glorious moment, when Pauline moaned about the racket they made, I suspected Sonia's new boobs had been fitted with circus horns. But clearly we're talking barnyard noises here. (Not chickens – their breasts are real!) One of them in that bedroom was nicknamed 'Donkey', and it sure as hell wasn't Martin.

It made you nostalgic for those innocent days when all Sonia blew was her trumpet...

Ishoos

Whereas *Coronation Street* was traditionally powered by its characters, *EastEnders* was the first high-rating British soap opera to be driven deliberately by social issues. Following the gritty lead of the pioneering Channel 4 show *Brookside*, *Enders* has tackled everything from homophobia to mental health via rape, prostitution, drug addiction and AIDS. They've done this generally in a number of wet, right-on ways and they haven't always been successful.

Let's consider some of the soap's big ishoos...

Race and racism

Is *EastEnders* racist? Certainly not intentionally, but there is something patronising, even unsavoury, about the way the soap treats its black characters. The Foxes and the Truemans (Patrick and Yolande), for example, all ended up herded together in the same house simply because they happened to be black. See also the way the Masoods seemed to just inherit the old Ferreiras' debt storyline, it was if the writers sat around scratching their heads asking, "What can we do with this crazy Asian family?" and some bright spark piped up, "Well, the money problems worked well with the last lot, but for gawdsake don't make any of them need a kidney transplant..."

The show could also reasonably be accused of reverse racism in that the white characters are painted as feckless trash, while baseless fears of 'negative stereotyping' confine the vast majority of black characters to tame and toothless roles. How frustrating must this be for the actors? There have only ever been two really meaty black bad boys in the show for any length of time, streetwise wheeler-dealer Dodgy Darren Roberts (Gary McDonald) and drug-dealing Paul Trueman (the great Gary Beadle). But you'll never see a black British equivalent of Trevor Morgan or Jack Dalton. Usually, black actors have had to settle for infidelity, like Tony Carpenter (Oscar James) with Angie or Patrick Trueman (Rudolph Walker) with Pat Evans. And ska-fanatic Patrick didn't even get to play 'Hey Fatty Bum Bum' in her honour ...

In 2008 the show's bosses rather insultingly let Angela Wynter (who played Yolande) go, saying that they had "run out of storylines for her" – a consideration that doesn't seem to apply to half the cast, particularly puzzling when you consider the Truemans were the only black married couple in a British soap. Yolande unconvincingly left Patrick behind to go off to Birmingham to work at Minute Mart HQ (the Minute Mart, which Patrick had once owned outright, had suddenly become part of a chain). Angela Wynter reckons the decision to axe her character may have come because the soap was exceeding its 'quota' for black and Asian characters: "If this is true, I am not hurt because I accept that fact that I live in England and it is not 'our' TV station where we can be over-weighted with black or Asian actors and have guest appearances from Caucasian actors – because 'we' are the guest."

Without her, and without his best mate Jim Branning, Patrick has pretty much been reduced to Denise's surrogate father. But they did give him a half-decent plot early in 2009. That February the soap broadcast its first all-black episode, with Patrick reminiscing about London in the 1950s to the Fox family. This was part of a wider story about the Notting Hill (actually Notting Dale) race riots of 1958, during which his fiancée Ruth had been killed by a blaze started by racist teddy boy Tommy Clifford, played in the present day by Edward Woodward. (In fact, no one had died during these unfortunate disturbances in West London.) A dying Clifford tracked Patrick down to beg his forgiveness and to find redemption in his dying weeks. Patrick duly obliged.

Oddly, the BBC didn't see fit to make much of a fuss about their historic all-black episode until after it was aired. My own view was that the Beeb played it down in advance because they knew it wasn't much cop. As I wrote in the *Daily Star Sunday*, having the Truemans chat about ancient bigotry is a poor substitute for a plot that brings modern social problems to light. I look forward to the Peasants Revolt episode, where the Walford plebs, inspired by Dot's memories of her night in the sack with Wat Tyler, will rise up against the tyrannies of Brussels rule, liberal hypocrisy, state snooping and unfair taxation.

It's certainly true that these days the soap writes Asian characters with more confidence than they did in the days of local GP Jaggat Singh, back in 1987. The Masoods have been built up as a core family, and the rather fierce and argumentative Zainab Masood (played by Nina Wadia) has quite bizarrely been put up for comedy awards. Even so, I've yet to meet a postman of any ethnicity or religion who manages to run a catering business in his spare time. And I still can't work out why their golden-boy son, Syed, looks more Mediterranean than Asian. Maybe Michael Jackson advised on skin care ...

Gays

As I write, *EastEnders* has just featured another gay kiss. It wasn't enough to spark the fury that their first one did in 1987, when Colin Russell pecked his barrow-boy lover Barry Clark chastely on the forehead, and *The Sun* responded with the furious front page headline, 'EastBenders!' After that, questions were asked in the House of Commons. But hey ho, they keep trying.

At the start the soap was following in the footsteps of *Brookside*, where Gordon Collins had come out years before. Two years later Colin kissed new fella Guido on the lips, without any passion, and again sparked a degree of public fury. In 2008 it took Christian Clarke publicly French-kissing his latest casual flame in broad daylight to provoke complaints, and even then the tabloids had been so progressively cowed by the militant gay lobby that their reaction was relatively muted. But had a couple of fellas carried on like that in Canning Town in real life then someone else would have thrown a bucket of water over them – if they were lucky. The soap wants to be gung-ho about homosexuality as a rights ishoo, but it can't bring itself to accurately portray what the public response would be.

In 2009, the soap attempted to kick-start another 1987-style orgy of outrage with a storyline involving not just a kiss but a love story between two men, one of them Syed Masood who is a) a Muslim and b) so far in the closet his back foot is actually covered in snow from Narnia. The main problem with this was not so much any potential shock it might cause, but rather the credibility factor. The whole saga is impossible to take seriously: Christian is not just gay, he's an über-gay – a hardcore, in-your-face, promiscuous Muscle Mary who is totally narcissistic, as underlined by his wardrobe (144 identical white vests). Previous stories have made it clear that Christian is the f***-'em and chuck-'em type. There's only room for one true love in his life, and he can see him every morning in his mirror.

Secondly, Syed is not in the least bit interesting. He is a personality vacuum – so what is it about this dull poltroon that Christian was supposed to find so goddamn irresistible? Not only that, but *EastEnders* completely bottled out by not having the gay Muslim Asian played by a Muslim – or indeed an Asian – but by Marc Elliott, suggesting that they realised exactly what the Islamic viewers' response might be to such a storyline. A recent survey result published in *The Guardian* found that, out of 500 UK Muslims, zero per cent thought that homosexual acts were morally acceptable. The world of fatwahs and jihads is clearly one that the soap bosses have consciously chosen to avoid. They want faux-controversy without the undiluted rage of the Leytonstone mullahs, which must be a blow for Muslim actors as well as for viewers.

How can we care about Syed's mental anguish, and the conflict between his duty, his faith and his loins, if we can't believe in the set-up? Especially when you suspect the soap's real agenda isn't to flag the problems of homosexual Muslims, but to drum up shock-horror press coverage and tick BBC boxes. (If Syed were in a wheelchair too, they'd have a full house.)

The announcement that the storyline would be 'nuanced' and involve various shades of grey will surprise anyone who has ever bothered to study the soap's approach to homosexuality. Their track record on lesbianism, for example, is truly poor: apart from Sonia Jackson's unconvincing love for Naomi and Zoe Slater's one-off, publicity-generating 'gay' kiss one new year's night in the Scottish Highlands, the only dykes I can remember in the show are Binnie Roberts and Della Alexander, whose Sapphic snog managed to generate nearly half of all complaints to the BBC about *EastEnders* in 1994. But the women were pretty dull and one-dimensional. Binnie spent most of her time trying to bully black Della into coming out; she finally kissed her publicly, but then the couple decided they'd had enough of Walford and emigrated to Ibiza. They were never seen again. It wasn't a patch on Beth Jordache in *Brookie*, or Zoe Tate and her truck-driving girlfriend (the 'van dyke') in *Emmerdale*.

Christian has forced other *Enders* characters to confront their prejudices. But he's not had to cope with the kind of jokes that a flamboyant solo gay resident in an East End square would attract and has only ever been teased about his vests once. Unlike John-Paul in *Hollyoaks*, tiresome Christian is defined entirely by his sexuality.

(Why are Walford gays so good-looking, by the way? They're always hunks. They never look like Peter Tatchell, Chris Smith or Boy George. This has led some observers to claim that, rather than reflecting reality, the soap is out to glamorise homosexuality.)

Literacy

Keith Miller was an unemployed lay-about, a square-eyed, sharp-witted rogue who'd never done a decent day's work in his miserable life. It wasn't until April 2005 that the character, played by ex-Hawkwind roadie David Spinx, was revealed to be illiterate.

The usually buoyant Keith was ashamed of the problem and, in a particularly stark moment, opened up about how he felt he'd let his whole family down, as he was unable to get a job to provide for them like a proper dad. The soap was congratulated for tackling the issue, even though they frequently undermined the storyline by showing Keith reading TV listing magazines, bank statements, *The Racing Post*, song lyrics on a karaoke machine and adverts for cheap booze.

Class

The middle classes are generally wrong'uns in Walford, unless they are health professionals or social workers in which case they are 90 per cent likely to be blameless ethnic minorities. But white upwardly mobile types – yuppies – are never on the side of the angels. The ranks of middleclass creeps have memorably included James Wilmott-Brown (rapist), Debbie Wilkins (bossy madam), Jan Hammond (Den's snobby mistress), Dr May Wright (mad bitch), Stella Crawford (solicitor and child-torturing nutter) and Magda Czajkowski (smug cow). The soap is determinedly anti-aspirational – Ian Beale has been persecuted for decades for having the temerity to run a business and expect to make a profit.

Down's Syndrome

In September 2006 they gave Billy 'Lucky' Mitchell a Down's Syndrome baby, Janet – this was trumpeted as a bold TV first by the Beeb, although the US TV series *Life Goes On* had run with a similar storyline more than 15 years before. At the time, Barbara Windsor told me, the plan was for us to watch the little girl grow up and understand the problems she faced and the joy she could bring; I told Bar the producers wouldn't stick with it. I was right. The soap took all the credit for introducing Janet and then got shot of her in September 2008, without giving her a single storyline.

(Down's Syndrome on *EastEnders* is not to be confused with Dawn's Syndrome – *Swannus Rejecticus*. That's where you stand around looking gorgeous for a year and nobody asks you out.)

Abortion/Contraception

The soap has handled abortion a few times. Over the previous decade, Vicki Fowler has terminated Spencer Moon's sprog and, more understandably, Zoe Slater got shot of Dirty Den's unborn child (she wanted to get pregnant to keep hold of the younger Dennis, who for some reason was more interested in his pouting orange sister than in East London's answer to Liv Tyler). But if their approach to abortion is generally sensitive, the soap's attitude to contraception is nuts. Experienced women of the world like Roxy Mitchell never use it, and when responsible teenage boys carry condoms, just in case, they are hysterically denounced. Derren Miller was monstered for possessing rubbers, and Whitney went postal when she discovered that her date, Todd Taylor, had a Johnny in his wallet. (Although what the hell gave her the right to go through his wallet escapes me.) Given the level of teen pregnancy in the area – Michelle Fowler, Sonia Jackson, Demi Miller – carrying condoms should be mandatory for any Walfordian who has gone through puberty.

Paedophiles

EastEnders' 'Gary Glitter' plot was generally as welcome as Harriet Harman at the Playboy Mansion. Tony King, who looked like Cartoon Head from the BBC3 comedy *Ideal*, had met struggling single mum Bianca Jackson off-screen in 2004, and ended up playing stepdad to her four brats. Unknown to Bianca, he was a paedophile. King started grooming her stepdaughter Whitney when she was just 12 years old. Whit fell for him and the dirty nonce took her to bed, although with low cunning he manipulated her into feeling like she'd made all the running. Their relationship only stopped when Tony was banged up for ABH on a kid who'd asked her out. All of this was back-story.

On 12 September 2008 King arrived in Albert Square, fresh from the jug. He bedded Whitney, now 15, almost immediately, putting a lock on her bedroom door to ensure their privacy. The sick creep hated Whit's more grownup appearance and made her take off all her make-up and jewellery, so that she would look more like the 12-year-old he'd fallen in love with. When she got a part in a local am-dram production he also ended up belting Peter Beale, who was playing Romeo to her Juliet.

In the resulting fallout, King realised that Whitney had outgrown her use and started grooming Lauren Branning, Bianca's cute 14-year-old cousin, instead.

His reign of terror ended before he could lure Lauren into his perverted trap. A lynch mob of largely white locals, including an extra with a noose, was headed off at the pass by various goody-goody ethnic characters. Whitney came clean but Bianca wouldn't believe the girl until she overheard Tony talking to her. King was arrested and good riddance to bad rubbish.

Jim Shelley in *The Mirror* was one of the many tabloid critics who hated the soap's fresh hell. He wrote: "Just when you thought the show couldn't get any more miserable, the writers come up trumps and produce a new way of making us depressed – a paedophile storyline. Thanks for that! I realise now this is what the family meal has been missing three nights a week: gathering around the telly to watch a grubby greasy-haired thug drooling over a 15-year-old who (as luck would have it) spends her entire life in her school uniform even when she's not at school. And they say family entertainment is dead."

Shelley called the BBC's claim that the storyline had educational value totally bogus, observing that, "at 7.30 or 8pm, the 'action' has to be so coded as to be pointless." *The Guardian* were all for it, as it mirrored their left-liberal worldview, but my response was different:

"Some say it was brave for *EastEnders* to tackle paedophiles a few years after *Corrie* did. I would say that instead of painting working class people as Neanderthal losers, a grown-up soap might consider why child molesters arouse such public fury. And lay the blame squarely on the wet, useless justice system that fails to adequately punish the guilty."

Child abuse is a serious thing, but *EastEnders* isn't. If they really wanted to confront reality they'd have a few characters worrying about their jobs and mortgages. And maybe show us some of that good old East End 'community fanaticism' so beloved of Islamic extremists.

Fascists

The Beeb always say that the soap has a moral duty to tackle everything that touches the lives of Londoners. So where are the BNP voters in the Square? There has been the odd racist, but they've either been young and dumb (Ricky Butcher's teenage gang) or ancient and doddery (Grandad Jim and Dot early on, Frank Butcher's old mum). I can remember fascist activists being featured just once back in the 90s – when Arthur Fowler saw them off with a rousing speech. But in reality, East London has long been a ripe recruiting area for the far-right since Mosley's day. Derek Beackon got elected in Millwall in 1993; they currently have 12 councillors in Barking and Dagenham and a member on the London Assembly. We may not like them – I certainly don't – but they're a fact of life.

So why won't the soap cover the BNP? They've had socialist activists in the past, they've had people singing IRA songs in the Vic, and I'm sure I remember Bert, Jim and Joe once serenading fellow drinkers with a quick burst of 'The Red Flag' (although the only thing scarlet raised high in Walford was probably Kat Slater's skirt for a kneetrembler). But they won't feature the British National Party. Why? Because they're terrified that viewers might agree with them. It's dramatic cowardice: rape they can do; paedophiles, yes; tackling homophobia comes easy. But racial nationalists? They're too risky. If Walford reflected the actual East End, one in eight of the population would be voting for the loathsome bunch and at least one of the hard-nut regulars would be running the local branch.

And to illustrate the point, in 2008 it was announced that Mike Reid's daughter had pulled out of standing as a BNP candidate in Essex. Angela Reid, of Braintree, had entered herself as a candidate in the district council's by-election in the hope of winning the Witham West seat. But the 50-year-old had decided to withdraw, officially informing the council just over an hour before the deadline for pulling out. A man who said he was Mrs Reid's husband said she was withdrawing because she was worried about being branded 'a Nazi', adding, "She has cancelled her candidacy because she's Mike Reid's daughter and people would call her a Nazi and slag her off." But the BNP's deputy chairman told the press, "I've just come off the phone to her and she is adamant that she's committed to the party's platform, it's not a question of politics. She is angry about a lot of things people are – overcrowding in this country, the country being run by a European federalist government, the amount of tax we have to pay, the fact the economy is taking a nosedive and the amount of crime."

Football hooligans

East London has been synonymous with football hooliganism since the 1960s, so it was perhaps inevitable that the phenomenon would finally hit Albert Square. Shame it was so unconvincingly done. In November 2007 a group of geriatric soccer yobs smashed up the Vic. It was farcical; Ronnie fought off one of the hulking great brutes by flapping her hands at him. It was like she was doing doggy paddle.

Mickey Miller became so squeaky that only Joe Pasquale could have heard him. While one of the thugs, Bird (short for bird-brain?), had the cheek to call the locals 'Dad's Army', even though most of his mob (Saddo's Army, perhaps?) were visibly older than they were.

It wasn't exactly the ICF – unless ICF now stands for, "I see f***wits." Just a few matters arising: why did the Vile End Mob trash the boozer when their target, Jason 'Truly' Dyer, wasn't there? Why didn't anyone surreptitiously dial 999 on their mobiles? Why do I ever expect this soap to ever make sense? There's more chance of seeing Sharon Osbourne shopping in ASDA...

Incest

Well near enough. Sharon '40' Watts married her brother in August 2005. Okay, she was Den's adopted daughter, and Dennis was his real son but it still felt wrong, although I expect they were cheering in Norfolk. Instead of turning their noses up, the Walford citizens turned out for a big street party. I'm not sure what was harder to believe. That Dennis preferred the spherical orange Sharon to Liv Tyler look-alike Zoe Slater, or that the registry office was open on a Bank Holiday.

Prostitution

In January 2009, Walford got a massage parlour. Hurrah! Naturally it was a front for prostitution. But has there ever been a less happy hooker than Marissa? Never has the phrase 'goodtime girl' seemed less apt. How desperate would you have to be to pay for grumpy-pumpy with this skinny, sour-faced bint? Not only was she as miserable as sin, she looked like pop star Feargal Sharkey in a wig (although it was odds on that the only teenage kicking she was used to involved a Class A drug habit).

Peggy was outraged and rightly so. There is no call for a massage parlour in *EastEnders* when Walford women give it away for free. Roxy, Ronnie, Stacey, Danielle, they're all anyone's for a bag of chips. If a bloke can't get a shag in Albert Square he might as well hang up his manhood.

Peggy's protest might have made sense if prostitution wasn't such an established local tradition. Her best mate, Fat Pat, ran a brothel; her stepdaughter, Janine Butcher, was on the game and Suzy might as well have been. Then there was Mary the Punk, Kelly Taylor, Donna Ludlow and very nearly Zoe Slater, who threw up over her first punter. I don't know why Dawn doesn't get in on the act – that girl must be sitting on a fortune.

Rape

December 2003, and the evil 'Crossword Rapist' struck again in Albert Square. (So called by the papers because he was always doing crosswords in the pub/caff, etc.) So it was a case of two down, one across …

I know rape isn't funny, but *EastEnders* is. A fortnight before they'd had people scrapping outside the church in a joke fight that made the Keystone Kops look like *The Shield*; now they were demanding that we take them seriously. Why should we?

They tried to dress up this latest horror-show as 'reality', but it was just a cynical ratings ploy. Poor Little Mo had already been raped and brutalised once – why do it to her again? Is her Frank Spencer voice a magnet for nutters?

The rapist was book-reading Graham who, like Wilmott-Brown before him, was good-looking, articulate and bright. So the dubious message is … what? That all men are potential rapists? Or just the white middleclass ones?

Euthanasia

Poor old Ethel Skinner fell terminally ill in September 2000 and asked Dot Cotton to help her pop her clogs. Of course, assisted suicide went against all of Dot's moral and religious beliefs and much agonising followed. At the – ahem – death, however, Dot decided that friendship mattered more than the faith that had sustained her all of her life, and so she helped Eff shuffle off this mortal coil.

That may have been unlikely, given Dot's commitment to the Good Book, but the soap handled the storyline with unusual skill. (Even if they did fail to consider non-religious arguments against euthanasia – which, if legalised, would be a green light for greedy relatives motivated more by avarice than altruism.)

Eff had been storing her morphine for months and planned to take an overdose before the pain got unbearable. But she became too weak and needed the help of Skeletor. After weeks of soul searching, Dot finally agreeing to help Eff kill herself on the night of her 86th birthday (though she said it was her 85th). She had a party at the Vic, blew out her candles and, with Dot's assistance, died with dignity. Or at least as much dignity as a woman in a wig on loan from the PG Tips ads could ever muster …

Mental health

Joe Wicks was the pioneer, teaching viewers that the giveaway symptom of schizophrenia is an urgent need to cover everything in

Bacofoil. Joe arrived in Walford in 1996, looking for his dad David, and was soon joined by his Bolton wanderer mum, Lorraine. He was glum, he was moody and by December he was as mad as a wet hen.

Joe's mental illness was triggered off by the anniversary of his sister's birthday. He started to hear voices in his head – probably his agent saying, "Get the hell away from this show!" – followed by hallucinations. He got to a point where he couldn't tell what was real and what wasn't – much like the writers. Then he started to think everyone else was crazy, which on balance was a reasonable deduction.

The soap was praised for its sensitive handling of the issue, but actor Paul Nicholls reported that it didn't have the desired effect on viewers. "Girls used to come up to me and say, 'Oh there's David Wicks's son,'" he complained at the time. "But now all I get is, 'There's Mad Joe!' I'm telling ya, that's all I get, 'There's Mad Joe!' If they start taking the piss I just scare them by going into character and talking to myself, and then I run to them and go, 'Yuurgh!'"

From then on Nicholls was always known as Mad Joe, even when he joined the cast of BBC1's flop drama *Bonekickers*. (Mind you, you'd have to be nuts to put yourself up for *that*.)

More recently, Stacey Slater's bipolar mum, Mad Jean joined the soap. At Christmas 2005, trappy Stacey found out that her mum was having problems and went to help her. Her old family home made Chateau Slater in Albert Square look like suburbia. There was a rusting old car, a filthy mattress, rotting sofas and a dilapidated pram. And outside was even more of a dump...

Jean, played by Gillian Wright, was in a dark, desperate place after being abused, humiliated, attacked and shunned by her callous neighbours. She was off her pills, off her food and off her head. It gave actress Lacey Turner, who plays Stacey, a chance to shine. "I'm never gonna leave you, Mum," Stacey vowed. "I'm gonna make sure that no one and nuffin' ever hurts or scares you again."

Stacey bathed, fed and cared for Jean, but it wasn't enough to prevent her from trying to top herself. The uncaring neighbours sniggered and Stacey snapped. "She's bipolar!" she shouted. "You probably think bipolar is where you get penguins and icebergs."

It was a terrific performance, and Jean ended up back in an institution for her own good. The storyline would win a Mental Health Media Award the following September.

Jean was only supposed to be a minor character, but the episodes were praised so highly that she inevitably became a regular, which had the double benefit of a) showing another side of Stacey and b) cranking up the soap's misery quota. At the time it was hard to see how such an intensely hard-to-watch character could be someone that viewers would put up with for long periods, and so it has proved.

But in May 2009, Stacey started showing signs of bipolar disorder too. Series consultant Simon Ashdown said that viewers would see Jean adopting a more caring, maternal role. Indeed we have, but only at the expense of ruining Stacey as a character.

Revolutionary ideas that EastEnders *might consider trying sometime*

- Happy people.
- Faithful people
- People who make a success of their lives by their own efforts.
- Football fans who actually go to games.
- Trade unionists.
- Golfers.
- Teenage boy boxers, or a resident cage fighter.
- Fundamentalist Muslims.
- A trip to the dogs or the races.
- Someone funny propping up the bar.
- A female who isn't nuts.

Soap Babylon – Actors Behaving Badly

Dirty Boy Den

The shocking story involving Leslie Grantham broke in May 2004, gloriously trumping anything that was happening on screen. On 2 May *The People* exposed the actor as a 'webcam pervert' who stripped naked in his dressing room at the BBC studios in Elstree, Herts, and sent photos of himself performing sex acts via a laptop computer. *The People* reported that the married dad of three "sent explicit messages about deviant sexual practices and slagged off his fellow cast members – using a phone funded by BBC licence payers." He also moaned about "the old dogs I have to work with."

Who *could* he have meant?

The paper happily told all, revealing that "the sleazy star" told his webcam pal Amanda that Wendy Richard, 60, who played his old enemy Pauline Fowler on screen, was one of the biggest 'wankers' on the show. (Given what he was up to online, I can't be the only one to have thought, "Takes one to know one.")

He called Jessie 'Kat Slater' Wallace a 'vile dog', Kim Medcalf, who plays Sam Mitchell, 'thick' and 'self-infatuated', and Shane Richie 'big-headed' (this remark not contested by anyone who knew Shane). The following week he went on to accuse Lynne Slater actress Elaine Lordan of taking drugs.

The sex chat was rather banal, with Grantham boasting about shagging in car parks, on commons and in hotel lifts. (Who hasn't?) He seemed obsessed with threesomes, implants and mutual masturbation. For the prurient Sunday red-top this amounted to sexual depravity.

It was bad enough that the story broke, but afterwards Grantham was inadvertently betrayed by the soap scripts – to the delight of the watching millions, Chrissie read out his star-sign prediction from the *Walford Gazette*: "Something's arisen and you must seize it."

Steve McFadden

In August the following year an even worse scandal broke. Steve McFadden, who plays Phil Mitchell, was embroiled in a lurid 'dogging' scandal.

McFadden's former common-law wife, Angela Bostock, mother of two of his kids, sold her story to the *News of the World*. She alleged that the soap star had forced her to take part in what the paper helpfully defined as a 'perverted sex craze' for ten years.

Angela claimed they trawled car parks and service stations in London, Surrey, Essex, Hampshire and Norfolk, cruising in Steve's camper van for strangers to have sex with. The allegations were rich in detail: Angela, then 29, said that the actor wore "bizarre disguises", including a spiky blond wig from *Peter Pan* when he was playing Captain Hook in panto, so that fans wouldn't recognise him. (It gave a whole new meaning to, "He's behind you!") He also wore glasses and adopted a stage-Irish accent before signalling to other doggers with torches.

Angela alleged McFadden made her have sex with a transvestite and a fellow dogger, so that he could watch and pleasure himself. She also claimed that, on another occasion, he 'demanded' she have oral sex through a car door with a stranger.

It was gutter journalism at its most compulsive: "Sleazy Steve McFadden stood in his camper van with his pants around his ankles as a French transvestite in a blonde wig and fishnet stockings prepared to have sex with his horrified girlfriend ..." *Ooh la la!* "McFadden even invited a passing cyclist to join in too." How very thoughtful!

Comedians had a field day with this. "Spare a thought for the other doggers while they watch Phil Mitchell give the missus a treat," said Jimmy Carr, "thinking to themselves, 'He's not just hard on the telly!'"

Described as "a tearful blonde", Angela told the *Screws*: "The father of my children is a pervert. He is addicted to dogging. Steve loved dirty old men watching us having sex in car parks. It disgusted and terrified me but he told me that it was normal, and that if we didn't do it he couldn't guarantee staying faithful to me.

"I clung on to the hope he would be there for me and our kids."

Cynics might have pointed out that to be forced to do something you don't enjoy once is understandable, to do it repeatedly for ten years is an entirely different matter. Had Angela only decided to spill the beans after McFadden had started dating his co-star, Lucy Benjamin, who played his on-screen lover Lisa Fowler?

Bostock was at pains to point out that McFadden carried on dogging after he had begun his relationship with Benjamin. She also detailed how the couple would drive to dogging hot-spots including one in Borehamwood, Herts, near the *EastEnders* set.

Other dogging sites frequented by the shameless pair included car parks off the A3, Epping Forest in Essex, the New Forest in Hants and outside of Paris.

The scandal put the *EastEnders* bosses in a difficult position. For starters, the allegations were obviously more extreme than Grantham's indiscretions. On the other hand they had recently signed McFadden, then 46, to a megabucks deal to return to the BBC soap after a two-year absence. His comeback episodes with Ross Kemp as his battling bruv, Grant, had attracted 13 million viewers. Losing Phil Mitchell would have damaged the soap in a way that axing clapped-out Dirty Den did not. Poor old Leslie Grantham was expendable; McFadden wasn't. So they stood by him, and McFadden's agent (Barbara Windsor's husband Scott) pulled strings to persuade the press to ease off on the coverage and the jokes.

But the scandal wasn't quite over. On 3 November 2005, Steve

McFadden was assaulted by Angela Bostock who was arrested and later released with a police caution. She also set up home with a lesbian lover, Jennifer Courtney, until then the wife of McFadden's good friend, 'celebrity gangster' Dave Courtney. (Dave and Jen have since reunited.)

Most observers agreed that Steve's off-screen activities were far more gripping than anything he'd ever got up to onscreen. And I'm pleased to report that the shame has not calmed him down. He's currently living with new partner Dr Rachel Green (nee Sidwell), a mother of three who he met on the school run. Dr Green left her surgeon husband for McFadden last year; in June 2009 brunette Rachel gave birth to a baby girl (a fourth child for her and Steve). She weighed in at 6lbs 3oz. Both mother and baby are said to be doing well.

Ross Kemp

Steve's screen brother, Ross Kemp, was also involved in some off-screen shenanigans; nothing as scandalous as panto-dogging, but intriguing nonetheless. In November 2005, Ross's then wife, the alabaster-white *Sun* newspaper editor Rebekah Wade, was arrested and held for eight hours after allegedly assaulting him. She was later released without charge. Scotland Yard said that Mr Kemp, 41, sustained a cut to the mouth but had declined medical treatment. The arrest had happened at their home in Battersea, South London, at about 4am – after the hard-man actor had called the cops. Strangely, *The Sun* seemed to miss the story, as it did the couple's break-up the following year amid unproven and unsavoury speculation. It was surely pure coincidence that the Steve McFadden story swamped that of Kemp and Wade, and just a matter of luck that the high-profile celebrity couple's break-up attracted such scant Fleet Street coverage.

Back in 2005, I asked in *The People*: "Is *EastEnders* cursed? No matter how hot the action gets on screen, the cast's real lives always upstage it. Lap-top sex, dogging, hard-men beaten up by girlies ...

"How can TV's biggest tough-nuts call the cops when they're

(allegedly) assaulted by women? It's a joke. The ultimate farce in fact. But there's no truth in the rumours that Ross Kemp is seeking sanctuary at Deepcut Barracks. Or that he uses Viagra eye-drops to look hard."

Rob Kazinsky

In January 2007, BBC bosses suspended Robert Kazinsky, the actor who plays womaniser Sean Slater, for bombarding a model with obscene text messages and photos. *The People* reported that sleazy Kazinsky, 23, texted Aimi Robinson a photo of his penis after meeting her online. He also spelled out his sexual fantasies to her in lurid detail.

Shocked Aimi, 28, said: "Maybe Dirty Den has been giving him tips. I can't watch *EastEnders* now. Every time I see him on screen I think of that horrible picture. It makes my skin crawl."

The mum of one added: "I realise he's a young boy and perhaps his hormones are raging. But you would have thought his bosses would have given him some advice.

"They should run a 'Keep it in your trousers' course for new *EastEnders* staff. His character on the show is a real dirt-bag, so maybe he's identifying with him too much."

Star-struck Aimi befriended Kazinsky on MySpace. They started chatting online on 15 October 2006, and later started to text each other. In one message he told her: "Might let you give me a blowjob one day." In another, he added: "Might film you giving me head one day."

As well as a picture of himself, he also sent Aimi a freakish image of a pig with a penis for a head. She said: "Just because I'm a glamour model doesn't mean I'm into all that stuff. I would rather have the real thing than a photo.

"I just thought, 'Here we go, just another creep.' What's that supposed to do for me? He was obviously boasting, and showing he is a natural ginger.

"It wasn't even done very well. He was wearing a horrible jumper and you could see a Dyson vacuum cleaner in the background.

"I hate to think what he was doing at the time. It's pretty obvious."

During their internet chats Kazinsky admitted he hates going out, preferring to stay indoors and cruise the internet for 'booty calls' – requesting home visits involving sex.

Aimi, from Battle in East Sussex, said that while she was happy to flirt she did nothing to encourage Kazinsky to send her X-rated material: "If anything, I was hoping for a proper loving relationship – someone to wine and dine me, like in *Pretty Woman*. Instead I got that. It was disgusting."

Their MySpace chat also included a savage rant against *Big Brother*-star-turned-glamour-model Michelle Bass, who had given a kiss-and-tell story about him to a newspaper. Aimi jokingly revealed Michelle would be at a party she had been invited to. Kazinsky replied: "I shall turn up and sledgehammer her over the f****** head."

To prevent disruption to the soap's storylines, Kazinsky was allowed to continue filming until February, and was then suspended for eight weeks. A spokesman said: "Following the story in the *Sunday People* on January 7 2007, *EastEnders* executive producer Diederick Santer has taken the decision to suspend Robert Kazinsky from early February for a period of two months.

"In addition, Robert Kazinsky would like to apologise for any offence caused to *EastEnders*' viewers and for bringing the show into disrepute."

Rita Simons' 'Drug Shame'

Roxy Mitchell actress Rita confessed to a 'wild' history of drug-taking, *The People* revealed. This consisted of snorting coke in clubs and smoking dope every night.

A friend (some friend!) told the paper in 2007: "Rita claimed she would snort coke every time we went partying, although no one ever saw her do it. She would sneak off to the toilets and then come back and brag about what she'd done, telling us how she'd just snorted the coke through a £20 note.

"She would boast about cocaine whenever she got the opportunity and seemed quite casual about it. She would say that if anyone offered her drugs she would also take what was on offer."

Rita – Alan Sugar's niece – also confessed on her MySpace page that she had got high "too many times". All a tight-lipped *EastEnders* press lackey would say was, "This is a private matter."

Lacey Turner

In 2005 Stacey Slater actress Lacey Turner was caught on camera having sex in a top-floor corridor of a posh West End hotel. *The Sun* reported that 'Lusty Lacey, 17' had left a party and jumped into a lift with a mystery man to find somewhere to do the wild thing.

They made their way to the 18th floor and threw caution to the wind, only for their romp to be interrupted by an astonished maid. CCTV film of the pair's X-rated antics was inevitably the talk of the five-star Carlton Tower Hotel in London's Knightsbridge.

It showed the couple emerging from the lift, waiting for the maid to go into a room and then bonking on a chair once the coast was clear. A hotel insider told *The Sun*: "The footage shows Stacey and the bloke really going for it hammer and tongs in the corridor."

Lacey was seen, in stockings and suspenders, straddling her lover before the shocked maid reappeared and caught them in the act. The red-faced couple then readjusted their clothes and made a hasty exit.

Lacey and her mystery lover had got raunchy after attending a party in the hotel's ballroom. The insider said: "She was done up to the nines and looked much more glamorous than she does in *EastEnders*. She was dressed in a black frock with fur trim, and stockings and suspenders. The guy had a massive grin on his face both before and after doing his deed."

The CCTV film of Lacey – nominated as Best Newcomer in that year's Soap Awards and presumably in the running for best all-round comer too – was taken at around 9pm. Ironically, that same evening she featured in a sketch for *Children in Need*, shot a fortnight earlier, in which she joked about not being stupid enough to be caught filmed having sex …

Other stars' antics pale in comparison, but it's worth recalling how Jessie Wallace's turbulent personal life included drunken fights with co-star Hannah Waterman (who played Laura Beale, wife of Ian), a drink-driving conviction and her extremely volatile relationship with ex-fiancé Dave Morgan who flogged details of her boozing and their sex life to the *News of the Screws*. Ex-cop Dave said the actress had banned him from seeing their daughter, Tallulah. Even Jessie's sister, Danielle Mason, went public about her fraught relationship, claiming Jessie had stolen her boyfriend (toy boy Tommy O'Neill) and then cut her out of her life.

"I can't believe my own sister did this to me," Danielle told the *Sunday Mirror*. "It was bad enough to find out my boyfriend had been cheating. But it was twisting the knife when I found out he'd been carrying on with my own sister. I feel I've been betrayed by the two people I should have been able to trust most."

Mason said that Jessie contacted her and started asking questions about her romance with Tommy. The next day, she called back and admitted that she had been dating him.

"It was like a punch in the stomach. She simply said, 'Oh by the way, I'm dating that guy Tommy.' I couldn't believe it," Danielle explained. "It was like she was talking to a stranger not to me, her sister."

It may not be any consolation, but that relationship didn't last either. Jessie's other short-lived flings included former co-star Joel 'Jake Moon' Beckett, divorcee Mark Stannett, who was accused of breaking a former lover's nose, and pot-bellied builder Chris Osborn.

Another scandalous Slater sister was Elaine Lordan, who played Lynne. Stories abound about her alcohol problem: while pregnant, she allegedly caused uproar after a drunken fight outside a pub in north London, and was apparently sacked by the soap for being drunk on set. Most recently, she collapsed twice on ITV's *I'm a Celebrity … Get Me Out of Here* and left the reality show after just one night.

The scandals that never broke

- One leading female star was filmed having sex on a snooker table with two of the country's best-loved light-entertainment personalities. The footage still exists ...

- At least two of the soap's most famous onscreen couples were shagging in real life – and had sex at the show's Borehamwood HQ. In fairness, this elder couple were married at the time; unfortunately, they were married to other people. The male star was also bedding a member of a famous pop family. (*Not* the Jacksons.)

- One cast member was blackmailed into marriage to keep his 'secret shame' a secret.

- Cocaine consumption in certain dressing rooms – to a degree that would have impressed Al Pacino's character in *Scarface*.

- One leading cast member grew marijuana plants by the sack-load at his mansion house. He used to store it in his shed in large black bin liners, which led to an unfortunate incident with his conscientious cleaner who put the bags out for the dustbin men.

- Two of the show's leading heterosexual pin-ups were actually as gay as a French horn.

Career Mistakes

Bobby Davro joined the soap in October 2007. A former giant of light entertainment, Davro is one of the country's best impressionists and his rapid-fire comedy patter has proved a hit all over the country. Bobby had seen how Shane Richie's role in the soap revitalised his career and how it made Mike Reid into a national icon. He must have thought his luck had changed when, at the suggestion of Barbara Windsor, *Enders* boss Diederick Santer decided to cast him as Vinnie Monks.

The character sounded promising, a loveable rogue and a 'cheeky chappy'. It was just a shame that no one bothered to tell the writers, who singularly failed to play up to Davro's strengths. Instead of giving him amusing plots and decent dialogue, they painted him as a rather dull non-character whose only role seemed to be love interest for Shirley Carter, an unpleasant alcoholic who'd abandoned her kids and lost any sense of morality years ago – if indeed she'd ever had any. Vinnie followed her around like a puppy dog, even buying a flat so that they could live together, but she treated him like dog dirt, leaping into bed with Phil Mitchell whenever he was drunk enough to oblige. Not even the arrival of his bird-bandit son, Callum, could make Monks' character interesting. Eventually, Vinnie realised that staying in Walford was pointless and, like so many hard-up middle-aged men, he decided to travel the world in a vintage car instead.

Bobby had the last laugh though, incorporating jokes about the soap into his stand-up routine. This caused 'offence' at a show he performed at London's O2 Arena in October 2008, when Davro joked that Shirley Carter "had a face like a bulldog licking piss off a thistle". He also claimed to have slept with Heather Trott. "I'm not saying she's big," he teased. "But I got on top of her and burnt my arse on the light bulb."

Chris Ellison, the actor best known for his brilliant role as tough, two-fisted detective Frank Burnside in *The Bill*, turned up briefly and pointlessly as Len Harker. I'd love to have been a fly on the wall when he took that call from his agent.

"Great news, Chris, you've got a part in *EastEnders*."

"Terrific, who am I playing?"

"You're onscreen in August."

"Great. What's the part?"

"You're breaking up, mate."

"Who-am-I-playing?"

"Fat Pat's love interest, must dash, meeting, laters."

"Arghhhhh!"

Len was apparently a quiet man with inner strength who made rocking horses for a living. Brightly painted, garishly adorned, wooden ... yes, you can see why he was attracted to Pat.

He gave her a lift. It was his first encounter with her and he hadn't been expecting company, but he had a picnic for two in the boot – so that was Pat sorted, but what did he eat? (I never leave home without a ready-packed picnic myself.)

Len even drove her 60-odd miles home for her to offer him coffee; by which point even the rocking horse stamped its hoof twice for "No!"

Pat was trying to trace her Down's syndrome sister Joan, institutionalised decades ago, but who was, as she discovered, brown bread. (If Joan had lived, imagine what she'd have said to her: "You poor love, fancy spending all this time in a grim, uncaring hellhole like Walford!") *Leave it aht.* Pat, at this point, had been around Walford for 21 years; surely she'd have mentioned her sometime before now?

Chris Ellison lasted a week in the soap and it seems he's unlikely to return. It'd be unkind to suggest the thought of being Pat's other half put him off, but frankly I'd rather sleep rough. (And I'm sure the feeling's mutual.) Len Harker was last heard of at Christmas 2007, when Pat received a rocking horse and a card from him. Sadly, decent male parts in this soap are as rare as rocking horse s***.

If ever an actor was destined for a part in *EastEnders*, it was surely **Phil Daniels**. He'd starred as Jimmy in the cult classic Mod movie *Quadrophenia* and did the spoken voiceover on Blur's 1994 Number One smash 'Parklife'. Islington born, Phil was a Londoner through and through with a lifelong attachment to cockney culture. Surely he could introduce some streetwise realism into the wretched soap?

In theory, yes. In reality, the writers handicapped him from the off by making his character Kevin Wicks mysteriously attracted to miserable Denise Fox.

Phil made his *Enders* debut on 17 February 2006; Kevin was killed off on New Year's Eve 2007, after Daniels refused to renew his contract the previous August, realising perhaps that he'd gone from 'Parklife' to no life. Kev seemed doomed from the off. He'd been married to sozzled love cheat Shirley Carter; Jimbo, his one son with her, had died; she'd had two other kids, Carly and Deano, by other men, but had abandoned them, leaving Kev to bring them all up on his own.

Kev moved in with his auntie-in-law, Fat Pat, with the intention of swiftly emigrating, but in the event his kids' troubles kept him in Walford and he ended up managing the car lot.

He and bad-tempered Denise bonded over her never-mentioned (before or since) interest in obscure French films. Why he persevered with the stroppy cow defied all male logic. She broke up with him as frequently as celebrity 'lovers' trying to generate coverage in *Heat* magazine. But the soppy mug stood by her, supporting her when Owen, her evil ex, came back on the scene, and finally marrying her – after she'd kicked him in the groin. Nice.

Kevin's barely credible storylines were not entertaining, so I'll keep this recap brief: ex-wife Shirley the Terrahawk came back on the scene, demanding contact with the kids and blackmailing Kev to get what she wanted, threatening to reveal to Carly and Deano that Kevin was not their real father. The truth eventually came out and both of the ungrateful brats shunned the man who stood by them during their formative years, after their mother abandoned them. Deano forgave him, but Carly would not. Understandably miffed, Kevin jogged on. He went on the missing list for months. Word finally filtered back that he'd cleared his bank account in Hastings and had gone to Dungeness in Kent with a view to ending up in France. Then some no-mark called Jed stole his ferry ticket (£44 return) and this, apparently, was enough to persuade Kev to give up all of his dreams of escape. For no good logical reason, he headed back to woeful Walford instead.

Spoilt cow Carly rejected him again, so he ended up shagging the un-alluring Shirley before going back to Denise. The ill-matched and ill-fated pair married in April 2007, but not before sneaky bitch Shirley attempted to ruin it all by blabbing about their bunk-up.

More family misery ensued as Deano got banged up for trying to pervert the course of justice. (He and Chelsea had attempted to frame Sean Slater for an attack on Patrick Trueman.) In December Kev started selling cars for Phil Mitchell, unaware that they were knocked off cut-and-shut affairs. Once again he was blackmailed by the Terrible Terrahawk, who he ended up kidnapping but, sadly, not garroting. Shirley goaded him to go crazy in one of Phil's dodgy jam-jars; he roared off, the car bonnet opened and Kev crashed, ending up impaled on a metal pole. He died moments before New Year Eve came to an end – another case of ring out the old, ring in more of the same old misery and despair.

Denise went on to scatter Kevin's ashes in the South China Sea, possibly off of the Spratly Islands – because you can't spell Spratly without the 'prat' that Kevin Wicks became.

VOX POPS

What real Londoners think of EastEnders

Hackney-born **Garry Johnson, former black cab driver and fulltime writer,** says of the soap:

"I can't abide *EastEnders*, it is as much in touch with reality as Michael Jackson was at the Neverland ranch. There's hardly any mention of West Ham United, just the odd token remark. Garry, Billy and Minty are fans but they never discuss the team and you never hear 'Bubbles' by the Cockney Rejects on the jukebox.

"It's all so far-fetched. I've just seen Ian Beale come back from Scotland wearing a kilt. What next, will he come back from a daytrip to France wearing onions round his neck? When they went to Ireland there were donkeys in the street; the writers can't see past old-fashioned clichés. They don't represent the real East End because they don't know it.

"You never hear a character talk about anyone from the area making anything of their lives, there is no mention of a successful pop singer or a sportsman coming from Walford because the loony left writers hate the idea of anyone having success. All they can preach is misery and failure.

"I liked the original Sam Mitchell, played by Danniella Westbrook – she was the only one who ever looked like a real East End girl, she was the sort of girl you'd have seen in Bethnal Green back in the day, done up to the nines and making something of herself.

"The BBC has every sort of person on here except for a real

cockney family. They never really have a proper Jewish family. You get the odd Jewish character like Dr Legg but never a real caring, sharing Jewish family with traditional family values. If I were Jewish I'd be insulted by that.

"The worst characters are the Welsh ones, they are always a waste of space. Huw was pointless; so was the Welsh punk who was around back when Wicksy had his band in the 1980s.

"Why are the gay characters always good-looking, by the way? Gay Christian, the Muscle Mary, never seems to have the sort of problems the straight blokes have because the soap likes to glamorise homosexuality.

"No one ever really talks about the type of people who duck and dive in the real East End either. Who is the local Mr Big now that Johnny Allen is off the scene? He was one of the few villains who wasn't a plastic gangster, they wasted his potential.

"Their idea of a criminal is Nasty Nick, the so-called hard-man who lived with his mum. He was such a useless bad guy he couldn't even murder poor old Dot, and how hard would that have been? He dressed more like a Goth than a gangster, in that big heavy leather coat. Who wears that at the height of summer?

"Little things annoy me too. Real EastEnders don't go to the café every day for breakfast. We're quite capable of making our own tea and toast, we're not as thick as the BBC would like to portray us. The launderette is a joke. We do have washing machines, you know, it's not the 1950s.

"And why does no one have a Rottweiler or a pit-bull? If you go down Bermondsey or Custom House you see loads of geezers walking about with dogs like that.

"Blokes on *EastEnders* never go to boxing matches. They don't go on beanos to Southend. They're a bunch of pussy-whipped wimps. No one plays golf or has koi carp.

"There has never been a decent police character in the show. There is never a mention of dockers – no one's dad or grandad worked on the docks, which is ridiculous. No one goes to the dogs, the betting shop seems to have disappeared. The bed and breakfast has more people living there permanently than it has guests. When they have karaoke nights there are more people on stage than in the audience. No one seems to read *The Sun* or the *Daily Star*, it's always the *Walford Gazette*. The show is a joke."

Gill Print, former market trader, born in East Ham: "*EastEnders* is a load of old s***; I'm sorry, but I can't put it any clearer than that. It doesn't come close to capturing the real East London. They need proper East End people writing it to make it true to life, not these funny sounding people with double-barrelled names. They should get Martina Cole in to come up with some real dirty deals and convincing villains. We watch it quite often, not because we enjoy it but because we like to take the piss out of it."

Mickey Pugh, cockney comedian (and Barbara Windsor's favourite funnyman): "What I dislike most about *EastEnders* – apart from the Dick Van Dyke school of cockney that you hear constantly – is that there is never a wag at the bar. In every London pub you ever go in you will find a funny regular who takes the piss and gets everyone laughing. You never have that in the Queen Vic. There's never any laughter. So why would you go? Everyone outside of London must think we're right miserable bastards.

"No one ever won the Lottery either. Not even a tenner.

"The whole of East London is a building site right now because of the 2012 Olympics, but there's no building work in Walford and no one has mentioned the Olympics. The only five rings you ever saw on *EastEnders* were around Keith Miller's bath."

Jeff Turner, singer, the Cockney Rejects: "I can't stand it, I find it unwatchable. It's just half an hour of moaning four times a week. The acting is dreadful and most of the cast aren't Londoners, so they never sound authentic. Come to Custom House, where I'm from, and no one pronounces their 't's.

"The dialogue is terrible. Most geezers in the pub will talk about the Championship League or who's buying what player. Pubs are a hotbed of football talk, but not in Walford. They don't talk about politics or bands or even boxing – and the East End is full of great boxing clubs. I only ever remember one boxing storyline, when Kelvin Carpenter became a boxer overnight. You never ever saw him train in the gym, he just did his roadwork running around the Square, like no one would ever do. He only had one fight and they were talking him up as the next champion. It was ludicrous. Then all these shady people start appearing laying on bets and he was under pressure to throw the fight, it just doesn't happen.

"The Mitchells were supposed to be the hard-nuts of the manor during the 1990s, but they never had any mates. They didn't have a firm around them, no team to go to work with. Like everything else about the show it was unreal."

David Essex, pop star: "The show is nothing like the real East End where I was born and bred. The real East End is full of characters who like a good time, the show is full of moody, boring people."

Terry Hayes, Poplar-born school caretaker: "I absolutely hate it. It's nothing like the real East End. It's contrived and ridiculous and full of unlikely situations and relationships you can't believe in. The gangsters are farcical. Most of the hard-men couldn't go a round with Tinky Winky from the Teletubbies. And the women are all barking mad. If this is the East End, where are the Eastern Europeans? They had a few token building workers in there for a couple of weeks, but there's no sign of any Poles or Serbs or Kosovans now. You never have any comedians in the pub. No one goes to see bands, or goes fishing or plays golf. It just isn't a reflection of the way white working-class Londoners are, and it certainly doesn't reflect the way Muslims are. It's terrible; stale, repetitive and out of touch with reality. It's just shocking."

Jimmy Greaves, former West Ham, Spurs and Chelsea footballer turned TV pundit: "*EastEnders* is a soap but it keeps trying to push out a message. It's very left-wing and miserable. It really is a load of rubbish. I'm fed up with the way it tries to ram homosexuality down our throats. BBC bosses should be forced to watch it themselves for a week. The trouble with television is that the people who make the programmes don't watch TV."

Ricky Grover, cockney comedian: "Bring back the old faces to *EastEnders*, it's gone to pot. I'm fed up with that ginger bald fella who keeps poling everyone. Sonia's acting is deplorable. Don't worry about Ricky – RICKY! We want KENNY! Put Kenny Noye on the Square! That's what you want, a bit of excitement, get a bit of road rage round the Square, beautiful. KENNY!"

A cast member who asks not to be named: "All soaps have highs and lows, but we have been struggling for quite a while now. We urgently need to get back to centering the stories on people viewers care about; the characters really are the soap's heart and soul. The rot set in with the rash of plastic gangsters we had a few years back. Viewers couldn't identify with them at all. At its best *EastEnders* is about recognisable people facing everyday problems. The fault is not in the cast, it is in the writing and in the class of the people who run the show. They're not working class and it shows."

Last word from a non-EastEnder ...
Morrissey, not a Londoner obviously, but a perceptive critic: "I just hate *EastEnders*. I would like to be a scriptwriter for it and slaughter the entire cast."

Seven Small Joys of *EastEnders*

1) Actor Peter Dean, who famously had trouble with his Rs, had annoyed the writers so they hit on a fiendishly clever revenge. They gave his character, Pete Beale, a girlfriend. Her name? Rose from Rotoroa ... or in Pete-speak, "Wose fwom Wotowoa." Then they killed him. Left him bwown bwead.

   (An interesting aside: Peter Beale was killed by an unsavoury character called Chapman who fixed the brakes on his car. Chapman was played by Gary Lammin, the former guitarist with East End punk band Cock Sparrer, and was described by Victor Lewis-Smith as "one of the most uncouth characters I've ever seen," the sort of person who orders "broken leg of lamb" for his roast dinners. After doing the dirty deed, Lammin tells me, "I couldn't go into a pub anywhere in London without people clocking me, and buying me drinks. A typical remark was, 'Well done, son. Thanks for getting rid of that f***er.'" After making such an impact you would have thought the soap might bring Lammin back, and they did. Only this time he wasn't shifty hard-man Chapman, they made him a nondescript plumber called – wait for it – Quentin. Says Gary, "Whoever heard of an East End plumber called Quentin? I expect he was in business with a plasterer called Tarquin, Crispin the spark and Tristram the chippie.")

2) The Queen Vic Jukebox – with its odd selection of vintage punk songs. We don't know which of the regulars are fans of

The Clash and The Jam, but I am grateful for their existence.

3) In the unlikely event of Garry Hobbs marrying Dawn Swann, only one good thing would come of it: she would then be Dawn Hobbs, or, to a cockney, 'Dawn 'Obbs' – which sounds like something out of a *Two Ronnies* sketch: "Dawn 'Obbs?" "No, Dawn 'Obbs, Dawn 'Obbs! Knobs for doors!" And just as easy to turn, I shouldn't wonder; she'd open for anyone, that girl. For similar reasons they should have engineered it for Peggy to marry Dr Legg, because then she would have been Peg Legg.

4) One of the tedious paedophile episodes was written by Justin Young. Honestly.

5) The catchphrases: the soap is famous for its many clichéd sayings. Here, remembered with affection, are my Top Ten favourites:

"On the 'ouse" – pronounced *ahse*. (Peggy Mitchell)

"Woss goin' on?" (All)

"We gotta tawk." (All female characters)

"Sorted!" (All male characters in the 1990s)

"Get outta my pub." (Peggy)

"I can't believe I'm 'earing this." (Pauline Fowler)

"What are you, some kind of pilchard?" (Frank Butcher)

"Rickayyyyy!" (Bianca Jackson)

"Oh I say!" (Dot Branning)

"What's on the other side?" (Ten million viewers since the 1990s)

One of executive producer Diederik Santer's first decisions after he took over the reins of the soap was to ban "Woss goin' on?" from the scripts. Killjoy.

6) A small joy you won't have heard about. When Frank Butcher had to run over poor Tiffany Mitchell he was driving a Ford car. Ford weren't at all happy about their vehicles being used to wipe out such a popular character and duly complained to the soap bosses, saying something along the lines of, "We're giving you our cars for free and you're using them to bump off much-loved stars." The 'for free' bit was the thing that made BBC execs sit up and take notice, as the middleman responsible for supplying the cars had been fraudulently charging the soap and

copping the dosh for at least two years. His relationship with *Enders* promptly ended.

7) And the smallest small joy of them all? The dwarf Australian teacher that the soap brought in as part of their diversity agenda. No one ever joked about her, suggesting that she'd been caught short, as would have happened in real life. No one except the reliably sarky Ally Ross even asked if her previous soap had been *Gnome and Away*.

Small Mysteries of *EastEnders*

- A ploughman's in the Queen Vic will set you back £6.25 – 75p more than the steak and chips. How so? It's almost as puzzling as who they employ to actually cook it ...

- Arthur Fowler always used to watch the telly in his allotment shed. How? It was the 1980s. Allotment sheds didn't have power points.

- The tans – cast members enjoy exotic holidays that their characters could never dream of. This means that the likes of Pauline 'the Growler' Fowler, Sharon '40' Watts and Ficky Ricky Butcher were frequently seen with magnificent but unexplained tans. It was as if their homes were doubling as nuclear reactors.

- In 2004, the video shop comically fined Den Watts for taking out *Porkies II* in 1988. Nice touch. Except Walford Videos didn't actually open until halfway through the 1990s.

- Why does West Indies fan Patrick Trueman never mention the cricket tests?

- Why does Shirley Carter buy *The Radio Times*? Clearly it's a nice bit of product placement for BBC Enterprises – there's always a copy in her gaff. But when Terrahawk Shirl isn't drinking or shagging herself senseless, she's working in the pub. When does she ever watch telly? And if she did, what would happen if she chanced upon *EastEnders*? Given the amount she knocks back, Shirley would probably just assume she was seeing double as usual...

- Women have breast implants – Zoe, Sonia – but no one ever notices and there is never an explanation.
- After the big funfair disaster of 2004, how did the Ferreiras manage to run Toucan Cabs from an office that had been destroyed with no radios or fare meters and no plates for their taxis?
- September 2008: the whole Square was suddenly decked out in James Bond outfits for a spontaneous Bond party. Where did they get them from? And who paid for the hire? The costumes start at £26 a pop.
- The strange case of Guido Smith: Gay Guido popped up in 1988 as a business contact of Colin Russell, the graphic designer and all-round wet liberal worry-guts. They ended up moving in together, but fell out because Guido had the temerity to tell the Old Bill that Junior Roberts was a thieving little toe-rag. After Colin left the Square he asked Guido to look after his flat; Guido actually moved out in February 1989. His leaving scenes were filmed but never shown, so viewers never saw him go and his exit was never referred to onscreen. When Ian and Cindy Beale moved in to the flat a while later, most viewers expected them to find Guido still inside with his feet up, eating cottage cheese and watching gay porn.
- Before she died, did Kathy Beale ever give Wurzel Gummidge his hair back?
- Missing shops: back in 1999 I wrote an article headlined, 'Why can't you get a ruby in Albert Square?' I pointed out that Walford was the only place in East London where you couldn't find an Indian restaurant. They fixed that a few years later by opening up the Argee Bharjee in George Street, but, bizarrely, Walford still has no Chinese takeaway and no kebab shop – and certainly nothing as cockney as a pie and mash shop. Until 2006 it was also the only place in London with no yellow lines.

- Shape-shifting tots: worryingly, Roxy Mitchell's baby Amy changes size every episode. Getting bigger isn't so much of a problem, but in 2009 the poor little tot has been noticeably shrinking.

- In December 2005, Patrick Trueman started managing the car lot for Phil. Patrick had no previous experience of car sales, but got by cheerfully enough ... unlike Frank Butcher, the very experienced former boss who was regularly reduced to apoplexy by the strains of the job. At other times, Patrick has successfully run a B&B with no guests and still makes a living from the corner shop.

- The tube station has been there since the beginning, but we've only seen a train once – in 1988, at Lou Beale's funeral.

- When Chas Slater came out of chokey after attacking Little Moan's rapist, how come he still had his black cab licence? Taxi drivers assure me that *any* infringement of the law means the cab authorities will take your licence away.

Into the Noughties – Year by Year Blog: A Decade of Decline

EastEnders entered the noughties with its best years firmly behind it. The pressures of trying to churn out four episodes a week with growing budget restrictions and under-performing writers reached a nadir with the dragging fiasco of the Ferreira family. Ronnie Ferreira's kidney was to symbolise the frustrating nonsense that had become the soap's stock-in-trade. In fairness, they did manager to create more giant characters – in particular Kat Slater and Alfie Moon, both of whom were dreamt up by the talented Tony Jordan. But, almost inevitably, their relationship was cocked up by abysmal writing and poor plotting. As the decade dragged on, desperate producers relied increasingly on hysterical melodrama to obscure the fault-lines. In rapid succession we suffered Ben Mitchell's torture by Stella Crawford (solicitor and sadist), respectable housewife Tanya Branning burying her womanising husband Max alive, mad Sean Slater terrorising saintly streetcleaner Gus Smith for no apparent reason and geriatric football hooligans running amok in the Queen Vic ... Even hardcore fans were shocked by the level of violence, and *The Radio Times* was obliged to defend the show from viewers who were understandably worried about the suitability of such horrors in a show aimed at families in a 7.30pm time slot.

2000 – *Who Let the Dogs Out? The Slater Sisters arrive...*

Mystery of the Year: What airline did Peggy, Frank, Roy and Pat use for their flight to Spain? From the outside the plane looked spick and span and modern, but inside it had a porthole like an ocean liner. It could have been a leftover prop that Barbara Windsor brought along from *Carry on Cruising*. Still, the cockney couples all had a bloody good view of the wings ... from their seats at the back.

Other mysteries:
- Where did Ethel Skinner get her wig? We can't be sure, but somewhere you felt there was probably a PG Tips chimp feeling the draught. (You know why they call her Ethel, don't you? Because even back in 1985, that's all she did...)
- Natalie's job on the *Gazette* involved six weeks training in Scotland. Why? Is it the *Walford & West Lothian Gazette* now?

Image of the Year: Frank Butcher turning up at Fat Pat's wearing nothing but a revolving bowtie. "Blimey," she must have thought, "the size of his ears!" The image was so horrific it's a wonder Benetton didn't snap it up for an ad.

I would have laughed if Roy had opened the door. How would Frank have explained that? "Easy, fella. Is this the right place for the Walford Naturist Club Meeting or am I some kind of pilchard?"

Their love affair was rekindled in Spain in the August. Fearless Frank Butcher shagged Patricia in his holiday bed. How did he ever think they could keep this monstrous betrayal from Peggy? For starters, surely she would notice as soon as she climbed in and plummeted into the big Pat-shaped indentation left in the mattress.

Pat revealed that she was 16 when Frank "took advantage" of her. Now she was sweet 16 stone and he was back for more. She described him as being "like a rollercoaster" – a big dipper, by all accounts, whereas Pat is more like a bouncy castle. (For the ghost train see Irene Raymond.)

But I was tormented by one big, burning question: what did Frank see in her? Their sex session can't have been that much cop. Afterwards Pat didn't have a hair out of place, no lipstick smeared, no make-up smudged, but she did lose an earring. Really? Have you clocked Pat's earrings? They're the size of ruddy anchors. She couldn't even stand up with just one on without it instantly jerking her off balance.

(Footnote: Frank only started fancying Pat when he stopped wearing his glasses. Coincidence? Unreliable Fact: the FX used for Frank and Pat's subsequent love-making scenes were pioneered on *Walking with Dinosaurs*.)

Elsewhere, the underwhelming di Marco family left Albert Square pretty damn quick. Who packed their bags, the Flash or Billy Whizz? Irene (who was once cruelly likened to Herman Munster in drag) gave Rosa wind chimes as a farewell present, saying, "Every time there is a breeze, think of me." Sweet. What a shame she didn't add, "And every time there's a lot of wind, think of Terry."

Oh, and Ian Beale copped a £103,000 tax bill on the profits of two chip shops, half a café and a general store nobody uses, mentions or works in. Ian has a live-in nanny, Laura Lard-Arse, a PA on £20K a year and he sends his son to private school. Who knew there was so much money in chips?

September saw a real landmark development – the arrival of the Slater family, led by mouthy Big Mo, a Big Daddy look-alike who made *Coronation Street*'s Les Battersby seem refined. Strewth, the woman was frightening! The last time I saw a face that hard it was in a documentary about the Alps.

Mo is muvva-in-law to Charlie Slater and Nan to his brood of daughters. They weren't so much Stepford Wives as Deptford Wives: loud, lairy and as rough as old Harry. Mum Viv – Mater Slater – had had the good fortune to have died the previous October. (That's nothing; Big Mo has been stiff since she started acting.) It was like the Addams Family had suddenly moved into Albert Square, or there had been a mass break-out of exhibits from the London Dungeon.

At the time I was singularly unimpressed by Laila Morse, who had been cast for the part primarily because she was the sister of Gary Oldman. I wrote: "Leila Morse delivers every line like she's reading it off an idiot board. The woman barely seems fit to play a corpse on *The Bill*." But a few years later Mo had become one of my favourite characters. I'm not too sure whether this was because her acting improved, or because everything else had got worse ...

One thing the character did bring back was the black market.

Standing in for me at *The Sun* when the Slaters arrived, Harry Hill reckoned that Big Mo "used to be a bit of a slut but now deals meat through her back door," and Little Mo "wants to learn how to drive a taxi, also learning to be a slut." Harry suggested additional characters like Middle Mo and Ho-Ho – "Middle Mo's boyfriend who turns out to be homosexual."

What else? In July another vice girl storyline began as Terry Raymond found a call-girl card in a phone box conveniently situated on the Walford/Soho border. And Melanie Healy's dad Jeff (the one who looked like the lion from *The Wizard of Oz*) publicly proposed to Pauline Fowler in the Queen Vic. "How could you do this to me?" she moaned. *Why* is more to the point? Last month she slung him out of the house just for trying to snog her. Proposing marriage revealed a commitment to masochism that was not to be equalled until Max Mosley.

June saw a late shot of social realism as soap bosses edited the June 19th episode to include the England v. Germany football result. Big Dan Sullivan hired in a TV set that was the size of Fat Barry. It was the first time they'd had 48 inches of entertainment on display in the Vic since Sharon Mitchell's plunging necklines.

(Dot didn't watch it. She was busy playing in the Number 2 shirt as Gary Neville.)

September saw some genuinely moving moments as Dot helped Ethel Skinner pop her clogs, assisting her to overdose on morphine tablets. This was one of the few occasions that the soap had dealt with a major issue – euthanasia – with genuine dramatic aplomb. True to her character, Dot was then tormented with guilt.

In October Mark 'HIV' Fowler got the all-clear – almost as

baffling as how he'd been smitten in the first place. And Frank and Pat's unnatural lust dragged on. He told Peggy he was away at a car auction, which was half-true as he was checking out an old banger ...

But here's what I couldn't work out: why was roly-poly Roy's dressing gown tight on Frank?

The following month, the apparently 'bright' Sonia Jackson went into labour without having a clue what was happening. (Medics call this a 'John Prescott birth'.) Brainbox Sonia didn't even realise she was pregnant. Her brother Robbie was devastated when she gave little Chloe away. It wasn't so much that he'd lost a niece, more a potential playmate.

(Robbie had never been a bright kid, but when he went on his roadtrip why would he need a map to find Southend? It's a straight road all the way from the East End.)

Also in November: a disgusted Roy Evans told Pat to go back on the game – presumably as a street waddler.

December 2000 was all you'd expect, yet there was one amazing moment. Just hours after Peggy had smashed up the pub, the bust of Queen Victoria which sits on the bar had completely repaired itself. It was a miracle, I tell ya, the miracle of George Street ...

Poor floppy Roy Evans was still praying for a miracle in his trousers; Trevor roughed up Little Mo; Nick Cotton's neck tattoo vanished and his dear old mum Dot was jailed for contempt of court, after shoplifting and smashing up a chemist's to ensure she'd be punished for her part in Ethel's death. The *Walford Gazette* ran the spectacularly dull headline, 'Local Woman Imprisoned After Court Outburst'. How rubbish was that? 'Old Smokey Gets Chokey' would have been better – or 'Dot Plot Rot'.

On New Year's Eve, Nasty Nick sent Martin Fowler on a bad trip – experts agree that it was the worst since the soap went to Ireland.

2001 – Who Shot Phil …
(or *why make up your own stories when you can
just recycle old ones from* Dallas?)

Image of the Year: Little Mo hitting Trevor with an iron.
Row of the Year: Kat and Zoe – as Kat revealed her big family secret. It was sensational.
Mystery of the Year: in 2001, Jamie Mitchell found true love with Sonia Jackson. Why? This rather plain and chunky girl was a graduate of the Anne Robinson Charm School. And Jamie had to snog her … no wonder he left later this year.
Other mysteries: how could Melanie Healy-Beale-Owen afford the clothes she wore on a barmaid's wages? And why did Kerry Skinner call Robbie Jackson 'tiger'? The leopard is the one with the spots.
Guest Star Casting of the Year: Susan George – she was the first straw dog seen in Albert Square since Kathy Mitchell arrived wearing Wurzel Gummidge's hair …

In January, Sonia Jackson gave away her baby and was portrayed as a suffering martyr. Pauline Fowler wanted to care for her granddaughter and she got painted as the soap baddie … only in *EastEnders* would this perverse morality be presented as normal.

February posited more mysteries:

- It was daylight when Roy Evans caught up with Fat Pat in a traffic jam but pitch black moments later. Did they go through a time warp? Or did Pat cause an eclipse getting out of the cab?
- Steve Owen married Mel despite knowing that she had slept with Phil Mitchell at Xmas. Why? He knew exactly what she was like now. He had a one-night stand with her when she was married to Ian Beale, and then she slept with her best friend's fella. If Melanie was a movie, it'd be called *Something Easy This Way Comes*. When the wedding

guests referred to the lovely spread, they might not have been talking about the sandwiches ...

In March, the great 'Who Shot Phil?' saga began. Critics were quick to point out that the soap had stolen this plot from *Dallas*, but on the plus side it did make a nice change from recycling their own stale plots. I was also able to compile a handy guide to the suspects.

("My money's on the big bloke – Pat Butcher," said Jonathan Ross. See, even JR was funny once.)

Topping my list was the magician Paul Daniels, because when Phil was shot the bullethole didn't appear in his shirt until after he'd fallen down the steps. Which means that either a practised illusionist was involved or Phil's a slow bleeder. And I thought Ricky Butcher was the only slow bleeder in the Square ...

Also that month, Jamie Mitchell went from henpecked wimp to Fight Club's finest street-rucker and Doctor Trueman was carrying on with Kat the Dog – he wasn't so much Dr Legg as Dr Leg-Over.

The big revelation came a month later: Lisa had shot Phil for sleeping with Mel – a clear case of Cock Shock & One Smoking Barrel. Oh, and Natalie found herself unexpectedly pregnant – that Fat Barry, always cocking things up ...

May was a particularly poor month. Michael Elphick turned up as the bloated Spanish bar owner Harry Slater (or, as the Spanish called him, 'El Sick'). What did Peggy see in this sad old drunk? Even his breath must have been a fire hazard. Charlie reached 60 on May 8 but Harry's waistline got there first.

Elsewhere, sleazy baker Ricardo (Dr Strangeloaf) tried to entice Kat into a threesome – it was the first time in years that she'd turned down a fresh roll. And Ian Beale had 'Muppet' written on his forehead. This was like an omen, because we'd all heard that Miss Piggy (a.k.a. Sharon) was coming back to sleep with Phil again.

Natalie nearly had an abortion in July. "I want a career," she whined. "I want to do something with my life." This was the same Natalie who was married to Fat Barry and who lived in Albert Square. Newsflash! It's too ruddy late, love ...

August was a month of mysteries and amazing facts. For

starters we found out that Melanie Owen's bladder has more power to absorb than a family-sized pack of Tesco Ultra kitchen towels: Mel was kidnapped on Tuesday, but she didn't need to use the loo until Friday. What a girl! She must have had insides like a camel's. She always did enjoy a good hump...

Elsewhere we had mysteries aplenty:

- Where had Janine Butcher's splendid new boobs come from and why had none of the local blokes noticed them?
- How did Harry Slater fix Audrey's plumbing problem by removing her ballcock?
- How did the fat bastard get into her attic in the first place without the aid of a hoist?
- How did Steve Owen hook up with Sharon Watts to buy the Vic? He didn't know her and had never met her.
- What happened to Martin Fowl-up? The kid had been missing for five months, apparently revising upstairs, and Pauline hadn't sent him up so much as a bacon sarnie. What a cow...

More seriously, would Mel really have torched the E20 with people in it? She might have been desperate but she wasn't a killer. It seemed to me that even the soap's writers had no clear understanding of what her character was supposed to be. One minute she was a hard-drinking, party-loving ladette; then she was Mary Poppins to Ian Beale's brood; then a gangster and after a twisted fire-starter. Her character was as about as consistent as Manchester sunshine.

September was a month to make you queasy, as Terry Raymond slobbered all over Janine Butcher and Steve Owen went overnight from being a small-time club owner to a criminal mastermind organising robberies. Where did that come from?

The big Slater family secret was finally exposed in October. So let's get this straight: Zoe's mum was now her sister, her sisters were her aunts, her uncle was her dad, and her dad had become her grandad... and her uncle. Phew! (Barry Evans was unaffected. He was still a complete pudding.)

Later that month, Beppe got a Halloween kicking for giving

lover Chris a nasty rash which she'd passed on to her husband. What a very tasteful storyline, perfectly suited to the soap's family audience. (What next, Fat Harry squeezing his genital warts on Big Mo's cornflakes?)

In November, Lisa had her baby. Ye gods, the size of it! Newborn Louise looked six months old and about a stone and half. No wonder Lisa did more pushing than a rugby prop, she must have had stretchmarks the size of Fat Pat's earlobes. Imagine giving birth to that, girls – I bet Little Louise was walking before Lisa was. In typically unlikely soap fashion Lisa had managed to keep schtumm about Phil Mitchell being the father for eight whole months, but then merrily blurted out the secret to his girlfriend.

Elsewhere, Mel was back. Hurrah. She was going into business with her ex-husband Ian, and what a vision she had. They'd be doing catering for "gallery openings, first nights, TV company do's," she said, adding, "I've got contacts."

As Frank Butcher might have said, "Woah, woah, woah, back up there a minute, sweetheart, what contacts are these then?" Mel was a vicar's daughter, a barmaid who married a fish-shop boss and once spent a day working in a long-forgotten health farm. Where and when did she get in-roads to the West End smart set? As usual, I was the only one asking.

Panto came to Walford for the first and last time in December 2001. Pauline was going to appear in it, which confused a lot of people because surely it takes two to play the cow? ...

Elsewhere, Beppe shagged Lynne Slater (why?), and then she married her loser fiancé Garry Hobbs (why?). Lynne and Garry's big day would have driven a Prozac salesman to clinical depression; they had the most miserable wedding speeches since Adolf and Eva in the bunker and the outcome was just as doomed.

At this point maybe we should return once again to the soap's claim to reflect 'real life': I know a lot of East End fellas, and not one of them would have stood by and watched the woman he was about to marry snog another bloke without trying to kick his door in.

Furthermore, if you were an experienced bird-bandit kissing someone else's bride to be, would you do it in a lit room with the blinds open so that any passing neighbour might see everything? Bah, bah, and triple bah. And besides – how many couples have their stag and hen do's in the same pub at the same time? Only in *Enders*, folks, only in *Enders* ...

Patrick Trueman's ska collection was the only thing bringing joy to Walford this Christmas season. Otherwise, there was a lot of cynical stuff about a sick baby, Jane was dying, Zoe Slater was sleeping rough and Trevor raped Little Moan after finding her wedding hat ... ("Harsh but fair" – James Willmott-Brown.) Charmless Trev had forbidden her from going. Finding the hat was the clue that she was defying him. Just one problem with that: no one else even wore a titfer to Lynne's nuptials, so why did Mo? (Granted, posh Belinda had a hat but she didn't go.)

Bad enough that the soap has to wag its finger at us like some lecturing social worker, but must it be so tiresomely predictable too?

A homing ground for losers and misfits and every form of human misery imaginable.

2002 – Janine's Drug Hell

In January, Sharon walked out on a pub she half-owns. In February, Janine Butcher became an overnight cocaine addict – although no one seemed to have told her, or the writers, that one immediate side-effect of cocaine consumption is SMILING. It perks you up and makes you chatty. (Rumour is Danniella Westbrook once sneezed in the Vic and the whole pub cheered up.)

Lee, Janine's dealer, looked like Jethro Tull's Scarecrow, or possibly Custer after his last stand. (Face it, Janine wouldn't be anyone's choice for a *first* stand.) The storyline was crap, of course. You can't get hooked on Charlie in three days, any more than Mark Fowler could have upped and emigrated to California without a trade or a green card. Or Zoe Slater would have burnt an £18K cheque. Or she'd have dated wooden Dr Anthony, or Jamie Mitchell would have proposed to Sonia, and Martin Fowler would have looked disappointed about it. . .

By May, Janine's cocaine addiction was completely forgotten. Grandad Jim scoring Patrick's 'natural Viagra' herbs was more entertaining, but sadly misguided. He wasn't going to get any – even on his wedding night.

Dot and Jim's nuptials brought a modicum of joy. But poor old Jim soon learnt that the wonderful couple wouldn't be enjoying any wonderful coupling ... Dot said, "I do," but she didn't. "I couldn't," she said. Well, she wouldn't. She shouldn't. Not in her condition. Dot had been clinically dead since 1997. If Jim had got too close to her he could have grated his chest on her ribs.

Dot, I observed, was so old that she had an F spot. Her first lover was Noggin the Nog, and her last period was Jurassic. Don't try and picture her and Jim starkers, it could put you off dried fruit for life.

(In January Jim was cursed with itchy private parts, which Patrick had to check out. Sadly, he didn't play any ska in the background – he could have gone for 'Big Six' maybe, or possibly Judge Dread's 'The Winkle Man' ...)

But the look on pop-eyed Jim's boat race as his 'private member's pill' kicked in was priceless.

February also saw Frank's 'funeral' in Spain (see 'Big Swinging Cobblers'), but these were the *Irritations of the Month:*

- The waste of Barbara Windsor. Over the years Peggy has changed from a tough but warm mum into a poisonous shrew. Why can't she be feisty and fun again?
- Chris Etteridge – the funny cop from *Goodnight Sweetheart* – as a heavy.
- The writers apparently thinking Sam Mitchell is 12 and not 27. Why is this grown woman hanging out with Zoe, 18, competing with Janine and flirting with teen losers Martin and Asif?

In March it was Steve Owen RIP – Roasted in Poplar. Steve's car blew like Janine in a cocaine frenzy after a thrilling death race. Thrilling, but unlikely – it was 3pm on a Friday afternoon, so where were all the mums on their school runs? There was nothing to slow Steve and Phil down, not even a speed hump. (Unless you count the one Steve and Sam had in a hotel.)

Steve had an hour to get to the airport with a pack of homicidal maniacs on his tail. So why did he go shopping? And why did he have the baby in the car? I'm not even sure how nightclub manager Owen had managed to raise nigh-on £200K in cash in five days, and the script made no attempt to tell us.

Elsewhere this month, Big Mo was calling herself Wanda Whiplash on a phone-sex line – Wanda Whipsnade more like. And launderette worker Pauline Fowler slapped Lisa – that's what I call a service bosh!

April saw Little Mo's trial for the attempted murder of the odious Trevor. She was found guilty of course, but the real people on trial were blokes. "All men are bastards" could be the *Enders* mantra. The soap's fellas are either wife-beating rapists, macho bullies, yobs or wimps.

Meanwhile, Angie was getting buried. Well, she couldn't have been cremated – Ange was so pickled with alcohol the flames would have taken out half of East London.

May saw the ludicrous back-story of Dot's abortion, Sonia's yawnsome baby-snatching escapade and Jamie's unconvincing heartache as the soap's plainest teenage gave him the elbow. We also met fireman Tom, who claimed to have gone to school with Ian, Mark and Sharon even though a) he's Irish and b) Den and Angie sent Sharon to boarding school.

June mysteries: how could Mo and Kat sack Zoe from her own market stall? Why is Beppe's car still parked in the Square while he's moved to Leicester? And how can Gus Smith turn up at all times of day when he's working in Dagenham, which is eight bloody miles away? Would *you* walk eight yards to date Sonia?

July mysteries: why did Ian Beale spend a night sleeping under cardboard when his aunt, cousin and best friend live just yards away? And can the Slater sisters really have had the same dad? You've never known such different girls: one posh, one common, one mouse, one grump ... no wonder Charlie's always crying.

Most amazing scene: Garry Hobbs punching Jason. He hit him with his right hand but managed to connect with Jason's right cheek.

Things hotted up in November with the Slaters' house fire. Tom, London's best-known non-working fireman, was brave, selfless and ultimately dead, yet little of the drama rang true.

When exactly did Trevor turn from a wife-beater to a suicidal psychopath? And who the hell has time to chat in a burning building? (Away from the fire, the episode's light relief came with a quick Full Monty – which, despite being impromptu and totally made up on the spot, appeared to be perfectly choreographed!) *Other ongoing mysteries:* what time does Walford market close? People stumble out of nightclubs to find the stalls are still open.

2003 – The Year of Dirty Den's Resurrection

2003 started cheerfully enough with Jamie Mitchell's funeral. Money-bags Phil paid for it (where does he get his dosh?) and Janine sent a last text to Jamie's phone: "XXX", it said. Shame he didn't text back, "XXXX off, I'm watching the football." Elsewhere it was hard to take the stories seriously. How could we sympathise with Lynne's pain over Garry knocking up Lumpy Laura when she had cheated on him with Beppe the night before their wedding? And she got jiggy with Jason last year – these are things Garry would have been banging on about from day one.

> *Mysteries of the month:* why is Garry so broke? Every bill in the Slater household (Chateau Tardis) is split seven ways and he clearly doesn't spend anything on clothes. Why is Gus still in the Square? He only came to date Sonia, and he works in Dagenham!

In February, it turned out that Anthony Trueman had knocked up Kat. Great – a doctor who's never heard of contraception!

Phil Mitchell had been suspected of murdering Lisa in Portugal for absconding with their baby Louise ever since he'd returned to the Square with the kid and Lisa's passport. Blood on his jacket was thought to be proof but in March it turned out to have been his blood from a nosebleed, and the cops cocked-up their undercover operation. What an anticlimax. Undercover policewoman Kate's emergency code word was 'Rainbow', possibly because the honey-trap storyline could have been written by Bungle and George. Why would streetwise Phil have been taken in by this shifty broad? Dim? Kate couldn't count her breasts and get the same answer twice.

Lisa's actual fate was revealed in special flashback episodes filmed on-location in and around Albufeira on the Algarve. These featured Patrick Balardi (Neil from *The Office*) and Duggie Brown (off *The Comedians*) in a spin-off that could have been called *Reborn in a Useless Soap*. (Lisa came back to Walford later in the year very much alive and waltzed off with the kid again.)

In April I congratulated the BBC for cheering us up when there was a war on. I wasn't serious. The wit and warmth of *EastEnders* must be right up there with the courage of Zachery Smith, the integrity of Clare Short and the whispered sweet nothings of Bianca Jackson. Every night was still a gloom-fest. Every episode saw Fat Barry throw another tedious tantrum. Roll up, roll up for the Incredible Sulk! He shouts, he pouts, he screams, he smashes up his own home with a hammer!

It's not just the dim equation of drama with misery that depresses, I wrote. It's the show's total ignorance of what cockneys are like. Would Peggy Mitchell really have told Pat Evans she was "a good wife to Roy" when Pat had cheated on him with Peggy's own husband? Never.

Would hard-nut Phil bond with soppy Sonia Jackson? Not in a million years. And why would Ricky complain about his ex-wife, a woman he slept with only last month, walking around in a towel? This is not how men are.

The ham-fisted stabs at comedy don't help. This month they had Fat Barry covered in custard – ho, ho, ho. Well, he was a big pudding. (And he was fighting for custody.)

This was the stuff of kid's TV. No wonder *Corrie* was romping ahead. Its big storylines were more gripping, its humour sprang organically from the characters and dialogue, the writing was a dream. Loudmouth Les Battersby was every bit as big a loser as Barry, yet the *Street*'s writers made us feel sorry for him.

At the time I predicted: *Corrie* will clean up at all this year's awards ceremonies, and rightly – the other guy blinked. *EastEnders* have taken their eye off the ball. They need big characters, decent writers (preferably some who could find Stratford East without a guidebook) and strong, credible stories. And for Pete's sake, let Alfie pull more than a pint ...

One sure sign of a soap on its uppers is that they start rewriting the characters. I didn't buy any of it: Fat Pat was a formidable figure, how would she have been driven off by a pair of pipsqueaks like Ian Beale and Barry Evans? If it had come to a fight she could have flattened 'em both with one hand tied behind her. And why would Alfie Moon, who started out as a fast-talking wide-boy, suddenly get all tongue-tied and tearful over Kat the dog? It's not as if she was Evangeline Lily. You couldn't help but suspect that this was a turning point for Alfie's character, the beginning of decline.

In a futile attempt to lift the mood this month they had bingo and, for added humour, streetwise Alfie Moon didn't know the rules. (Had he never seen *Lucky Numbers* with Shane Richie on ITV?) Bingo on *EastEnders*! We know one fat lady who couldn't call house – poor old Fat Pat.

Continuity clanger of the month: as Fat Pat queued for a bus, an extra walked up behind her in a check jacket. Laura went looking for Pat and the same bloke was in the Square. When Pat got on the bus, he was both already on board and simultaneously standing behind Laura. Cock-up or cloning, you decide.

May's Soap Awards brought some shocks. Don't get me wrong, Shane Richie had perked up Walford no end, he was Top Soap Newcomer by miles. But Sexiest Male? In that dressing gown? My arse – Alfie hadn't had his end away in the eight months he'd been there.

May mysteries: Why are there so few cockney accents in *EastEnders*? How many clubbers fit in four clubs and still get back to their local before last orders? Which clubs don't routinely check every banknote they get? And when would someone tell Kat that mini-skirts and macro-legs don't mix?

In June I asked if the *EastEnders* writers were using rejected *Harry Potter* storylines. Vicki had got magically pregnant without so much as kissing soppy Spencer. (For Hogwarts, see Barry.) Sharon had made Vicki an appointment with the doctor. How things change –

the last doc held consultations on the swings. Who was the GP now anyway? And more to the point, where had Anthony gone?

It's one of the big Walford mysteries, like exactly what kind of holiday was Patrick on? Was garage boss Phil turned on by Kate's spare tyre? And why has no one been swimming since Cindy Beale? (There was a woman who enjoyed a session up the deep end.)

Let's hope the doc had time to check out Alfie's Tuesday night date. Have you ever seen a woman so white? Check the cemetery, quick – now *Buffy* has ended, the undead have to materialise somewhere. And Dot could be their magnet.

EastEnders was now more popular with kids than children's programmes, according to a new study; possibly because this year's storylines could have been dreamt up by a retarded teenager. In no particular order of rot we had:

- Fick Rick recast as Poet Laureate. Suzie the floozy was so turned-on by rubbish verses like "Good on ya, Sonia" that they did it doggerel fashion all over his house. Talk about rhyming couplets. (Suzie called Ricky 'Shakespeare', but clearly preferred plenty of Dickens.)

- Little Mo, a woman who staved in her ex-husband's head with an iron, getting squeamish over a mouse.

- Gay Derek losing a job he'd never mentioned in a garden centre (an uphill one?).

- And, in a plot lamer than Don Brennan, we're meant to believe that jailbird Dennis had a fling with Phil's ex-cop girlfriend Geordie Kate while she was stationed in Brighton three and a bit years ago. (Den, Phil, who would she bed next – Frank Vickers from *The Vice*?)

- On Monday, Phil Mitchell left Walford at teatime to catch a late-night flight to see Grant in Brazil (at least 17 hours in travelling time) but was back in Walford on Thursday, which by the soap's time scale was actually 1pm Wednesday. You couldn't get to Alan Brazil and back that quickly. Imagine their bedside chat. Phil: "'Ello bruv, 'ow ya feeling?" Grant: "Grunt." Phil: "Good, gotta dash, plane to catch."

Back home things really took off. Kate convinced Phil that her desire to snog old flame Dennis – before letting him spend the night in their house while Phil was out of the country – was absolutely no different from Phil momentarily fancying a pretty girl at the airport. Of course!

And Phil, the notorious hothead, swallowed it.

But why get uptight? It's just soap, isn't it? Yes, except BBC1 always claim *EastEnders* is 'raw and realistic', when it isn't. It's dreary feminist nonsense underscored by an outmoded political correctness. It teaches kids that female sexuality is fabulous and fun, but male sexuality is dangerous. Why else would 'sex symbol' Alfie have gone without for nine months?

The lesson of *EastEnders* is: all businessmen are rats, all marriages fail and all men are bastards (except gay men).

> *Walford mysteries:* How did Mark Fowler's house expand to fit in all those Ferreiras? If they were Catholic, why had they got Hindu names? And why hadn't there been a Muslim family in E20 since the Osmans?

July saw another terrible crime, an atrocity that brought the soap to a new low – they tried to turn Janine Butcher into a sex kitten (possibly a bonking Bagpuss). As the thick-set siren sprawled over a car bonnet, it looked like she had airbags exploding in her stern. This wasn't so much *Cool Hand Luke* as *Some Like It Hog*. But it didn't stop Barry falling for her, or Paul from polishing her bumpers. Was it any wonder that Zoe was so bitter? She was the best looking woman in Albert Square and nobody wanted her. Sonia pulled more blokes than she did.

Elsewhere, owl-faced Jack Dalton – the Ollie Beak of organised crime – was gunned down by Dennis. After Richard Hillman in *Corrie*, I wrote that *EastEnders* bosses would rush through a killer of their own. They furiously denied it, but here's the proof. Unfortunately, the storyline never rang true; it was *Lock, Stock & One Scraping Barrel*.

Then there was Dr Trueman leaving Walford on a long journey, saying he didn't know where he was going to (how about acting school?), and US Independence Day on *EastEnders*. Gertcha! If we didn't get pearlies and Chas 'n' Dave for St George's Day it was gonna be picket-line time.

Here's a piece I wrote in August 2003:

HOW much longer will BBC1 allow *EastEnders* to be this BAD?

Their flagship show is sinking under the weight of abysmal casting, dismal characters and shockingly poor plotting.

WHY is Janine sleeping with Barry Evans, the wart-hog of love? It throws up deeply unpleasant images and makes no sense.

Barry is not rich, he's not successful. He's petulant and childish; a loser who ruined his dad's business and sells fewer cars than the Trueman guesthouse has guests.

All Janine can get from him is blubber rash and stretch-marks on her duvet.

Billy is thieving to pay back cash-strapped Charlie. But HOW did the Slaters run up a £321 phone bill? Who do they ever ring? They're either in the market, or legless in the Vic. Even Chunky Charlie can't order that many take-aways.

My guess is he's eating the handsets (along with Gus and Wellard who have vanished without trace).

Nutty nanny Joanne has rented out Phil's house to Tom Jones. But who believes streetwise Phil would have let a spurned, embittered mad woman he had just sacked stay there in the first place?

The Asian family is a disaster. (Ferreiras? Rotten!) Dan the ham is the worst, but there's no sign that any of them can act. Did you clock Ronnie's angry face on Tuesday? He looked constipated.

And when Kat said the Vic was out of lemons, I presumed Kareena had sucked them all.

Yes, Alfie is great, but what has he ever done? He's Jack

the Lad on bromide. Spencer is a wuss (where did he do time, HMP Trumpton?) and Nana going bananas looks set to drag on tediously.

The truth is the Cockney soap went 'reels of cotton' when Louise Berridge took over as boss. She's turned it from the Slater show into trash aimed at teeny-boppers, and let *Corrie* set the pace. It just isn't good enough.

The solution is simple: to save the show, Berridge must go.

Why is it always the wrong people having sex on *EastEnders*? Nobody wanted to watch Fat Barry slobbering over Janine, the dumpy ex-prostitute. Especially when Alfie hadn't had his leg-over since he got there ten ruddy months before.

Sasha was the latest woman of easy virtue to sashay into the Square. She called herself an escort, though old banger would be nearer the mark. She was taller than Adi, broader and certainly more macho. (Memo to the casting director: three words, laser eye surgery.)

Elsewhere, the soap's war on male sexuality continued unabated with grandad Jim painted as a pervert for watching women's wrestling. The poor sod is married to the most frigid, repressed old bat in London; let him grab his pleasure where he can. After all, even *Coronation Street*'s Martin Platt enjoys a half-Nelson. (For non-*Corrie* viewers: at the time Platt was getting jiggy with Lucy Nelson, a just-legal teenager 20 years his junior.)

No wonder those Walford teens wanted to film Mo's naughty knickers party, all the hot babes were there: Nana, Big Mo, fat Joanne, Jonathan Ross's mum ... (What, no Dot?) If Spencer and co were 13 and the women were all lookers, then maybe it'd happen, but Big Mo in a see-through nightie? Ye gods! Who'd want to see through to that? Those writers must have been smoking the stuff that Martin Fowler was busy growing.

Mercifully, the do changed from the hinted-at marital aids – "thingies", Little Mo called them – to negligees and undies; which was a relief. You dread to think what Big Mo might use as a sex aid – a battering ram, perhaps, or an epileptic dwarf. (Pauline didn't need to attend. The memory of Arthur's prize marrow will sustain her for a lifetime.)

On the eve of Dirty Den's return I noted:

EastEnders' cred is hanging by a thread thinner than Dot Branning on the David Blaine diet.

Absurd plot twists have undermined the strongest players. Alfie has turned from a fast-talking Jack the Lad into a wimp who can't tell Fat Kat that he loves her. While Lisa's hit-man raised his price to £35K when he learnt that her intended victim was Phil Mitchell.

Why? Phil's record would barely make a footnote in a true crime book: one robbery, minor arson, an accidental manslaughter. He lived with his mum into his forties. Where does his fearsome reputation spring from? And what did Kate, the police plant who turned out to be a cabbage, ever see in this charmless thug?

Den Watts came back to Walford in September with a lot of baggage – most of it under his eyes. Sharon was so shocked she threw up. (You and me both, love.) This should have been the greatest comeback since Lazarus, but it stank like the inside of David Blaine's box. Why? Don't blame Grantham. Dirty Den is a soap giant lumbered with a family of pygmies. Vicki is an irritating brat with a joke accent. Dennis (Shirty Den) should have come with a coat of creosote. While Letitia 'Sharon' Dean appeared to think she was auditioning for an am-dram production of *Pygmalion*. She's got a good head on her shoulders, that girl, but unfortunately no neck to keep them apart.

Grantham out-acted the lot of them effortlessly, yet even he couldn't lift the dismal, leaden dialogue that made the millions of extra viewers who had tuned in for his comeback episode switch off in millions.

It got better when Den got out amongst Walford's walking wounded, telling Ian Beale, "You look worse than me and I've been dead 14 years," and rattling Phil Mitchell's cage. I only remember Den having one fight in the '80s – that was with Angie, and he lost. But I could live with him being reinvented as a hard-nut as long as they kept him funny.

Humour is in short supply in the BBC's East London. Their market men couldn't sell life-boats on a sinking ship. More cheer, more cockneys, better writers, fewer plastic gangsters and less emphasis on dull teenagers would have restored the *EastEnders* crown in the long term, especially if boss Berridge moved away from shock plots and remembered that infidelity is the backbone of soap.

All of that yucky incest-lite may play well in Norfolk, but it's hardly family viewing. Den needed to be back in the Vic with a new Angie figure by his side. (A volatile brunette with a drink problem? Step forward Lynne Slater!)

That would have cleared the way for Phil to return at Xmas 2004 with that other lost giant, bruvva Grant (Ross Kemp, then serving with the SAS on ITV and one of the few actors who looks better wearing a balaclava). Then we'd really be talking soap heaven.

As it was, in September scowling Geordie DCI Geoff Morton came close to ruining his daughter Kate's big flat Walford wedding. He was a mean-spirited alcoholic with a face like a clenched fist. I liked the bloke. Geoff stomped around Albert Square cursing its wretched inhabitants. "Peasants breeding like rabbits," he called them, before dubbing Little Moan "a sour-looking trollop".

Sadly, Billy decked him before he got round to telling Kat how much she resembled Ronnie Wood if you'd roughed him up a bit and dragged him through Stringfellow's pants drawer. For his part, Geoff (Maurice Roeves) looked like something unearthed at Channel 4's *Big Monster Dig*.

As soap weddings go this was half-hearted fare. Apparently Kate had only got one mate in the world, the horsy-looking Sophie. Admittedly this is one more than PC Mick the Moron on *Corrie*, but why was she so unpopular? Was everyone she met as wound up as I was by the way she endlessly flicked her hair?

Kate even had to beg the Slaters to come to her hen party. (A tough choice for Zoe: hen do or Hindu?) None of Phil's family showed, not even Auntie Sal from *On the Buses*. There was no telegram from Grant, no phone call from Peggy bequeathing a round of drinks "on the ahse". His stag do – the Vic, the caff, the snooker hall – was exactly like every other night of his life.

Just give thanks that Minty's demented plan to strip the big pink guy naked came to nothing.

The gulf between *EastEnders* and *Corrie* had never been wider. The *Street* had five strong storylines on the go – Walford felt more like *Grange Hill* for adults. There was a nuisance neighbour, the feeble Ferreiras, Garry changing nappies, Nana going gaga (just like Frank Butcher's mum) and Kat and Alfie's endless will-they/won't-they non-affair. It might have made sense if they were teenagers, but not 30-somethings who'd been round the block more times than Postman Pat.

And why would Andy the well-spoken villain be after Kat? He craved sophistication; she was a mouthy slapper. He gave her a £4K watch and tickets to see *Swan Lake*. (*The Nutcracker* I could understand.) *WHY*? Even Ripley wouldn't believe that.

More Walford puzzles in October: Why had Pauline had her hair done like Dougal the sheepdog? Why didn't Martin move in with the Slaters? Everyone else does. Did Derek's wedding pictures include one of his Uncle Arthur (John Le Mesurier)? Why did gormless John agree to buy his gun back? How had Den got the dosh to buy a house outright? Why was Shirley persecuted by her loathsome neighbour? Why did Lisa need to sketch out her murder scheme? It was hardly elaborate. Where had Charlie vanished to? Was he the new Dr Legg? How would Mo and Billy fit into Chateau Slater? Why would the gamblers have handed over all their winnings to Dot's charity? And why was Den flirting with Fat Pat? 14 years underwater must have played havoc with his eyesight.

Memo to *EastEnders*:

Phil Mitchell is supposed to be a geezer. Geezers don't grass. A bloke like Phil would no more pick up the phone to the Old Bill than he would have a queer-eye-for-a-straight-guy makeover. It wouldn't happen.

November saw a tough choice for Kat. If she called off her wedding she'd have Alfie Moon, the man she truly loved ... If she went ahead ... three tiers of wedding cake!

I'm not making a big deal about Kat's weight, but don't most brides *diet* before their big day? The way she'd piled on the pounds you wouldn't have been surprised if her "something old" had been a frozen pizza, "something new" a bag of chips, "something borrowed" more chips and "something blue" a pound of cheese.

Still, she was soon over the moon now, not to mention under him – Alfie had an awful lot of celibacy to make up for.

Their on-off relationship seemed to last longer than *The World at War*. But it was almost worth the wait because, for once, *EastEnders* came up with an episode that was warm-hearted instead of mean-spirited.

Against the odds, it was even funny – and not just because some joker persuaded Kat to wear white. The dialogue sparkled. "Are you threatening me?" Alfie asked one of Andy's dodgy gangsters. "No," he replied. "But I can if you think it'd help."

And when Kat promised to rub his injuries better, Alfie quipped: "Did I tell you about my groin strain?"

Oddly, Shane was funnier as Alfie than he ever was as a stand-up. It was nice to see him out of that all-weather leather too; he always looked like he should be working the waltzer at Southend. (He could have done a double act with Ian Lavender – Pike and pikey!)

Only a heartless curmudgeon would point out how the producers cheated to make that week work. So please allow me:

- Kat didn't realise Andy was a (plastic) gangster until about five minutes beforehand, then she knew enough to shop him if he didn't walk away.
- It's hard to believe Kat didn't know he was a villain. Andy flew the Big Orange to the Big Apple, he showered her and her family with gifts – surely the subject of his earnings would have come up? She obviously forgot they met at Angie's Den when Andy dropped by to 'sort' a quaking Billy Mitchell.

- Who moved the church? When Frank and Pat tied the knot it was a brief trot away in a horse and carriage, now it was a frantic dash in a fish and chip van to get there...

After Alfie Moon's send-up of *The Graduate*, here are more Dustin Hoffman movies with an echo in Albert Square:

1) *Sphere* – Kat, if she doesn't diet.
2) *Sleepers* – Ricky, Gus, where are they?
3) *American Buffalo* – Vicki Fowler.
4) *Hook* – Den played him in panto.
5) *Marathon Man* – Fat Barry, but they're called Snickers now.
6) *Tootsie* – Adi's geezer-bird girlfriend.
7) *Rain Man* – Winston, he barely speaks.

This month we also learnt that Alfie would marry Kat in the Vic. (For the Nag's Head, see Lynne the bridesmaid.) Had he thought this through though? When the vicar asked if anyone had any objections, some wag was bound to shout, "I can't get served!"

And what if Alfie slipped up and said, "With this ring I declare last orders"?

Don't you wish you could fast-forward *EastEnders* by a month or two? I didn't give a monkey's toss about Shirley or the Ferreiras and I hated the way they'd turned Phil first into a grass and then into a sucker.

At least Garry Hobbs's unlikely love-life provided some comic relief. The mucky mechanic touched up Laura's bodywork, gave Lynne a full service and greased his big end in Belinda's sump. The only question remaining is which one of them would loosen his wing nuts?

December saw a Xmas miracle as Alfie's snow machine blitzed all of Albert Square in nine seconds. It even built snowmen, but it still wasn't enough to cover the rot in the plot.

Phil gave Kate his gun so she'd give him an hour's grace. Why didn't he just tie her up? He ducked a police manhunt by hiding in his own café. Then Loadsamoney Den bought him off with £200K from the robbery. (That much missing and Plod didn't suss he had an accomplice?)

Alfie's big dumb plan was to fake his wedding to Kat and then marry her properly later, without her realising what was going on. *Doh!* He wrote out the wedding vows for his fake service from memory. Then his solicitor bowled in and just happened to have the real registrar's home number on him...

Still, at least it was a happy ending for Kat, who has been more let down than Robbie Jackson's blow-up doll over the years. Normal misery and murder would be restored in due course. But before that, Alfie and Kat went on to qualify for *UK's Worst Honeymoons*: four days in Margate, in winter, with Nana ... the fun never starts!

But would Kat have kittens?

December mysteries: Why did Den give Lisa, who he hardly knew, 20 grand? And more puzzling than any of that, consider this: Den splashed out £260,000 cash on Phil's house; he was offering £100K cash for the Vic (making it the East End's cheapest pub). Why would anyone this loaded live in a dump like Walford?

But Walford's Santa is certainly consistent. No matter what you ask for, he gives you a black eye and a bucket of Prozac.

2004 – the year of Den's disgrace and the Ferreiras' mortgage arrears

> *Quote of the Year:* "One day Barry was dying, the next he's Peter Pan." – Janine Butcher. Actually, he was Muddles in *Snow White* with my old mate Dave Lee.

In January 2004 Fat Barry Evans fell to his death in Scotland on New Year's Day – or Hogmanay, as it's known there. (In Barry's case it's more like Hog Man: "Aayyyyyyyyyy!") No one had told Janine Butcher that in the Highlands you're supposed to toss the caber, not push the pillock down the hillock. As Ally Ross remarked, "not since Sue Barker has anyone gone down a cliff quite so unconvincingly."

Maybe it was for the best though. The twisted bitch had already broken Bazza's big soft heart, telling him how much she hated his "gross horrible body" on top of her. And all because he'd got the all-clear over his health scare. Barry had rung Dr Leroy for permission to bonk his bride. Luckily, both the GP and his receptionist were still at the surgery – *at ten past midnight on New Year's Eve!*

Unlikely? Maybe – but not as daft as Janine marrying the big lug for his money when he patently didn't have any. Lifelong loser Barry had done for the secondhand motor trade what Paul Trueman had been doing to Janine for months. He'd bankrupted his dad and hadn't sold a car since the clocks went back.

After murdering Baz, Janine somehow managed to have him cremated before there was a police enquiry. There wasn't even a holiday gap. We were left to assume that the quick fit fitters had started a quick-fry crematorium because, one episode after he'd died, Janine was bringing his ashes home in a Highland Shortbread bag. This was the final indignity – Bazza was more your deep-fried Mars Bar kind of guy.

(I saw Shaun Williamson, a.k.a. Barry, on stage in panto the day after he died onscreen. "Stay away from the edge," comedian Dave Lee ad-libbed to huge gusts of laughter and applause.)

Even this badly-written nonsense seems like *Six Feet Under* when compared to what the other EastEnders got up to in the Scottish Highlands. Mickey Miller had crashed his minibus rowing with Kelly Taylor. Consider the circumstances of the rescue: Gus Smith walked miles through uninhabited wilderness to find a phone. It had been vandalised. (Who by? No one lived there.) He held the wires together (how?) to call the emergency services. Here is exactly what Gus told them: "I dunno where we are, Scotland ... we came up the road and then we got lost." And that was enough! The ambulances got through!

The writers must think there are only two roads north of the border: the low road and the high road. BBC1 certainly took the low road when they leaked misleading publicity shots of Kelly and Zoe Slater's supposedly Sapphic snog. It was a cynical ratings-grabbing ploy. We might have known there was more chance of seeing Nessie than lezzies.

But here's what made me laugh: at 11.35pm, Paul Trueman set off in a cab in the West Highlands aiming to reach Edinburgh by midnight! This indicates geographical knowledge on a par with Robbie Jackson's mastery of Egyptian hieroglyphics.

Meanwhile, the soap's doomed attempts to make the Ferreiras interesting took an ugly turn when Tariq revealed that Dan was his dad and that he had dated his own sister in order to stay close to the family. Talk about rolling your own ...

This was sick. It was unsavoury. And you know what's worse? I still couldn't give a monkey's toss about any of them.

Also this month: Billy Mitchell washed his hands of Little Moan. Could you blame him? She'd said that she wanted to keep her rapist's baby. It was perverse; Billy said the kid might grow up to be as rotten as Graham; Mo argued that Kat was raped and everyone loved Zoë. Good point. I mean, if Zoë were like her real dad she'd be lusting after attractive young girls. Uh-oh ...

Mysteries of the month: the speed of Charlie Slater's court appearance. Chas was arrested, bailed charged and had pleaded guilty to beating up Graham all within hours of it happening. The day that the wheels of justice move this quickly they'll put speed cameras up outside the Old Bailey.

Little Mo did abort the rapist's baby. But how did her overcoat and pullover change colour during the taxi ride to the clinic? Why did Dan 'the World's greatest Elvis fan' Ferreira fail to mention Presley's birthday? And even more puzzlingly, why did his Elvis suit fit everyone who ever tried it on perfectly?

Finally the Ronnie Ferreira kidney saga began this month. At the time I noted:

Ronnie Ferreira needs an urgent transplant – to the History Channel, along with the rest of his redundant clan. Ronnie has a rare tissue type. I'm no medic, but my guess would be pure tripe.

(Cindy Beale would have been all right with a kidney

transplant. Her body never rejected an organ all the time she was in the show.)

In February, it transpired that Ronnie had lost his kidney after being stabbed in the stomach. How, exactly? Patrick Trueman disturbed a burglar in his house and made him a chicken sandwich – like you do. Even more extraordinary, Charlie Slater flogged his black taxi for £700. Eh? And Zoe Slater forgot her broken leg, whizzing around without her crutches. (Also forgotten: Big Mo's piles, Janine Butcher's fear of open spaces, Charlie Slater's dicky ticker ...)

Laura had a cockney night, but where could she get the eels from? The market, suggested Pat. Had you ever noticed an eel stall in that market? Me neither, but then Maud's book stall has crept up on me too. (What great works does Maud stock? *Janet & John v. Reg & Ron*? *Curious George Meets Bi-Curious Kelly*?)

Cockney night went down a treat with the locals, them being cockneys and all. So Laura decided on Indian and Mexican nights to follow. Great ... except, she's only got a cooker and a toaster; what was she going to do, send out for takeaways?

We'll never know, because Ian took over the caff minutes after giving Sam a cheque and Laura walked. That's the beauty of Walford, you never have to bother with contracts or conveyancing. Property changes hands overnight. Shirley got a month's pay and immediately emigrated to New Zealand, without so much as a word about selling her flat.

Mysteries of the Month:
- How did Sharon get pictures of the Valentine's night party developed and back by first post the morning after?
- Why did Ronnie's nurse tell the Ferreiras she wanted to "re-site his catheter"? Where to? They only put 'em in bladders.
- The biggest mystery of them all: how long would the writers have Adi bang on about dad Dan coming back when the big congealed ham who played him had been mercifully deported?

Why are Fat Pat and Big Mo always at each other's 'froats'? It was the question absolutely no *EastEnders* fan had been asking, but the BBC decided to tell us anyway with a Pat & Mo special in March.

The biggest joke was the casting. You could tell we were coming up to April Fools Day because the young Pat looked like the blonde one out of Bananarama. There was no Robert de Niro waiting for her though, just Mo's brother Stan. He'd got out of the Scrubs and told today's Pat she was "as lovely as ever", which just goes to show how much 15 years of porridge can addle your brain.

Imagine coming out of chokey and seeing Pat. Your first thought would be, "Is it too late to have a few more offences taken into consideration?"

The show revolved around Mo marrying Pat's soldier brother, Jimmy – clearly no stranger to battle-scarred tanks – 40-odd years before, and the memorial tree Pat was planting on his grave today. It was more like a twiglet than a tree but it still wasn't as thin as the plot. Young Mo was a foot taller than she is now, as plain as Kathy Burke's aris and with Basil Brush's teeth. But it didn't stop her being hit on by every man in town. She'd had a baby by a bloke who worked on the fairground waltzers (one good turn deserves another). She wed Jimmy, then had a fling with a nightclub owner and was grassed up by Pat, who had become a drunken brass on the rebound from Frank Butcher. Cue hatred, recrimination and ... was anyone still watching by the end?

I nodded off around the time the present-day Pat and Mo started line-dancing with a couple of cowboys who took them for cow-girls. Well, they were half-right.

The show raised some questions of its own, like: When did Charlie Slater get his taxi back? Why did young Pat only sound cockney when she had her earrings in? And is any BBC executive actually watching *EastEnders*? The soap needs to create strong new characters, not to milk old ones badly.

Still, we can probably expect more riveting spin-offs shortly, including *Wellard and Roly Uncovered*, *Kat – The Thin Years* and

The Ferreiras – Before They Were Boring (that last one is science fiction, obviously).

The big story of the month was the villainous Andy Hunter offering Kat a £10,000 loan in return for sex twice a week. Was he nuts? For £10K I'd want Zoë and Kelly on 24-hour call-out. (It's half-a-crown for Mo – and that's her paying you.)

This plot-line was as water-tight as a string vest. Graham wanted ten grand to drop all charges against Charlie. His brief told Kat that if it went to court they'd face costs and bigger damages. Except … wouldn't Chas get legal aid? He'd lost his livelihood! If he did have to pay out, it'd be in instalments.

Still, good old Alfie raised a grand on Thursday by going round the Vic with a bucket. Who was in, Bill Gates? Alfie's clientele included jobless Vicki, Pat (who gets paid a pittance), Paul (only source of income: a guest house with no guests) and Ash (too busy hanging around the bookies and fondling Vicki to ever go to work). It's a wonder any of them can even buy a round.

We couldn't be entirely sure who was masterminding the soap's big story arcs at the time, possibly a team of easily distracted gibbons, but the show was plumbing depths *The Man from Atlantis* could have only have dreamt about.

There was a particularly lame scene this month when Janine offered to cut up baby Jack's donut for him in the caff. The knife never left her hand, but Pat went nuts, shouting, "Janine! He could hurt himself with that." Eh?

The incident unsettled Paul Trueman so much that he went home and wrote down his suspicions about Janine's part in Barry's murder. Although, in fairness, Barry didn't suffer as much in Scotland as Shaun Williamson did on ITV's *24-Hour Quiz*.

Yeah, Paul had got Janine's number all right, and if she was really unlucky he'd give it to Leslie Grantham. ("'Ello, is that Janine? Just putting meself on 'old …")

I couldn't understand why she never worked. Janine had now come to be the sole proprietor of the car lot, which was her only source of income, and yet she was never there. She couldn't have been living on Barry's savings, he never had any. If Roy Evans really had kept a journal, every day's entry would have said: "Sold a car, ate lard, bailed deadbeat son out of trouble again," except for Saturdays when he might have added, "Took Viagra and bedded Pat, dreaming of Roly."

But Roy never wrote a word in the seven years he was in the Square. His diary was just an excuse for Pat to search Janine's drawers, find the bracelet and conclude (ludicrously) that Paul was cheating on Natalie with Janine – even though he'd only been nailing Nat for a week or two.

Elsewhere, Vicki and Ash played strip poker. (Well they couldn't exactly play Happy Families.) She also knocked on doors and ran away before getting caught in bed with Ash, very nearly going from knockdown ginger to knocked-up whinger in the space of three episodes.

Vicki also moved into the Ferreiras' elastic-walled house of fun. The only decent action happened off-screen when Charlie Slater – in the shovel for bashing Mo's rapist, Graham – smashed his cell and bashed a guard. Like a scene out of *Oz*, it was. (A bad scene that had never made it past the cutting room floor.) The writers were certainly earning their bananas this month.

Charlie finally came out of choky with one thing on his mind: a choc ice. How much does this fat bastard eat? He's the only man I've ever known to go to prison and put on weight. They played 'Welcome Home' when Chas reached the Vic; it should have been '16 Tons'. (A choc ice, I ask you. How much bromide did they put in his tea? After a month inside, I'd be more interested in getting my hands on some big juicy raspberry ripples.)

Elsewhere, the Ronnie hospital saga ground on remorselessly. He was stabbed in the stomach but had a bandaged throat ... Dirty Den came back from three months in Spain clutching one piece of luggage – an empty-looking hold-all. Oh, and Nana Moon went to Eastbourne on Tuesday, met Wilfred Aitkens on Wednesday and was engaged by Thursday. She must have been impressed by the miraculous way he opened that sealed window on the bus. If he could do the same with her legs (*cut! – Ed*)

March ended with a new bore: the Ferreiras had got mortgage

arrears. As thrills go this was almost as exciting as the saga of Shirley's noisy neighbour.

Continuity clangers of the month: Ian Beale walked straight into the nail bar moments after Kate had locked the door. Bookie Ash Ferreira paid out £500 on a £10 bet at 25-1. No wonder he was always potless.

In April it was time to hang out the flags; *EastEnders* finally had a knees-up for St George's Day. The Dragon has stalked the Square for years – hello Pat! – but this was the first time England's patron saint had ever been mentioned, let alone celebrated, in BBC1's cock-eyed vision of Cockney-land.

There were red and white banners in the Vic, patriotic songs, and old codgers you'd never seen before saying what a wonderful idea it was. It wasn't perfect; it was all a last-minute Alfie Moon scam and the music was archaic. (What, no 'Three Lions', 'World in Motion' or 'England's Glory'?) But the obvious delight of the Vic regulars was reflected in the real public response to GMTV's Friday morning phone poll.

Asked whether we should celebrate St George's Day, a whopping 95 per cent said YES! More to the point, why shouldn't we? Previously, *EastEnders* has partied for everything from US Independence Day to Diwali, while the BBC regions have cheerfully marked the saints' days of Scotland, Wales and Ireland.

So why try and deny English identity? The truth is simple. The people who run the BBC, recruited entirely via *The Guardian*, are the kind of intellectuals who George Orwell identified decades ago as loving every country but their own. The kind who cheerfully attempted to make heroes of the treacherous Cambridge spies who sold out to Stalin, but believe that English patriotism is too wrapped up in the sins of empire to be healthy. It's complete pony.

English achievements include the creation of trade unions and parliamentary democracy, as well as the victories of Nelson and the genius of the Bard. English talent was and remains a vibrant driving force in popular culture. We invented rugby, cricket and football – and it was the sea of red and white at Euro96 that lit the fuse for our patriotic revival.

It's not just England's old-timers who are proud of our country, and it's not all about nostalgia. Would it hurt the soap to do St Geo justice again? One day a year isn't much to ask for.

Also this month: Mark Fowler died off-screen, sadly. But at least death's release gave Todd Carty the chance of *Dancing on Ice*. Strangely missing from Mark's funeral were his sister, his two ex-wives and his best mates...

Andy Hunter was the only East London bookie who didn't take a Grand National bet. The Slaters emerged as the only family in England who have never heard of the CSA. And there was more high drama for the Ferreiras: a hinge broke on their kitchen units.

Elsewhere Vicki Fowler had her 18th birthday. (Hold up, she'd been drinking in the Vic for two years!) Wilfred spent three months at the B&B just so he could steal four medals. (Not exactly a master conman was he? He wouldn't have been worth a footnote on *The Real Hustle*.) And strangest of all was that trip to Bognor Regis to stay at Jollie's Holiday Camp, where Pauline Fowler pulled twice. Either there was a masochists' convention in town or a lot of Bognor men could have their heads turned by a radioactive tan.

May was the month of Leslie Grantham's internet shame (see 'Soap Babylon'). Angry stars threatened to strike unless Grantham was sacked from the show. My response was: "Let 'em!" How many of these losers would you have actually missed? I demanded that the BBC should call their bluff and bring in blacklegs. I fancied darts legend Bobby George running the Vic, former Page Three beauty Dee Ivens in the laundrette and Lloydy the comedy street trader giving it loads of old fanny in the market.

The show urgently needed (and still needs) a complete overhaul, fresh characters, writers with an ear for authentic dialogue and a big dollop of reality. Comic Ricky Grover would have made a more convincing gangster than Andy Hunter. That guy was so plastic it's a wonder he didn't melt in the sun. Jamie Mitchell had more personality in a coma than Martin Fowler ever did. Fowl-up had gone from bad boy to complete drip; they should have bought him a ticket to see *The Football Factory* at the pictures, to get an idea of what he should be like.

Meanwhile, the mortgage arrears story was still hanging about like Dennis Rickman's brown jumper. Ronnie, 'London's best DJ', tried to raise money by placing an ad in the Minute Mart shop window, doing a free gig and, uh, selling his decks – his only source of income. Nice going, Einstein.

And Janine was charged with murder and then questioned without a lawyer present. Hmm...

The other news was that Sonia was about to marry the bloke who killed the love of her life. Dennis had forgotten he was in love with Sharon. Laura died, although I was never entirely sure how her body was blocking the front door when she had been laying on the stairs. And a heartbroken Alfie Moon said that he knew that the tape of Kat bedding Andy had to be a recent one when he saw her ring.

Blimey! He must have zoomed in and hit frame advance. Alfie also went away on a course this month – probably of antibiotics.

Yes, a seedy sex tape led to a frantic Walford two-hander. They just couldn't get away from that Leslie Grantham story, could they? But was sleaze the reason that the soap's viewing figures were now plummeting? They had now added Kat's sex tape – not so much Paris Hilton as Pitsea lay-by – to their heady mix of rape, prostitution and sexual blackmail.

May saw the ITV Soap Awards. They are generally as unblinkered, truthful and unpartisan as a Soviet show trial. But the success of *EastEnders* across the board provoked me into paroxysms of rage. Here is my blog from the morning after:

The Ferreiras have put more people to sleep than Harold Shipman. Janine married Barry for his money. He never had any! Yet this is apparently award-winning fare! Go figure ... Den's resurrection was farcical. None of it made any sense. Den said that he'd pretended to be dead to fool Jack Dalton. But Dalton was the only one who knew he was alive.

True his off-screen antics brought viewers back but they won't keep them with stories like Andy's indecent proposal. Who'd offer £7K to sleep with Fat Kat? She's not exactly Demi Moore is she?

Yes Jessie Wallace is great as the trashy, gobby tart with a heart. But Sexiest Female, two years running? Come off it! *Corrie*'s Suranne Jones oozes animal magnetism, Kat looks like Terry Scott in a Ronnie Wood wig. Are ITV's judges blind?

Or just bent?

Other cobblers included Shane Richie, Best Actor. Why? He doesn't act! He's just Shane. Dennis Rickman (Best Newcomer) joined over a year ago. Natalie Cassidy (Best Young Actor) is 21 and she's been in the show 11 years. *Corrie*'s Chesney was robbed!

Worst of all was ITV brown-nosing BBC1 soap supremo Mal Young for "20 years of unbroken success". (Don't mention *Harbour Lights*, *Misery Beat* or *Red Crap*.) This idiot is to blame for our schedules being overstuffed with underper-forming overstretched soaps and rubbish light drama vehicles for ex-soap stars.

He shouldn't be honoured; he should be publicly flogged.

In June boss Louise Berridge came out and said that the BBC was "totally unworried" about *EastEnders*. Talk about, "Crisis what crisis?"! The soap had become a dog's dinner. Wide-boy Alfie Moon had come in like a breath of fresh air 18 months before and they had managed to turn him into the living dead. Kat had lost her spark. Unlikely villains abounded and Berridge wouldn't sack the flop Ferreiras.

On top of that we were supposed to believe that balding Den, an increasingly dingy figure, was a hot babe magnet while cheeky, handsome Mickey Miller couldn't get a girl.

Meanwhile, Wilfred did a runner with Fat Pat's 30 grand – but hold on a minute, where did she get 30K from? And who would give so much dough to a bloke they barely knew? Especially when they were as worldly-wise as ex-whore/ex-jailbird Pat Evans is meant to be. Why didn't she insist on a contract, or at least a receipt? And why didn't the soap give viewers even half a clue what his game was? It would have been far more effective than a last-minute personality transplant. (Wilfred managed to cash the cheque on a Bank Holiday weekend too; I'd like to know how...)

Yes, nice old duffer Wilfred turned out to be a ruthless hustler. So why did he waste half a year with Nana when she was potless? It was almost as puzzling as what had made Andy Hunter think marrying Sam in September would allow him to get his hands on the Mitchell millions. It was possible, if extremely unlikely, that he might have believed the family had made a few bob from their vast business empire (one pub, one garage and one deceased snooker hall), but it wouldn't have taken much to have simply checked their declared earnings rather than waltzing down the aisle with an airhead.

There were con artists at work in Albert Square, and much more serious ones than Wilfred. They were called the writers, and they were aided and abetted by their boss, Useless Louise Berridge.

Other 2004 irritants included the absence of England flags in the Vic for the football and the Ferreiras' mortgage debt storyline being replaced by an equally flaccid wholesale debt storyline. Next week, next month, next year: yet more misery, more deaths, more illogical nonsense and fewer viewers. But nothing to worry about for the feather-bedded BBC executives. Deep joy!

June was the month of the fairground disaster. Yes, the funfair finally arrived in Walford, bringing death and destruction inevitably in its wake. It was all Sonia's fault; a few minutes after she parked her lardy rump on the Dragon Ride, the whole thing collapsed. What a disaster! Pauline lived. Lynne lost her baby. Ian lost the use of his legs. Viewers lost the will to live. The only things left standing were the coconuts.

There hadn't been this much chaos caused by an unstable erection since, well, Leslie Grantham on his laptop. Tragically, not a single Ferreira died. Like cockroaches they survive everything. Broke and homeless, they'd sold their van and, from the proceeds, got themselves a flat, a car lot and three taxis...

On the plus side, the hall of mirrors did manage to make Fat Kat Slater look half-decent again. The only funny line was unintentional, the cry of, "Get Den Watts, he'll know what to do!" Yeah? Only if he can log on and get his cock out.

(They had a fortune teller at that funfair. I believe her name was

Pessi-Mystic Meg. She must have been the only one who didn't foresee it'd end in tears …)

Mysteries still unsolved: why would Dennis prefer Sharon '40' Watts over Zoe Slater, and why would Andy lust after Fat Kat? I can't tell you; I merely pose the questions. Although the biggest puzzle of the month was whose marriage would last the longest, J. Lo's or Sonia Jackson's? It beats me how the *EastEnders* characters ever keep a straight face when they take their wedding vows. Till death us do part? Even the registrar was going, "Yeah, right." These two were so mismatched they were frankly lucky to survive the honeymoon.

We knew what Martin saw in Sonia. She was plain, bossy and grumpy – "You're just like my mum," he said. But what did Sonia see in Martin? Leaving aside the fact that he killed Jamie, the love of her life, he wasn't exactly bright, was he? Martin thought D-Day was the day he got his GCSE results. He had less credible intelligence than Blair and Bush put together.

You could only hope his personality transplant didn't stick. Better a knuckle-headed yob than a weepy drip with Sonia's thumbprint on yer skull.

Elsewhere the Ferreiras – five adults, one of them a college lecturer – tried to evade bailiffs by switching door numbers. Beryl the Bailiff briefly brightened up the Square. And Alfie rejected Kat again, so she became an alkie overnight. (Wasn't this a woman's response to infidelity? Wouldn't a bloke want to take her back and, uh, 'put his brand on her' immediately?)

Also this year: Paul Trueman was assassinated; Billy torched Angie's Den; Sharon and Dennis enjoyed some light semi-incest.

And the rest of the ne'er-do-well Miller family arrived; their 13-year-old daughter Demi was pregnant and in November she gave birth to Britain's largest premature baby.

Stacey Slater turned up too – hurrah! And Grandad Jim was reliably funny ("Taiwan? I'll tie one round your earhole …") But the storylines just couldn't pull the soap out of the black hole it was falling into.

2005 – *Dirty Den Dogged to Death*

The repercussions of Paul Trueman's murder haunted the Square and Andy was showing signs of weakness. But it was too little, too late. Johnny Allen was on his case.

In February, Dirty Den's second and final death was the big story of 2005. His loving wife Chrissie bashed his head in with a cairn terrier doorstep, poetically enough, in the Queen Vic, where he was swiftly buried under the cellar. Walford CID was all over it like Miss Marple – if she'd been deaf, dumb, blind and legless, that is. But that didn't prevent the worry from getting to mastermind Chrissie and her criminal accomplices, Zoe Slater and Sam Mitchell.

Sam cleverly hid the murder weapon under her sink and a coat smothered in incriminating Watts DNA was hanging up in Zoe's wardrobe, but the killers got away with it – despite acting suspiciously for weeks on end. Chrissie, her perm showing clear signs of stress, could often be found conferring publicly and indiscreetly in not-that-quiet whispers with the other two stooges. To make things worse, Sam was now blackmailing Chrissie, who was busy writing huge cheques to buy her silence … even though Sam was an accomplice to murder and was frankly in no position to blackmail anyone at all.

An ever clumsier storyline ensued that would be complicated by a change of production team and cast availability. In a nutshell, Zoe had only struck the first blow but Chrissie, the real killer, let her believe it was her who had done Den in.

Sam knew and tried to get the Vic back in return for her silence. Both women played Zoe like a recorder (wooden and simple). Chrissie tried to convince regulars that Den had run off with another woman – faking phone conversations and throwing his clothes into the street.

Sam started binge-drinking and eventually told Zoe everything. The poor kid walloped Chrissie and hopped it to Spain. A frustrated Sam dug up Den's body and was nicked for murder (see 'Big Swinging Cobblers'). But Peggy knew something wasn't right about Chrissie (her perm?) and ended up slam-dunking the witch into Dirty

Den's grave at the funeral, landing her neatly on top of the coffin.

Chrissie confessed the murder to boyfriend Jake Moon. The Mitchell Bruvvas visited Sam in nick and convinced Sharon of who the real killer was. Jake and Chrissie rowed about it in Johnny Allen's nightclub, which naturally was caught on CCTV cameras. Johnny attempted to blackmail her into bed. After flogging the Vic to Ian Beale, Chrissie and Jake headed for the airport, but the Bruvs turned up with the Old Bill and Sharon punched her before the cops nabbed her for murder.

Then Jake lost her bail money (£25K) and blah-blah-blah ...

Chrissie actress Tracy-Ann (D)Oberman criticised her character's storylines after she left the show, saying the writers "must have been on crack" and blasting the death scenes as irresponsible. "It didn't make logical or emotional sense," she observed. "But they said, 'That's the soap convention, dear, get used to it.' I was worried when four-year-olds said to me, 'I saw you kill Den.' I don't agree with censorship but there has to be a level of responsibility."

Den was finally buried in the Watts family plot next to the wife he hated, presumably on top of the anonymous corpse that they'd fished out of the canal back in the 80s. It was better than he deserved.

(Oddly, Den's daughter Vicki couldn't make the funeral, which was particularly strange when her character's entire motivation had been 'fam'lee'.)

There were laughs with this storyline, but sadly they were all happening off-screen. (D)Oberman revealed that the cast and crew were cracking up during the murder scene when Grantham's hair got stuck to the floor. "We did lots of takes and poor Leslie was on his back for hours with fake blood all around his head," she said. "The liquid dried and his hair was glued to the floor. When he got up it ripped his hair out!"

Den's death was at least more exciting than Andy Hunter's – he'd been thrown off a South London fly-over by Johnny Allen for transgressing some unwritten gangster law.

Hot sex would have been a welcome distraction from all the murder and subterfuge. Only the soap didn't have any hot sex on offer, just Martin and Sonia and her new-but-never-mentioned boobs enjoying noisy congress whenever they felt like it, putting Pauline (and the viewers) off their tea.

It wasn't Martin's performance, or even Appalling's constant offers of "a nice shepherd's pie", that would derail their marriage, but Sonia going behind his back to see Chloe, the baby that she'd given away. (Cue months of tedious old codswallop and anguish.)

By November, Son had succumbed to a new temptation. Nurse Naomi (a.k.a. the Face of Boe) found her irresistible and made a move on her. It wasn't exactly *Sugar Rush* – Sonia's last sugar rush came from a jam donut. But Naomi was inflamed. The wine came out and so did she. Sonia was everything she ever wanted in another woman, plus two handfuls of blubber. It's up to you whether you think this was a cynical ratings ploy like the last fake-lesbian snog (Kelly and Zoe) or a bold move to blah-blah-blah...

All I know is, as titillation, it was a far cry from Beth and Margaret on *Brookie*. Or Zoe Tate and Frankie on *Emmerdale*. Or even Dulla and Lusty Binnie (the Square's last actual Sapphic couple). But it was still easier to believe in Sonia and Naomi than it ever was in Sonia and Jamie Mitchell.

Incredibly, Son's love-making wasn't the worst carnal image of the year. January had seen canal survivor and dirty old bastard Den pressurise the gorgeous Zoe into his bed. Pause here while the nation screws up its collective face in disgust...

In March, Pat tried and failed to drum up mourners for Hunter's funeral. She also tried and failed to get Adi Ferreira to provide a minicab for her and so ended up having to take her wreath on the bus, because there are absolutely no other cab firms in East London and, despite having spent years in the cab game she knew no drivers. It was also far too hard to dial 118888...

The riveting Ferreiras finally departed this year, but not until Romeo Adi had mucked up his uninteresting love life by inviting Sasha for a night out up west and then blowing her out for a ten-quid fare. She naturally repaid him by shagging Danny Moon. It would only be a matter of days before Johnny Allen forced them out of the Square.

Also in March, Johnny's new club, Scarlett's, opened and Mickey Miller dumped Kareena for shovelling Charlie up her hooter. Kat came back in May, fresh from prison, but Alfie was now in love with her sister Little Moan, "a cracking-looking bird" apparently. But Alfie and Kat were made for each other, and they finally got back together at Christmas for a rare happy ending.

(How Alfie got his Capri taxed and insured on Xmas Day is another story.)

Elsewhere, the Millers moved and their new living room had the same wallpaper as the old one. In June, illiterate Keith won a karaoke contest. But their lives were due to be blitzed by misery. Just two months later Leo, Demi's boyfriend, died of an overdose in a shameless *Romeo and Juliet* rip-off.

The year ended with Dennis Rickman stabbed to death and Sharon '40' Watts pregnant with his kid. (That's Sharon who'd been medically found barren years before. How she conceived was never explained.)

Johnny Allen had killed Dennis and implicated Phil in the murder. In return, Phil had paid Juley Smith to sleep with Johnny's daughter, the spoilt virgin Ruby. Den had beaten up Johnny, so his death was inevitable. Then Phil and Johnny set off to top each other, one with an ice-pick, the other with a revolver. (They'd left the lead piping and the candlesticks in the boot.) Ruby's near-suicide put all that on hold.

Also, Nana Moon died, after weeks of Alfie tormenting the poor old soul with day-trips, and Mad Jean made her first appearance.

Non-comic comedy of the year: Dot Cotton's driving lessons.
Bad idea of the year: Joe Macer dating Appalling Pauline.
Short-lived craze of the year: salsa!

2006 – Sex, Lies & Appalling Pauline

A year full of such unsettling images that frankly I'm minded to skip it altogether, but if you can face it, so can I. Ladies and gentlemen, I present to you the most chilling vision of the year:

Fat Pat and Patrick Trueman hard – I said *harrrrdddd* – at it.

Yes, February saw Patrick spread-eagled on the bed with the peroxide docker looming over him like a fridge-freezer – hard, cold and white – with lust in her eyes and rust in what passes for a heart.

Pat said she wanted to use pineapple and cream in their love making. Like you get a figure like that eating fruit…

There were also scenes of the two of them going for it in the car-lot portakabin on the pretext of doing the books (double entry, natch). Both were generally naked save for her fur coat and his pork pie hat. I can't tell you how relieved I was when this storyline was over…

2006 also saw pop-eyed lurv machine Grant Mitchell making the beast with two backs with Ian Beale's other half, Jane, a.k.a. Big Bird. And that wasn't much better. As Grace Dent in *The Guardian* noted: "Grant looks like he's limbering up for the Egremont Crab Fayre's gurning championship every time he pops by for chips."

The ex-para's yomping love style certainly did fish-shop temptress Jane some good. Finally she had found a battered sausage that could bring colour to her cheeks.

"There isn't a person in Britain that can fault Jane Collins for cheating on Ian Beale," Dent enthused. Except perhaps weasel-faced Ian himself, of course. The Gruntster turned on the charm. "You, Jane, are the most beautiful woman I've seen for a long time," he told her. Which surprised me. Who knew he'd been banged up in solitary? Such soppy talk didn't sound like Our Grant at all. "Oi, darlin', fancy a portion?" was more his line of seduction. His new touchy-feely 'noo man' approach was not right, but both of them seemed to enjoy it. Especially Jane – it must have made a change from Ian straddling her doggy style and doing the VAT return on her back.

Their panting passion was far more entertaining than Little Moan's latest traumas, as Little Freddie (her rape baby) was rushed to hospital, buggering up her planned night of passion with the GP, Dr Oliver, whose head had been turned by her dour expression and DIY mullet.

Freddie had a head injury – just like Trevor did when she parted his hair with an iron. Unfairly but inevitably, Mo was suspected of baby-battering. But she blamed Ben Mitchell, a kid with 'wimp' stamped all over him; Ben was the victim of the Beale/Mitchell custody battle; he got bullied at school; he wet himself; he was a loser through and through. He definitely had more Ian in him than he did Phil.

Ben Mitchell, a.k.a. the Milky Bar Kid, arrived in February. But, bizarrely, he hadn't got a South African accent. Even more bizarrely, half-brother Ian bought him a toy car – a nice touch for a kid whose mum (Kathy) had just been killed in a car crash.

January saw a slippery newcomer with a cheeky grin – Deano Wicks. He immediately nicked some of Den's flowers, lied about his dead dad and launched a money-making 'Save Wellard' campaign. (Gus's dog was due to be condemned for biting Ian Beale's arse.)

Deano's happiness was not to last. First his Aunt Fat Pat told him, "I'm not your cuddly auntie, so you can clear your shoes from under my table by Friday, latest." (This is the same Fat Pat whose house was home to all of Walford's waifs and strays.) Then randy pensioner Big Mo offered to put him up – in more than one sense. Mercifully, he declined. (Mo pounced on Dr Oliver too, but, true to form, her sexuality was still portrayed as healthy good fun – imagine if an old fella behaved like she does…)

February saw the sad off-screen death of Kathy Beale in South Africa – as southern Dubai is known to the writers – and the completely unlikely marriage of Joe Macer and Appalling Pauline moved closer. Joe's stag night was as exciting as he was – a darts match in the Vic.

On the plus side, Phil Daniels arrived as Kevin Wicks (see 'Career Mistakes'), presumed father of Deano and his sister Carly, and it didn't take long for his history of heartbreak to be revealed. It was the anniversary of the death of his eldest (and only actual) son Jimbo. Anguish ensued.

Kevin dropped by to give eye to Deano – a bit of a show-up for the kid, who'd told everyone Kev was dead. Luckily, Walfordians are used to people coming back from the grave and the wicked lie was swiftly forgotten.

Carly got herself a job as a mechanic down at the Arches, where her nails remained unbroken. Grace Dent observed: "Very 'empowering wimmin' of the scriptwriters but marred by the fact she spends most working days bent over a bonnet with her bum in the air and prancing to music, making lewd suggestions to Minty and Gary, a bit like Jodie Foster in the alarming opening scenes of *The Accused*."

Kev started running the car lot. Meanwhile, Billy's dishy-but-dim girlfriend Honey was pregnant. "I feel like a bleached whale," she remarked, in her entirely forced, unfunny, word-mangling way. Big Mo got jiggy with boring old Bert, Joe's ex-con northerner pal, and Rosie had her head turned by her ex, Mike Swann, the get-ahead father of Dawn – 'cos nothing says get-ahead more than this dowdy pub-bog cleaner. Rosie even and went and kicked out her live-in liability, Keith 'Stinky' Miller, forcing him to ponder what he'd done. (Nothing for over a decade. That was the point, mate.)

Grant and Phil returned again to take on Johnny Allen (see 'All the Small Things'). While May came and went without Hammers fans Garry and Minty noticing that their team had reached the Cup Final. Still, at least Joe, Bert and Jim had time to sing 'The Red Flag' in the Vic.

Elsewhere, Phil started battling Ian for custody of Ben, and Grant was battling Jane for custody of her vagina.

By June, Sonia and Naomi had split up (again) after having alienated the whole Square with three months of Sapphic passion. Shunned, Sonia took to drinking heavily in the park and realising it woz Martin wot she loved. Illiterate Keith was reading a World Cup guide, mad and suicidal Jean Slater was back and the only people shagging were Big Mo and Bert the Berk.

Grant's Brazilian missus, Carla, arrived, looking like a spare Sawalha sister. She'd been cheating on Grant – "SLAG!" – but was back to make up. Billy and Honey's wedding went on forever, riddled with tedious cock-ups and disasters – cancelled hairdressers, double-booked DJs, fainting brides, etc.

Oh and Kevin had fallen for the rather strict Denise – who had the potential to turn into an old boot just as hateful as Pauline. What is it with these wimpy men and their lust for strong women who'd be drummed out of the Gestapo for being overzealous? Anyone would think someone up there was a secret S&M freak, living out their fantasies through the characters.

By July, Sonia's alcoholism had disappeared, as had her lesbianism. She clearly still carried a torch for Martin but he was getting his big end touched up by car mechanic Carly. Sonia, meanwhile, was confiding in her ex, Gus.

Elsewhere, Bradley's long lost dad, Max Branning, arrived and moved into Johnny Allen's old house with his second wife Tanya and two daughters, Lauren and Abi. Keith and Rosie nearly got married.

In August 2006 poor old Grandad Jim had another rewrite and was exposed as a cruel callous bastard who had deliberately got his first wife drunk and left her to fall into a scalding hot bath before being allowed to be jovial old Jim again.

September saw Honey's Down syndrome baby (see 'Ishoos') and Denise's daughter Libby was abducted by the kid's feckless father, Owen. Peggy sprang a surprise wedding on Billy and Honey – whose waters broke during the ceremony. The real misery came later.

As light relief, tough-guy landlord turned big-hearted goon Minty was being made a fool of by his unlikely Aussie stripper girlfriend, SJ – who Garry accurately assessed as a money-grabbing con-woman tart of the first order. True to form, she made a play for Phil at Billy's wedding – driven mad by the allure of his pale bare legs. For the first and only time in his life, Phil was wearing a tartan kilt.

In October, lovesick Minty had failed to put the wheel back on Ian's jeep, causing him to career into Winston's stall. The shock was so great, Winston almost had a line of dialogue. Poor Ian. They say a car is a penis extension. No wonder his nuts came off…

The chip-shop magnate went straight round the Arches to tell Phil not to try to spoil little Ben's happy family life. "Happy family life!?" mocked Phil. "Is that why your Jane's been in bed with my brother Grant?" Whoops! Ian pretended to turn a blind eye to her infidelity, while secretly plotting one of his rubbish revenge stings – an expensive wedding in a swanky hotel with Grant as guest of honour. Yeah. That makes sense. For years he's been the tightest man in Walford. When he breaks wind, only dogs can hear it. So miserly Beale would spend a fortune to set up a sting that would reveal him to be a cuckolded twerp.

Elsewhere, Tanya opened a beauty salon. Yolande had been over the side with Aubrey (a.k.a. Jeffrey, the butler from *The Fresh Prince of Bel Air*). Patrick thought he was Denise's dad. He wasn't. And Bert and Big Mo were off to Lanzarote for some slap and tickle. What was more disturbing: the thought of Mo dropping her drawers, or Bert whipping off his socks at airport security?

In November, social climber Dawn was cavorting with Rob the wrong'un. Why couldn't she see through him? I suppose it's hard to smell a rat when you live with Keith Miller.

This same month, David Jason made the papers by claiming that *EastEnders* was aggressive and miserable. Surely not! He should have added contrived, poorly written and over the top.

One recent episode saw the Beales bawling and brawling in a downpour. (All together: "Minging in the rain, they're minging in the rain! Ian and Jane, sharing their pain, just minging and mud-slinging in the rain …") It was cringe-worthy. Drama only works if it's built on truth. This was about as believable as, well, Kevin planning a December holiday in Dorset …

Or Ian setting up a fake wedding involving his own kids, in revenge for Jane's unlikely fling with Grunt …

Or Peggy laying on that mega-spread in the Vic. (Who kept the pig's head? Charlie! It's on his shoulders, there's not much he can do about it …)

The soap's writers remain two-bob grief junkies, serving up a grim social worker vision of downtrodden cockneys. Death and despair are like heroin to them. Dirty Bert's dying ex was up next, but we don't care much about him, so why should we care about her?

Appalling Pauline was now a wicked liar and about as popular as trans-fats; we knew that she was destined to die on Christmas Day. There was more baby agony for Billy and Honey, and Max in the sack with his son's girlfriend Stacey ... an affair which, I noted at the time, would no doubt push Tanya into bed with that self-satisfied creep Sean. It's all horribly predictable and predictably horrible.

Heartache is part of life, of course, but so are joy, hope, ambition and redemption. No one is allowed to be happy here. No one stays faithful. Hardly anyone is likeable – Jane's mum (Nurse Gladys!) was like a toxic Mrs Toad.

The men are all wimps, cheats, thugs or fools. The dialogue is dreadful. Characters are absurdly rewritten. Even the non-morbid plots are pony. What would Whispering Phil see in Stella the scatty solicitor? (Going to the theatre? Phil hasn't been in one since he had his tonsils out.)

Do the BBC governors ever concern themselves with the negative effects their wretched show has on the national psyche? (Probably not, as they're unlikely to watch it.) The soap desperately needed a new Alfie, Angie or Frank Butcher, but there was no sign of one. It's moribund, a stretcher case, dying a slow, agonising death. Even Donald Rumsfeld would view it as torture.

Also this month: Jane's big secret was out. She used to be known as Leslie. (I thought I detected an Adam's apple.) Who was supposed to be marrying Ian and Jane, anyway? There was no registrar booked for the fake wedding but no one noticed.

Other Walford mysteries: if Mickey Miller converted to Islam, would his name be Seldom bin Layd? Martin was searching for Ian in a near-monsoon, so how come he only had tiny drops of rain in his barnet? And where did Rebecca vanish to when Pauline's house was alight? (She's the bungee-girl of soap, now you see her, now you don't.)

In December, Appalling Pauline spent the entire month pretending to have cancer. Peggy organised a festive sing-song to raise money for her brain tumour, but it all fell flat when the word got out that the old crow was lying. It all ended in tears, with Pauline slapping Peggy.

"But why, Pauline?" asked Yolande, speaking for all of us. "It doesn't make sense!"

"It's my business!" Pauline retorted before stomping off to sack Martin from his fruit and veg stall.

The soap was building up to its great gift to the nation: the death of Appalling Pauline, murder most Fowler.

She wasn't going down without a fight either. Pauline ended her soap life on blinding form, generally behaving like an 'as-been in need of an ASBO. As well as slapping Pygmy Peggy, she then smashed Jailbird Joe round the head with a plate. Not what most cockneys mean when they say, "Meet me old china," but good value nonetheless.

Nice-guy Joe had branded her cold, un-giving and "like ice in bed". Pauline retorted, "I don't love you … I can't bear to have you near me, you make my flesh creep," before sneering at his "clammy little hands" and referring mysteriously to his taste for bedroom 'filth'. (Sex with the light on?)

It seemed that it had finally dawned on the nitwit writers that this was the least likely soap marriage since Roy and Hayley Cropper.

No wonder Joe killed her on Christmas Day. But there were so many other people in the frame: Sonia, Martin, Joe, Mark Fowler's ghost, and nine million long-suffering viewers…

Pauline was fondly remembered by Joe: "I couldn't care less, the world's a happier place without her. I'm glad the old witch is dead." (Did Joe and Pauline Fowler ever consummate their marriage? He must have looked at her and thought, "annulled." As in, "What an old cow.")

Sonia, earlier in the year, called her a "dried-up, sour-faced rancorous old boot". Something tells me the writers didn't like her much.

Poor Pauline. She wasn't that bad. She'd just been in a lousy mood for the last two or three decades.

There was more fun when Bradley banned racy Stacey Slater from his City Boys party on Xmas Eve. Naturally she gatecrashed it anyway, looking for all the world like she was auditioning to be the third Cheeky Girl. Correctly identifying the occasion as "a room full of ponces", Stace proceeded to show herself up in revenge for not being invited. "I sell tops and knickers," she told Brad's boss. "I model the merchandise too, if you wanna have a look."

Bradley's idiot yuppie workmate couldn't wait. "She looks like a dirty little cow," he leered, before trying it on with her in the ladies. Classy. Stacey promptly threw up on him; an understandable reaction.

Dumped by Brad, she smashed his windscreen and invited his dad to "'ave a go". Something told me that Max would be stuffing more than one bird the next day.

Elsewhere, Billy and Honey provided the traditional misery quota with the heart-rending Petal storyline (if it dragged on much longer, I may have had to adopt her myself).

And Dr May slapped Dawn Swann. That's what GP stands for in Walford: Great Punch. (Next time, go BUPA, love. You'll still get hit, but faster.) But Dawn did try to keep Rob sweet. "I have rolled over and done exactly what he wanted," she said. No wonder she was up the duff ...

> *Quote of the Year:* "Sonia's a lovely girl" – Tanya Branning.
> Discuss with reference to alcoholism, bisexual adultery,
> underage pregnancy and accepted standards of beauty in
> Western society.

2007 – Here We Go Gathering Nutty May

2007 saw the soap – which as we know has always prided itself on gritty realism – tackle the widespread menace of family doctors who abduct patients in order to steal their unborn babes by forced Caesareans. Yes, it was Dr Psycho at your cervix. (Or *Myra Hindley's Casebook*, perhaps.)

And to think people say *Enders* can't do comedy.

The week started normally enough; a disorientated Dawn Swann was lying on a strange bed, writhing and screaming, her wrist shackled to the headboard. (Just like any other Monday night then.) It got funnier and funnier. Who among us didn't chuckle as Dawn wrestled with a bedstead even flimsier than the plot! Who wouldn't roar with laughter as Mad May popped up like a B-movie zombie! And who didn't split their sides laughing as the Millers extracted a proper East End revenge on May's cheating husband, Rob Minter, by holding him down and pouring gravy all over him. (By Reg and Ron, that'll teach him!)

Why did all these barmy bints want Rob anyway? He had less charisma than the Queen Vic bust, the inner strength of a soufflé and changed his mind a good deal more often than Keith Miller changes his pants. When he was with Dawn he loved May. When he was with May he lusted for Dawn. When he was with Dawn he betrayed her after finding dog's hair in the sugar bowl. Give me strength...

The storyline stank like Dawn's seat on the tube train after she threw up and wet herself. (Just like every other Saturday night for Shirley.) Soon, Dawn was feeling contractions – in the writing budget. But worse was to come, as Carly aborted 'Consider Yourself' in the delivery room and Dr May turned up at the hospital for a takeaway baby.

Keith had warned staff to bar Mr and Mrs Minter, but didn't think to add Dr May Wright, the work name of his own GP (Galloping Psychopath). *Doh!* Of course the writing was on the wall for Dr Mad, 'cos she was middle class. They're all wrong'uns in Walford (Wilmott-Brown, Cruella Stella). The soap's lifeblood is inverse snobbery. Cliché and melodrama they can do; believable human drama is beyond them.

The year had begun with Pauline popping her clogs. She died after being hit by a heavy object and a warrant was issued for Sonia's arrest. (Well, they don't get much heavier.)

Plus we found out that Kevin Wicks wasn't his kids' real father. They were one-night stands, geezers Shirley met in a pub and at a party. She wasn't sure of their names, given that blokes don't always chalk them up by the dartboard, but Carly's dad was a Dan (judging by her punch, maybe Danny Williams) though Shirl preferred to think of him as one of the Party Seven.

Also in January: Martin the Moron shocked and disappointed us all by kidnapping Ben and failing to throw him off the railway bridge. For a while CGI tube trains competed with Martin's MFI brain. Then he gave up and smashed up his living room, causing about £10 worth of improvements. That Friday though, Joe was able to offer Dot a cuppa, meaning that between bouts of despair, vandalism and abduction Martin had still been together enough to buy in some fresh milk.

Realism is this show's watchword – which is why Gus sat in the caff reciting a poem about sausages to Deano. It was apt, I suppose – his mum was a right old banger, though the only meat Shirley brings to mind is mutton ... dressed as kebab.

Oddly, this same month Phil Mitchell turned Phil-anthropist and paid for Sonia's brief. Wasn't this about as likely as Grandad Jim replacing James Brown as the Godfather of Soul? Why would Phil do it? He's not exactly loaded. He owns a pub that gives drinks away and a garage that's never busy. There's no reason for the transformation other than the writers are lazier than Keith Miller on ketamine ... the same reason Pauline's funeral service was held on New Year's Day.

In February, Stella took Ben to the London Dungeon. "Everyone used to gawp at the screaming mad people for entertainment," she told him. A sorry commentary on the soap's declining audience. One month later, Phil decided to marry her. Why? He hadn't even kissed her yet!

There were bigger mysteries to come. In May, Phil's Land Rover released its own handbrake, turned 180 degrees and drove itself through a forest before leaping to its death. The scene cost £1million. It was the costliest and most pointless stunt of the year. All that happened after that is Ben got water in his ear and Peter had a cough.

I was prepared to believe that Phil's car could drive itself into a lake. I could accept at a pinch that illiterate Keith Miller might just about be able to decipher a bank statement. But the idea that any woman could get herself and her kids ready to leave for an unexpected foreign holiday in under ten minutes, as Tanya did – that was the stuff of science fiction.

Phil Mitchell's other big storyline was his wedding. How many wives had he had in this soap? One of Ian's, one of Grant's, three of his own – most of them babes. So why was he getting webbed up with Cruella Stella, the pan-faced horror who tortures his son Ben? And why was Phil's kid as wet as Sheffield when the riverbanks burst.

What did he see in this needy, nerdy nutcase? Their relationship was more baffling than Max Branning's business hours. They had nothing in common; no chemistry, no passion. Besides, how many couples have their stag and hen dos in the same place? How many strippers actually perform to 'The Stripper'? And why would Phil feel the need to confide in Shirley, a sad, sozzled slut whose bed has been bounced on by more strangers than a DFS showroom divan?

It's just a relief they didn't leave the Argee Bargee for some rumpee pumpee.

It was all as baffling as Mickey Miller's June. Monday, Mick gets a massage, learns how to perform one himself and places an ad in the *Gazette* (a weekly paper) as a masseuse. Tuesday, the ad appears; he beds his first client and then Li, who wanted him to be a male escort to begin with, cops the hump. Eh?

Phil and Stella's wedding day was fun though, as Stella finally took the plunge – right off a factory roof. Her last wish, I speculated, was for her ashes to be mixed with itching powder and scattered down Ben's pants. Phil would better off marrying a bin Laden. At least the in-laws wouldn't be quite so deranged. (And were those premature age spots splattered over his skull? Or just an allergic reaction to his unlikely love-life?)

Look at the horrors this 'streetwise geezer' has had to marry: Nadia (Romanian bag-lady); Kate (undercover cop); Kaff of Kaff's caff (the believable one); and now Cruella Stella. Yet he failed to wed lovely Lisa. What's wrong with the bloke? What Phil, and *Enders*, desperately needs is a young version of Peggy. Instead, it's odds-on they'll have him back on the bottle for more endless gloom.

In July, Heather Trott, a comedy fat bird, arrived. And drink-soaked skank Shirley Wicks bedded a hunky young copper. As if he'd fancy her – Shirl was 52! She might not look it, but she did once ...

This year did see the soap include a token acknowledgement of East European immigration into the East End, when some Polish building workers turned up for a couple of weeks. Erek, the only one who really spoke, said Shirley Wicks was "the best-looking woman" he'd seen since he'd arrived in England. So either he's got a *Terrahawks* fetish or he'd just come round from an emergency cataract operation.

Also this year: Darren Miller rigged up hidden cameras to show 'live' footage of his dad festering in his living room. Wasn't the budding entrepreneur missing a trick? If people were willing to pay thousands to watch Keith rot, how much would they shell out to see Denise's daughter Squiggle jiggle?

Keith's new HD TV was the business though. Everything on it looked bigger and wider. It was like a Slater sisters reunion.

Mystery of the Year: how did Deano Wicks make a living from his market stall? Did you ever clock the contents? It was like the worst charity stand at a village fare. Deano's stock consisted of shopping bags, clocks, flea-ridden Dalmatian soft toys, toy donkeys that looked distinctly secondhand, handbags, one teddy bear and some ugly vases. Who would buy this cack? (The sort of bums who can't afford washing machines, I suppose. Incredibly, the launderette was recruiting staff! When it's 8pm in Weatherfield, it's 1957 in Albert Square.)

Arrivals of the Year: the Mitchell sisters. Cheering from the sidelines, I acknowledged that the soap had been in need of a couple of fit blondes for quite some time. Maybe the Mitchell girls could help them find some ...

Ronnie (Sam Janus) may have turned heads ten years ago. Sam Janus claimed to be mistaken a lot for Sarah Alexander – presumably in the dark. But now, with her angular features, strangely taut skin and boomerang chin, she looked like a cartoon preying mantis. While hard-faced Roxy was as down to earth as the straw in her kennel.

Bow belles, you say? Bow Locks! Yet Ronnie and Roxy – named, for a laugh, after the Kray twins – were here to stay.

Of course, it all made perfect sense. You're running a bar in Ibiza. You fly over to see a cousin you've never met get wed. You find chaos, death and hostile locals ... who wouldn't forget their business, renounce the sunshine and move in permanently?

The soap's logic is as lopsided as Stephen Fry's hooter.

The feisty women were obviously this year's Slater sisters and they immediately tarted up the Square, flashing boobs at taxi drivers – "Consider that your tip," said Ronnie (I'd consider it small change) – and putting Ian Beale in his place. But the funniest thing about them is that Peggy calls them 'Woxy' and 'Wonnie'.

Poxy Roxy flirted with Dumbo Wicks and gave Sad Brad a makeover. Her first impressions of Brad were, "you'd be good in a pub quiz." Our first impression of her is she'd be good in any available bed. Roxy looked easier than Junior Sudoku and, as it turned out, we were right.

Both women seemed tough and upbeat. So how long, I asked, would it be before the writers weighed 'em down with doom, drudgery and despondency? Odds-on they'd need a second taxi for all their emotional baggage ...

The sisters' arrival helped misdirect viewers from the holes in the plot. Why would Phil tell the cops that he'd killed Cruella Stella when he hadn't? How did Ian forget that he'd seen Ben's bruises months ago? And why would Peggy have persisted in having a champagne wedding reception with the bride brown-bread, the groom nicked and her grandson traumatised? She even left up the balloons with Stella's face! It was completely nuts. Even more baffling, why didn't Walford Plod wipe the CCTV footage and bang Phil up for a ten-stretch?

(Peggy was displaying quite a bit of cleavage this week though, despite her mastectomy – a credit to her surgeon, Adam Dunn.)

> *Steal of the Year:* the soap ripped off the illicit drinking den scene from *Some Like It Hot.*

> *Low of the Summer:* a week when the soap's highlights were cockroach racing, a live sheep, and a bad drag act ... All of which begged the question, were they outsourcing the scripts to India? This might be someone's idea of a good night out in Bangalore, but it didn't exactly scream, 'Working-Class Britain 2007'.
>
> Then again, much of Walford life rings as true as Gordon Brown's smile. The soap's writers have no grasp of how real Londoners live or love or laugh, or indeed the number of people who can fit comfortably into a three-bedroom house.

Pat's place was now so overcrowded no one even noticed Squiggle had gone missing. The Brad-Stacey-Mekon love triangle was ridiculous. The alarm bells should have gone off for Brad when Stace said she "didn't feel ready" for sex; she's normally as ready as the condoms in his pocket.

Equally, Garry and Dawn's relationship seemed as likely as Venus Williams playing a quiet game of tennis. It came from nowhere, and yet next month he proposed. On the plus side, Shirley was rewritten as a worldly-wise wit – just as Minty the nasty slum landlord was turned into a loveable old goat.

And on the XL plus size there's Heather, this year's 18 stone of idiot, who's suffering with hypoglycaemia: "Yeah, it's a curse."

More verbal humour and less heavy-handed slapstick might have helped ...

> *Day Trip of the Year:* In August Shirley tried to lift Heather's spirits, which admittedly is a lot easier than trying to lift Heather. Unexpectedly, the Soap of Gloom was almost fun in Brighton. The close-up of Heather's face at the end of her roller-coaster ride was hilarious – although her insane craving for Garry Hobbs might have been easier to believe

if it hadn't been six whole weeks since she last saw him.

(Heffer or Dawn: a tough choice for any man. No, don't scoff. If your plane crash-landed in the Andes and you had to survive on human flesh, Hefty Heather would have weeks' more meat on her. You could fondle her all night and never touch the same place twice.)

Understandably Garry preferred the prospect of Swann-upping. But Dawn likes her blokes well-endowed – with cash.

Heather's been brought in to make Shirley look less like a selfish, sozzled slut, but she's too dim for the relationship to ring true. And her 'comical' cheese obsession reeks like year-old camembert.

Tantrum of the Year: Furious Bradley Branning told the whole Vic about Stacey on the Christmas Day *EastEnders.* "She is a slut," he announced. To which the casual observer might well have responded: Well, duh! She's a Slater! Poor Brad. It was like walking into the Kremlin in 1930 and accusing the doorman of being a bit of a Bolshevik. It's the Vic. They're all slappers!

Although, in fairness, Stace had a long way to go before she caught up with shameless trollops like Sozzled Shirl and Poxy Roxy. (Shirley Carter's Xmas card message: "Did I sleep with you this year while I was smashed? If so, season's greetings. [See reverse of card for STD clinic number.]")

Still, if bawling misery was what you were after in the season of good cheer, *Enders* delivered brilliantly. Brad chinned Max, Tan slapped Stacey. It was compulsively watchable, an emotional train wreck, well directed and performed. It's just a shame it wasn't immortalised in song for the Walford Carol Service.

All together (to the tune of 'Good King Wenceslas'): "Bad Max Branning dropped his kecks for his son's girlfriend / And because he played away, two marriages will end / Bradley smacked him in the jaw, Tanya took a tumble / Won't be long till sneaky Sean is in there for a fu-um-ble!"

Ghost of the Year: The spirit of Cindy Beale was haunting Albert Square. So was Cindy alive? No. Had *The Sixth Sense* come to Walford? (I see dud people …). No! The only spirits here were in a flask in Phil's back pocket.

Entry of the Year: in October Bobby Davro made his debut by knocking down Shirley in his Merc. The whip-round to buy him Fat Nav and a ten-ton truck for a free run at Heather starts here. Davro was playing Vinnie Monks, although really he's Alfie Moon II. Trouble is that Alfie had a great writer in Tony Jordan; Vince had the same ready smile, twinkling eyes and comic timing but his script and storyline lacked wit, sparkle and all sense of reality.

Alfie was a streetwise cheeky chappie, Vince was a bit of a plum; a nice guy but a mug – Alfie Part Duh. I mean, what sober bloke would look at that sozzled, hard-faced old slapper Shirley in the cold light of day and think, "Whoa, cut me a slice of that!"? Even Vince's nodding dog was nodding sideways.

Shirl could count her lovers on one hand (with a calculator) and never mind Vinnie, Harry Monk is her speciality. (Ask a cockney. It's rhyming slang.) Still, Linda Henry is terrific as Shirley, and if Vinnie helped bring more depth to her character then so much the better.

But it'll take more than comedy casting to bring sense to this soap. What was that Stephen Beale storyline all about? Mind games, kidnapping, assault – all because, "I just didn't want Mum forgot." Yeah? Well, buy a memorial stone, you plank, or put an advert in the paper.

(So a cheating wife has another man's baby and dies abroad in mysterious circumstances. Her cuckolded husband gets painted as the bad guy and, ten years later, mad people are still banging on about her. Remind you of anyone? Me neither, Your Majesty.)

Where did all the hatred come from? Five years in New Zealand stunted Stephen's growth, turned his blond hair dark brown, his blue eyes brown and fried his brain cells (but didn't affect his accent in the slightest).

In revenge for God knows what, he'd lured Ian to a block of flats which, despite being derelict, had full power. (The lights were on but no one was home – a perfect metaphor for the soap's writers.) Ian was trapped here for two weeks, apparently without attempting to escape; even though the door and windows were covered with flimsy metal grills which he could have bent with, say, a wooden table leg.

There was a balcony out the back with a drainpipe to shin down … but no, tightwad Ian just sat in the dark growing a beard, definitely more Huge Meanie than Houdini.

Where would this happen? This isn't *life*. *Enders* can book who the hell they like but, until they sort out the writing, good casting is just gilding a turd.

Reality Check:
- In October Jack contemplated buying a French chateau. There was no credit crunch in Albert Square. He and Tania planned to leave almost immediately, without taking even rudimentary steps such as finding school places for the girls …
- What was Dawn supposed to see in Jase? She always went for go-getters. Jase was potless, charmless and looked like a partly-shaved ape. John the grasping estate agent would have been more her type …
- In December, Vinnie Monks used Pat to make Shirley jealous. That's Fat Pat – a 65-year-old, 16-stone, hard-faced pensioner; a woman so frightful her first husband died on purpose. It was as baffling as a) Vinnie fancying Shirl while he was sober and b) Vinnie then turning the trashy, tipsy Terrahawk down when she wanted him. (So it'll be next year before he changes his name to Vinnie Garstrokes, then.)

Crash of the Year: New Year's Eve, Walford, and the only thing emptier than Ronnie's club was the writers' ideas box. Another crash! This soap has seen more car carnage than

Police Camera Action. Still, it gave Phil Daniels his finest soap acting scene – as a corpse. I was moved to tears, of laughter, as Kevin croaked. He wrote off his cut 'n' shut Golf with his nut 'n' slut ex. As Shirl leant over him, Kev went cross-eyed. Was it the pain or an involuntary response to her breath – a heady mix of fags, phlegm and other men's cock … tails? (Let's not dwell on the speed of his funeral or the lack of a post-mortem.)

Wretch of the Year: Billy Mitchell. Poor Bill rose effortlessly to the top of my *EastEnders* misery-ometer in December. No job, no home, reduced to robbing charity boxes … if Billy rung the Samaritans and said he felt like topping himself they'd tell him it was probably for the best. He's the sort of bloke who could contract an STD from a wet dream. If he was in the Taliban his cave would be repossessed. The soap's perpetual whipping boy was sacked from Fat Barry's old part-time job as a Christmas elf. (Give me strength!) He ended up rolling home as pissed as Shirley's mattress and disappointing Honey, his simpleton missus, but worse was yet to come.

Keep punching, Billy son, you'll get knocked out soon enough.

The only also-ran loser was Ian Beale's son, Uneven Steven, who took to smashing up his own stall for no convincing reason…

2008 – The League of Walford Gentlemen

March saw the start of what Ally Ross called the soap's *League of Gentlemen* period, with Gus Smith tortured, Mad Jean Slater abducted and Max Branning buried alive in their very own, highly unlikely bush-tucker trial.

But there was a fate worse than death for one popular character this month. It was pure shock-horror. You watched with mounting disbelief as the nightmare unfolded – Minty really did snog Heather Trott! It looked like wedding bells next.

But why though? Why would he? Why would *anybody*? She's not exactly a F.I.L.F. (Fatty I'd Like to F***). She's not even his type – Minty's last girlfriend was as thin as a rake. His lovelife has turned into an episode of *Supersize v Superskinny*.

Heffer has no personality and no brains. Dim? She thinks global credit crunch is a high-carb breakfast. Could anybody really fancy her? Frankly, you'd rather dig up Nana Moon.

Elsewhere, there was more unlikely horror as ginger love god Max was in a coffin from Good Friday to Easter Monday, but still had more fun than anyone stuck at home watching BBC1. It was big-time melodrama, of course, but it did raise at least one big question. To wit: If you were being buried alive by your wife, would you call a) 999 or b) your dippy nine-year-old daughter? Max chose b. *Doh!* (This despite having a mobile that didn't allow emergency calls in bad reception areas – like, for example, a shallow grave.)

Beauty salon boss Tanya's transformation from loving mum to would-be killer was not in the least bit convincing. She had never so much as broken a client's nail before, and now suddenly it was *Murder She Waxed*. The change rang as true as Tanya's relationship with swivel-eyed nutter Sean Slater. What long-term future would a get-ahead businesswoman see in this scruffy layabout? (Especially as Rob Kazinsky's acting style is somewhere between method and manic depression.)

Max, a vengeful bloke, could have had Tanya charged with attempted murder. More likely, he could have hit on her for make-up sex. Instead he meekly accepted responsibility – *it's a fair cop, I'm to blame; I cheated on you so I deserve to be almost killed.* And then he walked away. 'Reality' indeed. (He'd been on his back, feeling trapped and dirty – isn't that how Fat Pat started?)

Another crime was committed here, too – grand theft, the shameless nicking of *Coronation Street* plots. When Tracy Barlow found out her fella Charlie Stubbs was over the side, she took him back, faked a relationship and topped him. Sound familiar? There's more …

Stephen, Stacey and gurning creep Christian (a.k.a. the Vest Ham) would soon be caught up in an unlikely bisexual love triangle – just like *Corrie*'s Michelle, Sean and Sonny. *Enders* nicks from everything these days, from *The Simpsons* to *Some Like It Hot* via *Friends* and old black and white movies. When caught out, they claim it's a 'tribute', but in reality they're completely out of ideas. Random recent cobblers has included budgie-napping and gold-digger Clare targeting Walford. (Why? The West End is a few tube stops away.) The 'long-lost' relative has now become a core feature. (Peggy's never-mentioned nieces, Pat's unmentioned sister, Tanya's druggy sister, the entire 'long-lost' plot ...)

No one in the Vic is Irish, yet they celebrate St Paddy's Day. Ian Beale hasn't mentioned the Queen in 33 years, but suddenly in 2008 he became an ardent royalist. Lucy heard a bit of Sham 69 and, in the very next episode, teenage Mohicans were wrecking her house to antique punk tunes. It was like 1980s kids running amok to the happening sounds of Bill Haley.

Behind Tanya, the second biggest transformation came with Deano Wicks, who returned to Walford, head-butted Sean and roughed up his mum. It was prison that transformed wimpy Deano into a hard-drinking, whore-humping tough-nut.

After 12 weeks. Imagine if he'd done a year. He'd have come back like a cross between Charles Bronson and Uday Hussein.

More 2008 madness: competing for the nuttiest storyline of the year, or any year, was Minty Peterson's marriage to Heather Trott. Heather in her wedding dress looked like the Alps. Were we really supposed to believe Minty wouldn't realise he'd have to sleep with his morbidly obese bride until their wedding day?

How old are the people who write this garbage? 12?

The whole storyline was like some fat girl's fantasy. In the real East End, there would be a wag at the bar coming out with one-liners: "Watch out Minty, when she drops her drawers her arse will still be in them ... She tried computer dating once and it matched her with Romford ... Imagine that naked, she'd look like a giant dumpling with eyes ... If you knock her up, how will you tell? She's already eating for two."

Poor Heather. You'd have trouble getting in a lift with her, let alone a bed. Let's hope it's over soon and she goes back to the real love of her life – Colonel Sanders. But Cheryl Fergison is great as hefty Heather, and I understand she's RSC trained. (Not Royal Shakespeare Company – *Ready, Steady, Cook*.)

Runner-up madness: Ian Beale's gay date. But the real gay storyline was reserved for his bonkers non-son.

Mo had bullied Steven Beale into bed with Stacey. "Leave it much longer and she'll think you're a bit of a Doris Day," Mo advised sensitively. But when it came to the crunch, Steven couldn't get a John Bardon. His Queen Vic failed to rise to the occasion. Turned out he had the Angie Watts for Christian instead.

The storyline was a predictable fiasco, as Steven's quest for his first Donald Duck became public knowledge. Christian caught him starkers and observed, "Quite some light you've been hiding under your bushel." (I'm touched, but not in the way Steven wants to be.)

He even got intimate advice from his dad, Ian, who told him sex is like riding a bike. And he should know, he married one. Ian also told him to avoid 'over-excitement' by mentally reciting the entire England team. (Wouldn't have worked with the goalie we had in the 1990s.)

Finally, the supposedly cool Christian eavesdropped on Steven and Stacey's private conversation, crassly and completely unbelievably denouncing him as "still a virgin" in a crowded club. Before you knew it, Steven was outside snogging his step-uncle.

So was this Barry and Colin all over again, I asked? Or Tiff's bisexual brother recycled? The *Enders* writers do love plagarising their own past. (And film scenes – the 'dog-eating' twist, when Sean Slater tricked Gus into believing he was eating Wellard in a spaghetti dish, came straight from a Vincent Price movie.)

Hold up, though; back in the 1980s, gay storylines were bold and challenging. But society has changed. Homosexuality is no longer an issue. Apart from a few fanatics, no one cares how adults entertain each other in private. But we *do* care about soap stories making sense and characters that remain consistent.

We also want our soaps to have a sense of morality – something *EastEnders* has long forgotten. Sean Slater is a spiteful bully who is guilty of attempted murder. He must get his comeuppance. As should Janine the murderess, self-centred thief Chelsea and Tanya, who is also guilty of attempted murder.

Bianca has been rewritten as a crass, selfish trash-mother who thinks the world owes her a living. There are plenty of women about like her, of course. But why is there no one in Albert Square prepared to pull her up about her mouth – sorry, *marf* – and her attitudes? No one made her have four kids by different blokes.

As for Steven, he's gone from psychopathic nutter to sensitive artist to overnight gay. Who gets him though the night doesn't matter, but it does matter that we can't believe in him. It's hard to credit that even a schmuck like Steven wouldn't know he was gay at his age. (Mind you, no one's pointed it out to Graham Norton yet. Imagine the shock that'll be for his wife and mistresses!)

2008 was also a funny old year for Charlie Slater. First he was referred to in a script as 'middle-aged'. Eh? How so? Derek Martin is 75 this year. He's 66 in the show. News flash: not many people live to 122, you morons! Perhaps the folk who write this junk are swigging Dwain Chambers' old urine samples.

Apart from his love-life, Charlie's other major storyline was his encounter with a spider hilariously on the loose. Chas thought he'd been bitten by it. "He's swollen up like a drowned hippo!" squawked Big Mo. So, condition normal then?

That spider was the scariest thing with eight legs to hit Walford since the Slater sisters arrived – though not quite as predatory. It turned up with Billy's bananas and crawled into Charlie's shirt. "What's this horrible hairy thing?" said the spider. The biggest miracle is that Roxy didn't bed it, she's shagged everyone else. (Or maybe she has already. If the birth is filmed live on a webcam, don't be too surprised.)

This year's most welcome return was Mad Dr May. It made me ask if May Wright was really that bad. Consider the evidence: she locked Jane Beale in a storage cupboard; for that relief, much thanks. She branded Dawn a stupid bitch – no argument there. And she walloped Mickey round the head with a crowbar. (It's okay, he didn't dent it.) To be honest, I liked the woman.

Summer Swann's little face certainly lit up when she saw her, too, although that may have been the gas explosion. In May, the Square's former GP (Galloping Psycho) ended her demented quest to abduct Dawn's baby by blowing herself up. You may think it odd that a woman this resourceful didn't settle for the relatively safer option of adoption ...

But I enjoyed her ninja-like ability to creep up on Mickey undetected. And her compulsive need to diagnose her victims. "Superficial haematoma, scalp laceration," she cooed after clubbing him, before telling Dawn that, "Rest, ice, compression, elevation," was the best way to treat her newly fractured leg.

It's just a shame the disgraced doc never got to treat cheating husband Rob: *May breaks his neck, mutters, "Vertebral fracture." She rips off his balls, curtly noting, "Uterectomy with bilateral castration ..."*

May's gas explosion made a mess of the Millers' entire ground floor, although the untrained eye might strain to spot the difference. Locked in an upstairs bedroom with smoke pouring under the door, congenital nincompoops Mickey and Dawn took a full five minutes to hit on the idea of opening a window. *Doh!*

And five minutes more to think of throwing Summer out of it ...

But Dr Mad did some good. She galvanised Keith Miller, that useless lump of human flotsam, into risking his life to save Dawn. Well done, mate. (Normally, when Keith wants to get his hands dirty he just runs them through his hair.)

And the Costco-size can of grief she dumped on Dawn distracted us from tiresome nonsense like Pat's lost wedding ring and Shirley's Best of British day. Strangely, the Vic was the only pub in East London that didn't celebrate St George's Day, but everyone took a sneaky day off for the union. Who writes this stuff? Gordon Brown?

Still, at least Heather's twin turned up for the party. Oh, I'm sorry, that was a bouncy castle ...

There was much more grief to come for Dawn Swann in 2008, as her fiancé Jase the apeman was topped by the football hooligan gang. And the soap seemed to blame Dawn for his downfall 'cos he'd returned to a life of crime to pay for her dreams. Hmm.

Dawn's crime was to want a better life after their marriage. Because of this, the writers stripped her firstly of friends, and secondly of her dignity (tragically forgetting the third step of stripping her of clothes).

Dawn spent her hen night, absurdly, in her £1690 wedding dress being lectured by Shirley the lush. "You are the sum of what you buy," she sneered; which by my reckoning makes Shirl two parts vodka, one part gin and three parts Mad Dog 20/20.

"You used to be one of us," she went on – the 'us' presumably being that community of selfish tarts who desert their children but don't commit the cardinal sin of wanting to move to Essex. For *EastEnders*, written mostly by middleclass graduates, hates working-class aspiration. "Oi, plebs," it says, "know your place!"

Elsewhere, more madness reigned:

- Sean Slater was auditioning for *Grand Theft Auto V*. Or maybe he was just defending his title as the world's most pointless psychopath. Either way, for no apparent reason, he was planning to murder nice Gus Smith. He'd tied him to a chair and left a fake suicide note. (How would he tie himself up and then top himself, Einstein?) Luckily, sister Stacey arrived and talked Gus out of calling the Old Bill, 'cos "we're mates" ... Pure BAFTA-nominated realism. (Sean also passed off baking powder as cocaine. See, you can have your coke and eat it too.) My ode to Gus: "So farewell then to Walford's bard / No one will miss you 'cept Wellard / Your leaving story was a farce / You can stick your poetry up ... on the wall of Keisha's van."

- Chelsea was getting as high as gas prices, becoming an overnight coke addict (just like Janine was) despite snorting less gear than Amy Winehouse spills on a night out.

It was huge swinging cobblers of course, but it faded to insignificance compared to other Walford bilge. Like the Millers' demented reaction to a five-number Lotto win – worth about £2K, and not enough to pay off the average credit card bill. Maddest of all was Ricky Butcher passing a kid's IQ test. This is Fick Rick we're talking about, after all, a man who would lose a game of snap to a banana.

Elsewhere, reality continued to shine as Billy wore a suit and tie to be interviewed for a roadsweeping job, Bianca fed a dog chocolate with the wrapping paper on, with fatal consequences, and Ian pretended to have a butler while living in an East End hovel ... Yes, welcome to Walford, land of dog post-mortems and instant market stall acquisitions, where strangers waltz into jobs and accommodation. And if the small elements add up as well as a flustered Honey Mitchell on *Countdown*, then what chance have the big storylines got?

Say you had a dodgy gold bar, would you a) bury it in a public place, or b) stick it in a safety deposit box? If you were Phil Mitchell, would you a) hide it badly in a beer cellar used by bar staff and accessible from the street, or b) put it in your safe?

If your answers were both a), congratulations, you too could be an *EastEnders* writer. No knowledge of life in general or Londoners in particular required.

The idea that neither Phil nor any of his shady underworld contacts knew how easy it is to shift stolen gold didn't just defy credibility; it beat it to a bloody pulp. As for Jase, if you were planning to illegally relieve a lump of £100K would you really want Billy 'the Jinx' Mitchell as your getaway driver? This guy is so unlucky he makes Jonah seem blessed. His wife is gorgeous but she's as thick as Chris Hoy's thighs, his daughter has Down's syndrome, but he can't hold down a job or – uniquely for a Mitchell – hold up his fists. If Billy met the Dalai Lama, the old man would probably mug him.

Who could believe in this parallel London, where market inspectors employ council roadsweepers, chocolate wrappers are poisonous and sons forgive fathers for poggering their wives? *EastEnders* was originally built around the Fowlers and the Watts, solid families drawn from reality. We recognised their dramas, traumas, hopes and dreams because they were our lives too. Not anymore.

Now the Square was awash with sisters and cousins never previously mentioned. There was a new girl in the Square, teenage Danielle, so I wrote in the *Daily Star Sunday*, "whose long-lost relative will she turn out to be? Is she the daughter Christian never knew he had, or the one Ronnie gave up for adoption?"

Okay, call me Mystic Meg...

More things I couldn't believe this year:

- Garry Hobbs turned down a drunken Dawn Swann. No wonder we saw her crying for a rabbit ... But WHY would Garry do that? Yes, Dawn was grieving, but Garry's an opportunist. He doesn't do sensitive. He would have grabbed a bereavement shag with both hands. The reason he didn't? A woman wrote that episode. Later that year, Garry spent the night with Dawn and "didn't take advantage". Muppet!
- Bradley's instant James Bond party. Within hours the club was transformed into Pinewood. But where did all the locals get their costumes from? And who paid for them? The guests came as Bond characters, but sadly there was no Holly Goodhead (Kath), Honey Rider (Billy – unseated) or Plenty O'Toole (Phil Mitchell, by all accounts). Brad got the idea from Dirty Den – *You Only Live Twice*.

Farewell/Comeback of the Year: EastEnders turned into *I Love the 90s* as the Butchers returned. And wasn't it ter-rif-ic? All it needed was for someone to torch the car lot and the retro joy would have been complete. The Butcher brood were back for their dad's funeral. It was his second, but this time Frank was as dead as the great Mike Reid who played him. Francis Aloysius Butcher was a giant character, larger than life, with a voice like a cat burglar sliding on gravel. Even dead he stole the show. Yes, Frank was a two-timing loser – "wotten thwough to the core," said Peggy. But Reid made him loveable and believable. A proper cockney.

(We heard about Frank's death on the Monday; on the very next day they buried him. Never mind *The Apprentice,* Alan

Sugar should hire the bloke who organised that funeral.)

In contrast, Pat and Peggy at the gay wedding felt as real as a Hilary Clinton war story. The blokes were the least convincing couple since David Gest married Liza Minnelli. Ricky and new squeeze Melinda seemed just as unlikely. Even Fick Rick wouldn't tolerate this dippy Daddy's girl; mercifully she didn't last long. Pre-funeral, we got Albert Square's greatest hits with Pat and Peggy slapping each other for the umpteenth time, and Peggy trotting out her catchphrase: "*Get ahta my pub!*"

It took Bianca Jackson, the human foghorn, to drag us out of nostalgia mode and reignite our interest in the present. She started by getting evicted, and ended the week getting nicked for punching a cop. Happy days ...

The Jackson family always were a DNA disaster area and Bianca was no exception. She turned up with four kids by three different blokes and, if I'm not mistaken, the same jacket she left in nine years ago. She is destined to be a Butcher, of course. (Play join the dots with her freckles and they actually spell, "*Rickkkayyy!*") If only the soap put the effort expended on the Bianca trailers into the actual episodes.

And if only they'd realise what made Frank such a great character. 1) He was a genuine Londoner. 2) Comedy was in his blood – even Frank's wives were little and large. 3) He had an ear for cockney patter.

They should replace him with another real East London comic, like Barbara Windsor and Ross Kemp's favourite London funny man, Mickey Pugh. (Don't expect him to shag Fat Pat though ...)

Gifts that Frank should have left his kids: Ricky – a brain. Janine – some underwear. Diane – a personality.

Question arising from the Butchers' back stories: how could Bianca ever have been a brass? She's loud enough as it is. If she was faking an orgasm she'd stampede cattle.

Runner-up Farewell of the Year: Shabnam Masood, a.k.a. the pretty one, a.k.a. the normal one, a.k.a. the only one I half cared about. In October, Shabs left the East End for Karachi. But she's a bright, Westernised woman. What has Karachi got for her that East London hasn't? Well, washing machines maybe! Culture! A lower crime rate! But surely she couldn't be stranded in such a primitive, backward place? ... said the Pakistanis. I'm just relieved that Mrs Masood's Post Office shut down before any of the dim local villains worked out that it didn't have a security window. It was the only Walford business that hadn't been robbed.

In this demented soap, life-changing decisions are made on a whim, and the laws of physics are meaningless. Eight people were currently living upstairs at the Vic, and only Peggy was sharing a bedroom. It's like the Tardis in there. Elsewhere, Jack Branning turned into Swiss Toni from *The Fast Show*, and Callum Monks claimed he had "moving costs" – how come? He turned up with sod-all. What's he got to move?

If the small stuff was baffling, the big stories were just bonkers.

Jason's son Jay was so eaten up with hatred that he nearly fried Dawn and his baby stepsister alive. Of course! Your Dad died 'cos he's a thug; how better to honour his memory than by murdering two people he cared about? Mercifully, Billy nixed Jay's sick Summer barbecue. But the obnoxious brat had been seconds away from arson.

And guess what? Two episodes later they were all mates again. Dawn forgave him. Jay wasn't charged; he won't have to see a shrink; he won't be punished at all. That's how it is in wet, woolly Walford – anything goes as long as you've got a story that'd make a social worker's heart bleed.

Forget personal responsibility. It ain't your fault, son; *society's to blame*.

In March, Tanya buried Max the Mekon alive. But it wasn't her fault, either, apparently. No, it was down to him being a cheating control freak, so no one mentioned it afterwards. Not even Max!

The work-shy but mysteriously wealthy insurance salesman also forgot to tell his brief that his ex is a lying, scheming tart that gets through plonk like Kerry Katona on a medication bender. It's almost as if her tree-trunk legs are hollow.

Should we feel sorry for Jay? Of course – but don't forget he was a mouthy oik with a chip on his shoulder even before his dad was (understandably) beaten to death for betraying his criminal firm. It's hard to think of a better advert for bringing back the birch.

The stench of murder hung over Albert Square again in November too. A disturbing crime had almost certainly been committed. I am of course referring to the continued unexplained absence of Corky the parrot. The poor bird hadn't been seen since the Masoods opened that curry stall. Coincidence? I think not. (See also Wellard, Terence, Albert, Gilbert the chinchilla and the Slaters' missing cat.)

Elsewhere, the mystery of who ran over Max the Mekon was exciting us like the prospect of a Heather Trott striptease. We were supposed to think it was Jack or Bradley, so obviously we could rule them out. Tanya had previous, having tried to top Max already. But I was offering 20/1 on Jeremy Clarkson, 10/1 on any punter fleeing a Jane Beale comedy show and 2/1 on Archie Mitchell, who might well have done it as one of his many cheeky wind-ups. He's a wag, that Archie.

> *Mysteries of the month:* how did Jack Branning get his hair cut between leaving the Square and arriving at Walford nick? Why didn't anyone tell Suzy the floozy that her brother was in intensive care? Where did that bog in the caff come from? How did Ian lock himself in when the buttons are on the outside? And if Shirley didn't go to the dogs on Friday, who was in trap five?

The year ended with a riot of old cobblers. December was a memorable month for all the wrong reasons, as Jane Beale made her debut as a stand-up comedienne (see '15 of the Most Ridiculous Storylines Ever'). Elsewhere in 'realistic' Walford, people were still giving away money, men were turning down offers of sex and Nick Kamen's 1985 launderette strip was re-enacted by a tramp – no, not

Roxy; she was busy hiding her top-secret DNA test results under a box of pub snacks.

Natch, someone (Archie?) nabbed them and, due to a paperwork mix-up, now believes baby Amy's real dad to be a bag of Lay's … which is not far from the truth.

Later that month, Janine Butcher tried to marry a trainee corpse. Using the altar ego Judith Bernstein, she conned some old schmuck into a synagogue wedding – until Fat Pat scuppered it.

Why, Pat? It would never have been consummated. The groom looked like he'd have spent the honeymoon getting out of the car. He was so old he'd need Viagra to raise his hand, he must have gone to school with Moses.

The upshot was that murderess and renowned ceiling inspector Janine ended up back in Walford permanently. She's just the girl next door type, if you happen to live next door to a brothel …

We also learnt that it was Lauren Branning who had run over Max, her father. That's Lauren, 14, who had never driven a jamjar in her life. Not only did she manage to instantly adjust the seat so her feet could reach the pedals, she also worked out in seconds how to put it in gear, operate the clutch and drive without the car jerking and shuddering like a Moroccan milk-float.

She'll be presenting *Top Gear* next.

Christmas 2008 saw the climax of the 'Who's the Daddy?' storyline – which BBC1 cleverly blew in a trailer before *Gavin and Stacey* on Christmas Eve … Jack Branning was the real father of Amy, not Sean Slater. The reveal was still uncharacteristically entertaining, however, as Sean read the results of the DNA test which Suzy had concealed in Ben Mitchell's homemade crackers. Well, Xmas is a time of giving and the chesty slapper managed to give most of the Mitchells a nasty turn. Naturally, a devastated Sean attacked Jack before going on a rampage and, for no clear reason, kidnapping the blameless babe. Merry Christmas everybody!

> *Query of the month*: if Suzy was pregnant with Phil (or Archie's) child, then technically did she have a bum in the oven?

Mystery of the month: how come Max was sprinting upstairs just eight weeks after getting run down; have his limbs been reconstructed using the same technology that made Steve Austin the Bionic Man?

Elsewhere, Hefty Heather turned detective this month (she was Walford's answer to Wallander: Whale-Ender) but could she, I wondered, find out what had happened to Jay? He'd been missing since October. Maybe he'd been hiding on Minty's boat, with Corky and Walford Town FC. Scientists will find Higgs Boson long before they can get around to working out how four adults, two teenagers and two kids are living in Fat Pat's three-bedroom house with only the kids sharing and no one kipping on the settee.

Then there was the year's most unwelcome development, the paedophile storyline. Step forward Tony, the toxic creep. Has there ever been a duller soap villain? He was like a black hole in human form. Even his ears annoy me. Are they so big and red 'cos Whitney's been hanging off them? Torpid Tone managed to outdo Stacey in the glum stakes. (When he was little his local park had mood swings.)

Tony had a lot of time on his hands, but hopefully he'll have more soon – ten years in Belmarsh. BBC1 justified this sick storyline by saying, "it happens." But a lot of things happen in real life that we don't see in Walford. People stay faithful; crack jokes; smile; some even commute to work. And if Toxic Tony was caught fiddling with Whitney in any working-class area, he'd have got the kicking of his godforsaken life.

Minor Irritations of the year:
- Aunt Sal claiming that she was 'a looker' when she was younger. Eh? When Sal was younger she was Olive from *On the Buses*. Not so much a looker, more looker-the-state-of-that.
- The family soap having Christian and Lee vigorously French-kissing in public. Perhaps this happens all the time

in Hampstead. Perhaps the BBC's 'Director of Vision', Jana Bennett, trots out her kids to give exhibitionist gays a round of applause and an orange to suck at halftime. But carry on like that in the real East End and you'll get a bucket of water thrown over you. If you're lucky ...

- The credit crunch by-passing Walford. Callum turned down a grand, Brad casually bet £10K on the gee-gees. They've always got money to burn on *Enders*. Billy gave away Jase's filthy lucre, Stacy turned her nose up at Max's 40K ... It's a sure sign that the people writing this garbage have never gone without in their lives.
- The continuing 'all men are bastards' theme. Writing in the *News of the World*, Ian Hyland pointed out something connecting all the latest characters: New boy Callum – controlling, manipulative, womaniser. New boy Archie – controlling, manipulative, bully. New boy Tony – controlling, manipulative, paedophile. The only surprise being we haven't had a wife-beating drunk rapist for a while, as Hyland said.
- A soap producer with the good old cockney name of Dominic Treadwell-Collins.

Some Enders *rhyming slang:* Max Branning = needs hanging. Dot Cotton = this soap's rotten. Ronnie and Roxy = the women are poxy.

2009 – *The George Michael Year*

New Year's Day 2009 saw Sean Slater's pilot for a great new TV game show: *Dancing with Death on Ice*. His plan was to drive himself, Roxy and Amy onto the frozen lake so they would crash to a watery grave. Lovely! A bit like a weekend in Frinton but maybe not quite as cold.

Mercifully, baby Amy survived Sean's sick suicide scheme. Considering her likely fate growing up in Walford, it would probably have qualified as a mercy killing, poor mite. Amy wasn't really born premature; it was an attempted prison break.

Previously, Sean had returned to the Vic and convinced Roxy to leave with him and Amy to make a new life together, although his plan was always suicide and murder. Somehow – sixth sense, telepathy, an unmentioned tracking device? – Ronnie and Jack managed to trail them to the lake of doom.

When they arrived, Roxy coaxed Sean out onto the ice. With Ronnie and Jack watching, the ice broke and the pair went under. Sean freed Roxy from the weeds she was tangled up in as Ronnie dived into the water to rescue her. The Mitchell sisters escaped, but there was no sign of Sean.

Roxy then spotted him crawling out of the water while Ronnie and Jack were warming up back at the car. She urged this demented maniac, who had tried to kill her and her baby, to escape. Sean walked away into the darkness. Viewers were impressed. All over the country we responded with a collective cry of, "What an ice-hole!"

(Fact: soap bosses had originally intended to kill off the Sean Slater character, but were persuaded to leave the door open after pleas from actor Rob Kalinsky who plays him.)

Also in January, poor Jean Slater was sent back to the nut-house. (When she finds out where she is, she'll go f***ing mental!) And Walford got its first Book Club. If that lasts the year, I'll eat the book you're reading now with a topping of curry sauce.

The Walford Book Club inspired me to speculate on what the most popular works might be: possibly *Back Passage to India* (the Dr Fonseca story), *The Hoarse Whisperer* (Phil Mitchell), *The Di Marco Code* and *1984* (the last year the soap made sense – the year before it was launched).

Mystery of the Month: Billy Mitchell was freaked out by Janine's dead cat. Why? He's never said a word about the one Peggy wears on her head.

February was like *Carry on Stalking*, as 'comedy' duo Heather and Shirley embarked on a desperately unfunny mission to hunt down George Michael at his leafy mansion. (See 'Big Swinging Cobblers'.) The week ended with Shirley booking Heather a male escort for the night, which was frankly taking her obsession with the former Wham star much too far.

Songs George could have sung to Hefty if they'd actually met: 'Careless Whopper', 'I Want Your Snacks', 'You've Gotta Have Cakes', 'I Knew You Were Weighty', 'Last Christmas Pudding', 'Let's Go Outsize'.

February also saw the soap's first-ever all-black episode (see 'Ishoos'). The storyline was to end a couple of months later with Edward Woodward's character, Tommy Clifford, begging Patrick's forgiveness for killing his girlfriend in an arson attack during the Notting Dale race riots of the 1950s. No one was actually killed in these disturbances.

Also this month: Garry Hobbs went missing for one weekend and his brains-trust mates decided he was brown bread. Eh? Dr Legg disappeared for months on end and no one raised an eyebrow. Two days! Heather Trott has taken longer craps. On the plus side, a whole bar watched the report of Garry's 'death' on TV. It was News 24's biggest-ever audience.

Mysteries of the Month:
- Ricky took a DNA test to find out whether he is little Tiffany's father. Considering her cheek, her hair colour and the fact that she was conceived in Manchester, wouldn't it be worth testing *Coronation Street*'s ginger malingerer Eddie Windass?
- Ian and Jane Beale had a porn session. Was it an adult film or just an amateur disc downloaded from Dirty Den's laptop?
  (The worst-selling blue movies in Walford: *Dorothy Does Dagenham*, *Mo Does Mile End*, *Last Tango in Plaistow*, *Bell-Enders*, *Albert Bare*, *Wellard and Willing ...*)

In March, Dismal Dani's insipid presence was irritating the hell out of me, as well as many long-suffering viewers. She "has been in Walford for nine months and still hasn't told her mum who she is," I noted, asking, "Why? The Hundred Years War, the fall of

Communism, the erosion of mountains, the evolution of land mammals ... these monumental events are but the blink of an eye compared to this endless old malarkey. This story is dragging so much it has almost made me nostalgic for the 'Michelle's two sons' snooze-athon on *Corrie*. Almost. Danielle's new nickname? The Mouse That Bored."

Danielle had one topic of conversation – if and how she should tell Ronnie who she really is. At one stage she got hold of Charlie's paint and daubed the words 'Evil cow' on Ronnie's flat. If she'd just written 'Mum, I'm home' we would all have been a lot happier, and the daft teen might have lived.

Also this month: Roxy and Ronnie were mistaken for hookers. Ridiculous! Hookers have far more class ...

Peggy started running for councillor on a true blue, clean-up-Walford ticket. And St Patrick's Day came a day early in the Vic because Hefty Heather, as well as being fat, is also exceedingly thick. Laugh? I nearly bought meself a Guinness.

In April, Peggy Mitchell's wedding to Archie Mitchell had as much chance of a happy ending as a mid-season episode of *24*. It was gloriously ridiculous. Peg and Archie rowed through their vows, the best man's speech was abandoned and the groom was exposed as the biggest liar this side of *Question Time*. No wonder her son Grant didn't bother coming – his flight from Portugal would have lasted longer than the marriage.

The big day climaxed with the bride screeching, "*GED AHT!*" at her guests and the dismal Danielle brown bread. Yes, the dreary Danni storyline was finally over, and for that relief many thanks. Betrayed by her scheming grandad and denounced by her secret mum as "a pathetic little freak", the wretched waif was run down by Janine and died in Ronnie's arms – bringing the number of Albert Square car deaths to six (Tiff, Jamie, Debbie Bates, Andy O'Brien and, saddest of all, Roly the poodle). Dramatic stuff, and of course you'd need a heart of stone not to laugh. But did any of it make any sense?

Millionaire Archie abandoned his seaside mansion to live above a grotty East End pub ... just to control his daughters. But if he was that obsessed with them, why didn't he move to Ibiza when they were out there for donkey's years?

He and Peggy got engaged within *two days* of meeting up again – the shrewd decision-making you'd associate with a self-made man. (Although it's possible that he'd only gone down on one knee to look her in the eye ...)

Dani stepped off the pavement and saw Janine driving towards her, just standing in the road like a rabbit trapped in headlights. Archie contemplated murdering his granddaughter. Eh? He'd always been a selfish manipulator, but a killer? Where did that come from? Up until now his biggest crime was scheming to improve Peggy's dress sense. Suddenly he was ready to tie the knot in Dani's scrawny neck.

The motivation for Archie's reign of misery and terror remains lost in the ether. Then there was the small business of Ronnie suddenly believing her father, even though she'd denounced him as a lying toe-rag for two decades. None of it made any sense. Fans of Dani were distraught. Thousands of them petitioned the Beeb to bring her back from the dead and give the forlorn teenager the dramatically satisfying happy ending that the poor mite deserved, and that young fans in particular had been expecting.

Happy ending? Are they mad? This is *EastEnders*. There's never a happy ending for anyone.

You don't even get one in the massage parlour.

There was more joy to come at her funeral as Stacey Slater had a nice old chat with an open grave. Why? It wasn't as if Dani's coffin was there; it was just a hole in the ground. Nevertheless, it still made for a better conversation than talking to Uncle Charlie ...

There was snow in Albert Square in April. "See," I wrote, "Hell is freezing over." I know they film episodes six weeks in advance, but would it have been too much effort to have cleared the snow away? It looked ridiculous.

Also this month: all the cakes went at Shirley Carter's buffet. Heather never misses one. She has profiterole vision.

But it was very disturbing news in May: Heather Trott found

out that she was pregnant. This was the soap's follow-up to 'Who Shot Phil': 'Who Upped Tubs?' It was also an echo of the famous Michelle Fowler, whose baby storyline was a lot more interesting because she was a 16-year-old schoolgirl at the time and we actually cared who the father might be.

The obvious favourite for Heather's tot is her nightclub chubby chaser. Outsiders include Gumbo the dog, Phil Mitchell (unlikely – even Phil's never been *that* pissed), Billy Mitchell (seen snogging her earlier this year) and at 100-1 her husband Minty.

(I had a fiver on Neville Staple from the Specials. According to reports he's shagged everyone else.)

She was no stranger to men though. Heather has been closely linked in the past to Ronald McDonald, Colonel Sanders, the Burger King ... And Hev did go to bed with two Indians once. (A madras and a balti.) I had to laugh when a nurse said to her, "You won't have had your breasts scanned then?" Nope. Not even by Minty.

The big dramatic scenes of the month all revolved around Stacey Slater. Poor Lacey Turner. Stacey's love life has bafflingly consisted of bouncing between the beds of ginger mingers Max the Mekon and his perma-frowning bore of a son, Bradley Branning. As a child she devoted herself to caring for her schizophrenic muvva Jean; more recently, she's been looking after Jean, her equally mad brother Sean and her flaky friend Danielle, who she recently and traumatically watched die in a road accident.

If that wasn't bad enough, she has to live with fat Uncle Charlie and almost as fat Big Mo, who she calls 'Nan' even though she isn't. That would surely be enough misery to last most people a lifetime.

But for *EastEnders* that was just a starter. Now they'd decided she would be bipolar too. In other words they'd decided to turn one of the show's most promising characters into a junior imitation of the worst – screeching harpy Jean.

The wretched Stacey's descent into madness was apparently set in motion by watching dismal Dani die, but was triggered by her staring at a poster asking, 'Deprivation, how long can you stay awake?' It manifested itself by her acting like a slapper (bedding a builder, throwing herself at Max) and running up huge credit card debts on wild spending sprees. Uh, wasn't that pretty much condition normal? Charlie ordered her out of the house for good after she smashed a window – "I want you gorn!" – but, by the time she came back a month later, the big soft pudding had forgotten all about that.

Light relief this month came from Steve McFadden's wonderful turn as drunk Phil Mitchell – no-one plays pissed like McFadden. Rat-arsed Phil accurately referred to Shirley Carter as a "sour-faced tart" and congratulated his loser cousin Billy on "50 years of failure". It was great stuff. I was hoping that he'd go on to call Charlie an emasculated slug, kick out his weedy son Ben and make Heather play Russian Roulette with her asthma pumps. (Five full of Ventolin, one of strychnine. Deep breaths, Hev.)

Also this month: the Square got a new GP, Dr Al Jenkins, who at time of writing is already giving consultations in the pub and the launderette. (Wot? No swings?) Plus Syed, the Masoods' eldest son, turned up – they "expected him to be different somehow". So did we. We thought he'd be Asian.

Elsewhere, Theo helped Jordan with his algebra. (Maths is not little Dotty's strong point either. When her teacher asked her what three sixes were, she replied, "The birthmark I had removed.") And Jack Branning chased Ronnie Mitchell to Stansted airport. This certainly made a lot of sense. Ronnie has PMT – she's a Permanently Miserable Tart, a lunatic control freak prone to depression and bouts of destructive rage that make Drogba look demure. What man could resist her?

The month ended with a strong image: Ronnie, desperate to get pregnant, left Jack a trail of casino chips leading to her boudoir. Luckily, he'd learnt his lesson on the slot machine – or Roxy, as she's affectionately known – and wouldn't oblige her. (How like a man to turn down a shag!)

Continuity cock-ups were in abundance in May. Jack Branning saw Charlie Slater locking up his black cab. He ran over and asked if he could give him a lift to Stansted airport. Jack then followed Chas into Chateau Slater while Charlie said, "Okay then Jack, I'll just go and find my keys." Eh?

We also witnessed the miracle of the disappearing cake. Bradley Branning's new squeeze Syd cut Dot a slice and, as she walked into the hallway, noticed that Dot was at the front door and about to leave. Syd put the plate on the stairs behind her. A moment later we saw her and Brad climb up the staircase. But not one of them stepped in the cake, neither did they eat it. What happened to it? We can't be certain but surely they'd have heard Heather?

Mystery of the Month: Big Mo Harris had her comedy pig Chops slaughtered to pay off Stacey Slater's café tab. She was later seen giving Ian hundreds of pounds, begging the question, how much tea does Stacey get through? She'd only been running the tab for a few weeks. Maybe Dani's death didn't send her loopy after all, it may have been a caffeine overdose.

(Tsk. Chops slaughtered, Corky the parrot forgotten, Gumbo the dog for sale ... is this a soap or is it Farmageddon?)

Minor query: the new doctor's vest, does he have it on a time-share with Christian?

June 2009 – The Present Day

Good news for this book at least – as we leave the soap for now, there is no sign of it getting any better. Indeed, the climax of the latest Nasty Nick Cotton storyline was the Great Café Disaster, one of the most ludicrous incidents for years. (See '15 of the Most Ridiculous Storylines Ever'.) Other nonsense from this episode included a drugged-up Panto Nick feebly chasing young Dotty around Dot's kitchen, which was like a scene out of a bad Chuckle Brothers show.

Also this month: Walford's betting shop has disappeared entirely (like the Queen Vic pool table), so it's just as well that no one wanted to have a flutter on the Derby or Royal Ascot. Craving the glam lifestyle, Chelsea snogged a coke-head in a grotty nightclub toilet. (Living the dream, girl, living the dream!) Amira fell out of Syed's wardrobe, but we know she's not the only one in his closet. And Ronnie Mitchell started putting tiny pricks in

Jack's condoms (insert your own joke here). Although why she didn't just tell him she was on the pill is beyond me ...

On Tuesday 16 June, *EastEnders* recorded viewing figures of just 5.92 million. *Top Gear* beat it. (That's the car show, not Chelsea Fox's favourite white powder.) The soap has lost its power to shock. Could it finally be losing its ability to mildly interest?

Mystery of the Month: Who has Patsy Palmer upset in the *Enders* wardrobe department? That pink-'n'-print jacket that Bianca has suddenly started to wear looks like the lampshade in a Shadwell whorehouse. And her red tea-towel top isn't much better. Bianca, babes, you've mixed and matched and missed.

Other mysteries: how come Whitney's mum was a foot taller than her? Was her dad Ronnie Corbett? And how is the Masoods' curry stall still in business? The dish that Parveen emptied over Syed's head looked like congealed vomit.

Quotes of the Month:
- Jane Beale: "Am I the only person who is watching this car crash?" No, love, but if the viewing figures keep tumbling you soon will be.
- Roxy Mitchell: "How can things get any worse around here?" Dunno, babe, but the evidence of experience suggests that they will.

After the sad death of Wendy Richard in 2009, BBC1 broadcast a special tribute show featuring the cast looking gloomy and depressed. For the same effect, why didn't they just repeat any of the previous 1,000 episodes?

Epilogue

Where will they go next? They've had homosexuality, bisexuality and incest. 'Orrible 'Arry abused his niece. Steve snogged his mum. They've had love that is cross-racial, cross-class, and even cross-species (Jamie and Sonia). What next? Bestiality? Orgies? Dot Cotton, lap-dancer – with cries of, "Put your fag out for the lads"?

Small things are forgotten – Jane's colostomy bag, the Naturist Society, Walford Town Football Club, the Masoods' debt mountain ...

Devoid of inspiration, the soap goes around and around like a loop tape from hell: here we go again with Jack-Ronnie-Roxy and Max snogging Tanya, the wife who buried him alive just one year ago ...

There is no consistency in the characters or logic in the storylines. Stacey couldn't find a fella (ain't she heard of Bebo and Facebook?) but never tried socialising anywhere outside of the Square. Now they've ruined her by making her nuts. There is no end to this storyline, it's permanent. They can't conveniently make Stacey's bipolarity go away – although I suspect they'll try.

Soap plots come thick and fast these days, and the faster they get the thicker they become. There is no joy, no sense of reality and no escape.

The strain is starting to show. On Tuesday 23 June 2009, viewing figures were down below five million again to 4.84m.

People are realising that there is life beyond the Square and are switching off this hideous televisual carbuncle in search of a brighter reality. There is lush green grass beyond George Street. There is a clear blue sky above the Vic, and fun and laughter to be found everywhere from Aldgate East to Barkingside.

Life is beautiful. Even in London. Let future generations of viewers cleanse it of all dreary *Guardian*-think, unfettered misery and man-hating violence. Hold hands, *EastEnders* fans; hold hands and contact the living.